COMPLETE WRITINGS

PHILLIS WHEATLEY

EDITED AND WITH AN
INTRODUCTION BY
VINCENT CARRETTA

PENGUIN BOOKS

PENGUIN BOOKS
Published by the Penguin Group
Penguin Group (USA) Inc., 375 Hudson Street, New York, New York 10014, U.S.A.
Penguin Group (Canada), 90 Eglinton Avenue East, Suite 700, Toronto, Ontario,
Canada M4P 2Y3 (a division of Pearson Penguin Canada Inc.)
Penguin Books Ltd, 80 Strand, London WC2R 0RL, England
Penguin Ireland, 25 St Stephen's Green, Dublin 2, Ireland
(a division of Penguin Books Ltd)
Penguin Group (Australia), 250 Camberwell Road, Camberwell, Victoria 3124,
Australia (a division of Pearson Australia Group Pty Ltd)
Penguin Books India Pvt Ltd, 11 Community Centre, Panchsheel Park,
New Delhi – 110 017, India
Penguin Group (NZ), 67 Apollo Drive, Rosedale, North Shore 0632, New Zealand
(a division of Pearson New Zealand Ltd)
Penguin Books (South Africa) (Pty) Ltd, 24 Sturdee Avenue, Rosebank,
Johannesburg 2196, South Africa

Penguin Books Ltd, Registered Offices: 80 Strand, London WC2R 0RL, England

First published in Penguin Books 2001

20 19 18 17 16 15 14 13

Selection, introduction, and notes copyright © Vincent Carretta, 2001
All rights reserved

CIP data available
ISBN 978-0-14-042430-0

Printed in the United States of America
Set in Stempel Garamond

CONTENTS

Extant Poems Not Published in *Poems on Various Subjects*

Variants of Poems Published in Poems on
Various Subjects

Letters

Variant Letters

Proposals for Volumes of Poetry

Appendix A: Possible Wheatley variant of "Hymn to Humanity"; Possible new Phillis Wheatley poem, "The Voice of Freedom"

Appendix B: Lucy Terry Prince

Appendix C: Jupiter Hammon

Appendix D: Francis Williams

INTRODUCTION

Born around 1753 somewhere in west Africa, probably between present-day Gambia and Ghana, the little girl who would become Phillis Wheatley was brought to Boston, Massachusetts, on July 11, 1761, aboard the *Phillis*, a slave ship commanded by captain Peter Gwin and owned by Timothy Fitch. At the time, approximately one thousand of Boston's more than fifteen thousand residents were slaves, with perhaps twenty free people of African descent in the total population. About seven or eight years old (her front teeth were missing), the sickly child was soon bought from the slave dealer John Avery by John Wheatley, a prosperous Boston merchant, for his wife, Susanna. Named after her new owners and the vessel that had brought her to America, Phillis Wheatley was taken to the Wheatley home at the corner of King Street and Makerel Lane (present-day State and Kilby Streets) to help the Wheatleys' few other domestic slaves care for their mistress and master, as well as their eighteen-year-old twins, Mary and Nathaniel. The Wheatleys were members of the New South Congregational Church. Susanna was also an active supporter of the evangelical missions of the Calvinist Methodist minister George Whitefield and others. John was gradually turning over to his son the management of his real estate, warehouse, wharf, and wholesale businesses, and the *London Packet*, a three-masted schooner, used to trade between Boston and London.

Mainly through the tutelage of Mary Wheatley, the obviously precocious Phillis gained an extraordinary education for a woman of the time, and an unprecedented one for a female slave. According to John Wheatley, within sixteen months Phillis was proficient enough in the English language to be able to read even "the most difficult Parts of the Sacred Writings." She was taught English and Classical literature (especially poetry), geography, and history, as well as the Bible, some Latin, and Christianity. Her poems and letters show that she became familiar with works by Alexander Pope (her principal poetic model for the use of heroic couplets), John Milton (her most admired modern poet), William Shenstone, Horace, Virgil, Ovid, Terence, and Homer (the last through Pope's translations). None of Wheatley's surviving writings, however, indicates a familiarity with Classical sources that could not have been gained from translations alone.

Phillis's first known piece of writing, a now-lost letter to the Mohegan minister, Samson Occom, was written in 1765, when she was about twelve years old. A Wheatley family friend, Occom had gone with Nathaniel Whitaker, another minister, to England and Scotland in 1766 to raise money for the education of Occom's fellow Native Americans in New England. The school that resulted from their efforts was Dartmouth College, named after William Legge, Earl of Dartmouth, another of Phillis's correspondents and the subject of one of her poems. Her first published work, the poem "On Messrs. Hussey and Coffin," appeared on December 21, 1767, in a newspaper, the *Newport Mercury*, no doubt through the support and contacts of Susanna Wheatley. The poem's combination of Christian piety and Classical allusions anticipates the themes and expression found in most of her subsequent verse. The subscription proposal for Phillis's first volume of poetry indicates that she was composing poetry as early as 1765. The surviving variant versions of many of her poems demonstrate her desire to improve her verses and her ability to fit them for various audiences. For the next several years, Phillis published a number of occasional poems, that is, poems on recent events, culminating in her 1770 funeral elegy addressed to Selina Hastings, Countess of Huntingdon, on the death of her chaplain, Whitefield. Wheatley probably heard Whitefield at least one of the four times he preached at the Old South Church in August 1770, a month before his sudden death in Newburyport, Massachusetts. Since Susanna Wheatley corresponded with the Countess, Whitefield may well have been a guest in the Wheatley house. On August 18, 1771, Phillis was baptized by Samuel Cooper into the Congregationalist Old South Church (not the Wheatley family church).

Phillis Wheatley's elegy brought her both international fame and the Countess's attention when it was published in London, as well as in Boston, in 1771. Her reputation was reinforced by the publication of her poem "Recollection," initially in March 1772, in the *London Magazine: Or, Gentleman's Monthly Intelligencer*, and subsequently in both American and English periodicals. Wheatley's community of women supporters soon extended beyond her American and English patrons to include her fellow Bostonian poet, Jane Dunlap. In her *Poems Upon Several Sermons Preached by the Rev'd and Renowned George Whitefield While in Boston* (Boston, 1771), Dunlap mentions Wheatley's elegy, referring to "a young Afric damsel's virgin tongue." In *An Address to the Inhabitants of the British Settlement in America, upon Slave-Keeping* (Boston, 1773), mistaking her status and how long she had been "in the country," Benjamin Rush observed that "[t]here is now in the town of Boston a Free Negro Girl, about 18 years of age, who has been but 9 [*sic*] years in the country, whose singular genius and accomplishments are such as not only do honor to her sex, but to human nature. Several of her poems have been printed, and read with pleasure by the public." In France, Voltaire told Baron Constant de Rebecq in a 1774 letter that Wheatley's very fine English verse disproved Fontenelle's contention that no black poets existed. Wheatley, however, was neither the first black woman poet, the first published black poet, nor the first black poet to gain international notice in British America. Those honors belong, respectively, to Lucy Terry, whose poetry remained unpublished until the nineteenth century; Jupiter Hammon, who published his first poem at the end of 1760; and Francis Williams, who wrote poetry in Latin. (The poems of Terry, Hammon, and Williams are included in the Appendices to this Penguin edition.) But in contemporaneous and subsequent recognition, reputation, and influence Wheatley far surpassed her black predecessors, whose works she appears not to have known: unpublished, Terry was almost completely unknown until the following century; never published in London, Hammon remained a provincial poet; and unpublished and untranslated, Williams was largely unknown and inaccessible, especially before 1774.

By 1772 Wheatley had written enough poems to enable her to try to capitalize on her growing transatlantic reputation by producing a book of previously published and new verse. Consequently, subscriptions were solicited, probably by Susanna Wheatley, in the *Boston Censor* on February 29, March 14, and April 18, 1772, for a proposed volume of Phillis's poems to be published in Boston. Unfortunately, despite Wheatley's local reputation as a poet, sufficient support for the project was lacking. Having failed to find backing in Boston, Susanna turned to London for a publisher, using Robert Calef, captain of the Wheatleys' *London Packet*, to seek out Archibald Bell, a relatively minor publisher and bookseller of primarily religious texts in the City of London, in the fall of 1772. Bell agreed to publish Wheatley's *Poems on Various Subjects, Religious and Moral* in 1773, on the condition that the volume be prefaced by a document signed by Boston worthies certifying the authenticity of the poems for an English audience. Through Bell, Wheatley gained the patronage of the Countess of Huntingdon, who agreed to allow Phillis to dedicate the book to her. As Phillis and her mistress knew, Huntingdon had already sponsored the publication of James Albert Ukawsaw Gronniosaw's *A Narrative of the Most Remarkable Particulars in the Life of . . . an African Prince, as Related by Himself*, published in Bath at the end of 1772. Huntingdon subsequently supported the publication of religiously oriented works by other black authors, including John Marrant's *A Narrative of the Lord's Wonderful Dealings with John Marrant, a Black . . . Taken down from His Own Relation* (London, 1785), and Olaudah Equiano's *The Interesting Narrative of the Life of Olaudah Equiano, or Gustavus Vassa, the African. Written by Himself* (London, 1789). Gronniosaw, Marrant, and Equiano all knew Whitefield, as well as Huntingdon, having heard him preach, either in England or during one of his seven trips to North America. In a letter Wheatley wrote to Huntingdon during her six-week visit to London, she acknowledges Gronniosaw as her literary predecessor, thus recognizing a tradition of English-speaking writers of African descent, as well as Huntingdon's role in enabling such writers to gain access to print.

Wheatley went to England to recover her health, to meet her aristocratic patron, and presumably to see her book through the press. She achieved none of those goals. After Susanna Wheatley had written to the Countess asking her advice about finding proper housing for Phillis in London, Phillis left Boston with captain Calef aboard the *London Packet* on May 8, 1773. They reached London on June 17, just as the publicity campaign for the forthcoming book, coordinated by Susanna Wheatley and Bell, was beginning in the London press. Before she had a chance to meet the Countess, who had retired to her home in Wales for reasons of health, and before her *Poems* was published, Wheatley left England with Calef on July 26 to return to Boston to nurse her ailing mistress.

Soon after Phillis left Boston for London, a copy of her poem "A Farewel to America" appeared in *The London Chronicle*, with a cover note to be published with the poem, intended to stimulate interest in the soon-to-be-published volume, and indicating that Phillis was already known to English readers:

Sir,
You have no doubt heard of Phillis the extraordinary negro girl here [i.e., Boston], who has by her own application, unassisted by others, cultivated her natural talents for poetry in such a manner as to write several pieces which (all circumstances considered) have great merit. This girl, who is a servant to Mr. John Wheatley of this place, sailed last Saturday for London, under the protection of Mr. Nathaniel Wheatley; since which the following little piece of her's [*sic*] has been published.

Although advertisements for the book itself began to appear in London newspapers as early as the 6 August notice in *The Morning Post and Daily Advertiser*, Wheatley's *Poems* was not registered by Archibald Bell with the Stationers' Company to protect his copyright until September 10. As the remarkable advertisement in *The London Chronicle* and *The Morning Post and Daily Advertiser* attests, *Poems*, the first book by an English-speaking black writer, went on sale the following day, while Wheatley was still at sea:

Dedicated, by Permission, to the Right Hon. the Countess of Huntingdon. This day, Sept. 11, will be published, Price Two Shillings, sewed, or Two Shillings and sixpence neatly bound, adorned with an elegant engraved like-ness of the Author. A Volume of POEMS ON VARIOUS SUBJECTS: RELIGIOUS AND MORAL. By PHILLIS WHEATLEY, Negro Servant to Mr. John Wheatley, of Boston. London: Printed for A. Bell, Bookseller, Aldgate; and at Boston, for Messrs. Cox and Berry, in King Street. To the Public. The Book here proposed for publication displays perhaps one of the greatest instances of pure, unassisted genius, that the world ever produced. The Author is a native of Africa, and left not that dark part of the habitable system, till she was eight years old. She is now no more than nineteen, and many of the Poems were penned before she arrived at near that age.

They were wrote upon a variety of interesting subjects, and in a stile rather to have been expected from those who, a native genius, have had the happiness of a liberal education, than from one born in the wilds of Africa.

The writer while in England a few weeks since, was conversed with by many of the principal Nobility and Gentry of this Country, who have been signally distinguished for their learning and abilities, among whom was the Earl of Dartmouth, the late Lord Lyttelton, and others who unanimously expressed their amazement at the gifts with which infinite Wisdom has furnished her.

But the Publisher means not, in this advertisement, to deliver any peculiar eulogiums on the present publication; he rather desires to submit the striking beauties of its contents to the unabashed candour of the impartial public.

The "elegant engraved like-ness of the Author" featured in Bell's advertisement had been added to Wheatley's *Poems* as a frontispiece, at the urging of Huntingdon. It may have been designed in Boston, perhaps by Scipio Moorhead, a black artist to whom Wheatley addresses a poem, and engraved in London. Humbly dressed as a servant, the poet looks upward, as if seeking inspiration. Significantly, Wheatley is shown with a book, perhaps intended either to be her own *Poems,* or to indicate that hers was an educated as well as an inspired "native genius." But perhaps as significantly, the frontispiece emphasizes Wheatley's African heritage and her inferior social status by having her likeness contained by an oval whose framing words appear to limit the extent of her gaze. The enslaved poet is euphemistically identified as "Phillis Wheatley Negro Servant to Mr. John Wheatley, of Boston." The artistic quality of her frontispiece is as modest as her domestic status.

Wheatley's *Poems* includes a Preface, a letter from John Wheatley to the publisher, and an "Attestation" by New England dignitaries, all intended to authorize and authenticate Phillis Wheatley's achievement. She is conventionally described as an author who did not write for publication and who has agreed to have her poems printed "at the Importunity of many of her best, and most generous Friends." Her volume's title is reminiscent of other first books by poets, including Pope's *Poems on Several Occasions* (London, 1717), Laurence Whyte's *Original Poems on Various Subjects, Serious, Moral, and Diverting* (Dublin, 1742), her friend Mather Byles's *Poems on Several Occasions* (Boston, 1744), her London acquaintance Thomas Gibbons's *Juvenalia: Poems on Various Subjects of Devotion and Virtue* (London, 1750), George Roberts's *Juvenile Poems on Various Subjects* (Limerick, 1763), and Samuel Taylor Coleridge's *Poems on Various Subjects* (London, 1796), all titles appropriate for works intended to display a new poet's talents in various forms of verse, such as the hymns, elegies, translations, philosophical poems, tales, and epyllions (short epics) found in Wheatley's *Poems*. Several of the arguably anti-British poems advertised in the 1772 subscription proposal are not included in the 1773 collection published against a background of rapidly growing tensions between Britain and its North American colonies. And several of the occasional poems are given more general titles, better suited to a London audience unfamiliar with the particular Bostonians addressed or mentioned in them. Wheatley's *Poems* became available in New England and Nova Scotia in early 1774.

Her opening poem, "To Maecenas," appropriately thanks her unnamed patron, loosely imitating Classical models such as Virgil and Horace's poems dedicated to Maecenas, the Roman politician and patron of the arts. Maecenas had long been proverbial as the greatest patron of poets. John Wheatley and Mather Byles have been suggested as Wheatley's patron and thus the subject of the poem, but a more appropriate and likely candidate, despite her being female and Maecenas male, is the dedicatee of *Poems*: the Countess of Huntingdon. Only in the poem's concluding stanza is "Maecenas" explicitly gendered male when addressed as "great Sir" and solicited for "paternal rays" of protection. But the reference to *"Thames"* in the stanza's opening line clearly suggests that the dedicatee is English, and the closing request that "Maecenas" "defend my lays" echoes Wheatley's comment in her July 27, 1773, letter to the Countess that through her patronage "my feeble efforts will be shielded from the severe trials of uppity Criticism." As an aristocratic widow, Huntingdon had virtually all the authority and power of a male. With no classical models of female patrons available to her, Wheatley's decision to address the Countess in the guise of a male would be understandable. Emphasizing in a footnote that the Classical Roman poet Terence "was an *African* by birth," Wheatley implies that her "Maecenas" has enabled her to claim a place in the Western literary tradition, which has included Africans since its beginning:

> The happier *Terence* all the choir inspir'd,
> His soul replenish'd, and his bosom fir'd;
> But say, ye *muses*, why this partial grace,
> To one alone of *Afric*'s sable race;
> From age to age transmitting thus his name
> With the first glory in the rolls of fame?

Indeed, her invocation of her African predecessor marks the poem's turning point. Prior to naming Terence, the speaker of the poem is immobilized by her humility in the face of the epic achievements of Homer and Virgil:

> But here I sit, and mourn a grov'ling mind,
> That fain would mount, and ride upon the wind.
> . . . .
> But I less happy, cannot raise the song,
> The fault'ring music dies upon my tongue.

As an enslaved black woman poet entering the commercial publishing market, Wheatley's interest in the reality of strength

underlying apparent weakness, and in confidence beneath pro-
fessed diffidence, may also account for her including in *Poems*
the epyllion "Goliath of Gath," whose title masks its true hero,
David. Unlike the overly masculine "monster" Goliath, "[o]f
fierce Deportment, and gigantic frame," who mistakenly relies
on his own physical strength, David is a relatively feminized
hero, a "stripling," "in youthful bloom," who has "left the
flow'ry meads,/And soft recesses of the sylvan shades," and who
relies on faith in God for his moral strength. Wheatley may even
have been consciously writing within the tradition of associating
powerful women with David traceable to the Renaissance
iconography surrounding Queen Elizabeth. In her poetic per-
sona, Wheatley repeatedly and quite conventionally character-
izes herself as "[t]he languid muse in low degree" ("An Hymn to
Humanity") or the "last [newest] and meanest [lowest in social
rank] of the rhyming train" ("Niobe in Distress for Her Chil-
dren"). But such characterizations are belied by her assumption
of the role of "*Afric's* muse" in the former poem, by the publica-
tion of her *Poems,* and by her efforts to sell the book in America.

Elsewhere in her poems, Wheatley appropriates the persona
of authority or power normally associated with men and social
superiors. For example, in "To the University of Cambridge, in
New-England," first composed when she was about fifteen years
old, Wheatley speaks as a teacher to students, or a minister to his
flock, in addressing the young men of what was to become Har-
vard University, many of whom were being trained there to
become ministers themselves. Confident that "the muses" will
"assist my pen," she asserts her authority as one who has "left
my native shore/The land of errors" and "those dark abodes,"
who has known "sin, that baneful evil to the soul," and rejected
it to embrace the "Father of mercy." From a position of moral
superiority gained through experience she speaks as an "*Ethiop*"
to warn her implicitly complacent students—"Ye pupils"—to
"Improve your privileges while they stay." Audaciously, the
teenaged, enslaved, self-educated, female, and formerly pagan
poet assumes a voice that transcends the "privileges" of those
who are reputedly her superiors in age, status, abilities, author-
ity, and gender.

Perhaps in part because of Huntingdon's patronage and protection, Wheatley's *Poems* was widely and generally favorably reviewed in British literary magazines, many of which included exemplary poems from the collection. Wheatley benefitted from the growing interest in the later eighteenth century in temporally, geographically, socially, and ethnically exotic origins of sentiment and literature, such as James Macpherson's Ossianic forgeries of ancient Gaelic epics (1762), or the poems of the supposedly unlettered Scot Robert Burns (1786), and of the uneducated milkwoman Ann Yearsley (1785). For example, after reproducing the text of "To Maecenas," the anonymous writer in the *Critical Review* (September 1773) remarks, "[t]here are several lines in this piece, which would be no discredit to an English poet. The whole is indeed extraordinary, considered as the production of a young Negro, who was, but a few years since, an illiterate barbarian." Political considerations also affected literary judgments: several British commentators shared the opinion expressed anonymously in the *Monthly Review* (December 1773): [w]e are much concerned to find that this ingenious young woman is yet a slave. The people of Boston boast themselves chiefly on their principles of liberty. One such act as the purchase of her freedom, would, in our opinion, have done them more honour than hanging a thousand trees with ribbons and emblems."

In the posthumously published *Letters of the Late Ignatius Sancho, an African* (London, 1782), Wheatley's first black critic later shared the *Monthly Review*'s concern about her status. Sancho, a free man who had been a slave and servant before becoming a Westminster grocer, considered Wheatley's presumed return to Boston as a slave to have been a tragic move. Sancho, who never met Wheatley though some of the places she visited while in London were within blocks of his home, never learned of her manumission. Sancho wrote on January 27, 1778, to the Quaker Jabez Fisher of Philadelphia to thank him for sending an anti-slavery book by Anthony Benezet and a copy of Wheatley's *Poems*:

> Phyllis's poems do credit to nature—and put art—merely as art—to the blush.—It reflects nothing either to the glory or generosity

of her master—if she is still his slave—except he glories in the *low vanity* of having in his wanton power a mind animated by Heaven—a genius superior to himself—the list of splendid—titled—learned names, in confirmation of her being the real authoress.—alas! shews how very poor the acquisition of wealth and knowledge are—without generosity—feeling—and humanity.— These good great folks—all know—and perhaps admired—nay, praised Genius in bondage—and then, like the Priests and the Levites in sacred writ, passed by—not one good Samaritan amongst them.

Jupiter Hammon, a slave in Connecticut, seems to have been as unaware as Sancho that Wheatley had gained her freedom by the time he published *An Address to Miss PHILLIS WHEATLY* [sic], *Ethiopian Poetess* (Hartford, 1778) in response to "On Being Brought from Africa to America" in her *Poems*. Neither the anonymous writer in the *Monthly Review*, Sancho, nor Hammon recognized that Wheatley's trip to London not only transformed her literary identity, but also offered her the opportunity to transform her legal, social, and political identities as well.

Accompanied by Nathaniel Wheatley, Phillis Wheatley arrived in London on the eve of the first anniversary of what many Britons, especially those of African descent, considered the emancipation proclamation for English slaves: the Mansfield decision in the *Somerset* case on June 22, 1772, which was greeted by euphoria in London's African-British community. Lord Mansfield, Lord Chief Justice of the King's Bench, the highest common law court in England, had ruled that James Somerset, a slave brought to England in 1769 from Massachusetts by his master, a Boston customs official, could not legally be forced by his master back to the colonies. Somerset had run away from his master in 1771 but was recaptured later that year and put on a ship bound for Jamaica. Two days after the recapture of Somerset, Mansfield, at the urging of the abolitionist Granville Sharp and others, issued a writ of habeas corpus ordering the captain to bring Somerset before the court. Sharp convinced several lawyers to argue Somerset's case free of charge. Although Mansfield's ruling technically established only that a slave could not be seized by his master and forced against his will to leave England and that a slave could get a writ of habeas corpus to prevent his master's action, Mansfield's judgment has been widely considered as the moment slavery was abolished in England.

If the Mansfield ruling did not abolish slavery *de jure* (by law) it certainly undermined it *de facto* (in effect) by indisputably denying slave masters the coercive power of removal to the colonies. Even if the ruling did not render slavery illegal, lacking that power, slave owners could no longer enforce their claims of possession because slaves on English soil could legally emancipate themselves by flight. To many people, prior to Mansfield's decision the legal status of slavery in England had been established in 1729, when attorney-general Sir Philip Yorke and solicitor-general Charles Talbot unofficially offered their opinion that slavery was legal in England, that a slave's status was not affected by baptism, and that "the master may legally compel him to return again to the plantations." But the authority of the Yorke-Talbot opinion as legal precedent was disputed and challenged by other pre-1772 rulings. And the *de facto* status of slavery was unclear even before 1772. For example, Jane Collier, in *An Essay on the Art of Ingeniously Tormenting; With Proper Rules for the Exercise of that Pleasant Art* (London, 1753), confidently asserts that in Britain "[p]urchased slaves are not allowed."

Somerset was the latest and most important victory in Sharp's campaign to gain a legal ruling overturning the Yorke-Talbot opinion, thus rendering slavery illegal in England. While waiting for a suitable case, Sharp published his own refutation of Yorke and Talbot, *A Representation of the Injustice and Dangerous Tendency of Tolerating Slavery; or, of Admitting the Least Claim of Private Property of Men, in England* (London, 1769), which also includes a denunciation of the hypocrisy of the American colonists who practiced slavery while objecting to political oppression. Sharp became a well-known figure in London's African-British community because of his successful legal intervention in 1765 on behalf of Jonathan Strong, a castoff slave whose owner sought to send him from England to Jamaica. Consequently, he was appealed to in the cases of the kidnapped former slaves Mary Hylas in 1766 and Thomas Lewis in 1770, both of whom were physically and legally rescued through Sharp's efforts. But none of those cases led to any judicial ruling whose implications extended beyond the particular case. With the *Somerset* judgement, Sharp appeared to have moved from having won individual battles to winning the war against slavery in England. So famous was Sharp as a defender of the rights of enslaved people that less than a year after Wheatley's visit to London, Olaudah Equiano sought his aid in preventing a friend, John Annis, from illegally being taken from England back to the West Indies as a slave. Unfortunately, they were not able to act fast enough to save Annis.

But how aware was Wheatley of the contested status of slavery in England before she arrived in June 1773, and how willing was she to take advantage of the opportunity it offered her? Although not incontrovertible, the circumstantial evidence that she knew what lay ahead is compelling enough for conviction. By August 1772, the Mansfield decision was being reported in colonial newspapers, a medium used since 1767 for the publication of Wheatley's poetry. For example, on Monday, September 21, 1772, *The Boston Gazette* pointed out the perceived implications of the Mansfield decision for any slave owner contemplating taking a slave to England: "*June* 22. A Correspondent observes, that as Blacks are free now in this country [England], Gentlemen will not be so fond of bringing them here as they used to be, it being computed that there are about 14000 blacks in this country." Given the press coverage of the ruling and its possible significance, as well as the local connection to Boston of Somerset and his master, Mansfield's judgement was the talk of the town and would have been known to Wheatley either in print or by word of mouth.

Although we lack incontrovertible evidence that she knew of the ruling, we do have the October 18, 1773, letter Wheatley wrote to David "Worcester" [Wooster] in New Haven, Connecticut, after she had returned to Boston. She tells him that in England she had been treated as a touring celebrity, visiting Westminster Abbey and the British Museum, among other London attractions. She mentions meeting Benjamin Franklin, the

Earl of Dartmouth, and other members of English high society. Wheatley's owner had taken a great risk in allowing her to go to London to recover her health and oversee the publication of her *Poems*, a risk much increased by Wheatley's befriending "Grenville [*sic*] Sharp Esqr.[,] who attended me to the Tower [of London] & show'd the Lions, Panthers, Tigers, &c. the Horse Armoury, Small Armoury, the Crowns, Sceptres, Diadems, the Fount for christening the Royal Family." It is very difficult to imagine Wheatley and Sharp looking at caged African animals, as well as the emblems of British regal glory, without the subject coming up of Sharp's recent judicial triumph in extending British liberty to African slaves. Not to have encouraged Wheatley to seek her freedom would have been completely out of character for Sharp. Wheatley and Sharp may have met more than once: on July 21 he gave her a copy of his *Remarks on Several Very Important Prophecies, in Five Parts* (London, 1768). Although *Remarks* is not one of Sharp's anti-slavery texts, it may not have been the only book he gave Wheatley. A slave owner could not have thought of a more dangerous tour guide than Granville Sharp for a slave newly arrived from the colonies.

Wheatley's letter to Wooster looks both back and forward, with her recent manumission after her return to America marking the transition from her opening account of her experience in England to her plans for selling *Poems* in America. Mention of her manumission also marks the point at which she shifts from using the passive to the active voice, from describing herself as the beneficiary of the agency of others to being the agent of her own enlightened self-interest in the publication and distribution of her book. Unless we see the implicit control I think that she reveals in the first paragraph, the tone of her letter appears to shift sharply and inexplicably at its mid-point.

What most likely enables Wheatley to express her agency directly in the second half of the letter is her new status as a free woman, the same status that would have enabled her to publish in the newspapers in March 1774 her most direct attack on slavery and her clearest expression of ethnic consciousness in a letter to Occom from February 11, 1774. But that status, rather than being a gift passively received from her master "at the desire of

my friends in England," may well have been a concession manip-
ulated by Wheatley from Nathaniel Wheatley in exchange for
her promise to return to Boston to care for his mother, her mis-
tress: one promise for another. In this negotiation, Wheatley had
the stronger hand. In England the year after *Somerset*, with her
master's son keen to have her return to Boston, and in the pres-
ence of Sharp and other "friends in England," to whom she
could attribute the idea for her emancipation, and in front of
whom she could insist that her master's son give his word that
she would be freed if she returned, Wheatley could neither
legally nor practically be forced back to the colonies. In effect,
the choice of freedom, the terms, and the place were Wheatley's
to make. On January 28, 1774, John Andrews, a Boston mer-
chant who had just received a copy of Wheatley's *Poems*, wrote
to his friend William Barrell in Philadelphia to tell him that he
had "at last got Phillis's poems in print . . . These don't seem to
be near all her productions. She's an artful jade [young woman],
I believe & intends to have the benefit of another volume."
Events would prove Andrews correct about Wheatley's plans for
future publication. Such an "artful jade" could exploit her legal
as well as entrepreneurial opportunities.

Other artful and trusted American slaves made travel plans
with the recent *Somerset* case in mind. On August 27, 1772, *The
Virginia Gazette* (Williamsburg, Virginia) published a full ac-
count of the Mansfield decision and subsequently reported sev-
eral cases of slaves seeking the promised land of England. By
1773 even illiterate rural slaves were aware of England as a sanc-
tuary. On September 30, 1773, slave owner John Austin Finnie
advertised for two runaway slaves, "a Wench, named AMY, of a
very black Complexion, about 27 Years old," and "a Fellow,
African born, named BACCHUS, about 19 Years of Age, [who]
speaks somewhat broken [English]." Finnie noted that he had
"some Reason to believe they will endeavour to get out of the
Colony, particularly to *Britain*, where they imagine they will be
free (a Notion now too prevalent among the Negroes, greatly to
the Vexation and Prejudice of their Masters)." At least some
white colonists also anticipated the application of the Mansfield
judgment to America. For example, on January 8, 1774, the Loy-

alist Richard Wells wrote anonymously in *The Pennsylvania Packet*, "I contend, that by the laws of the English constitution, and by our *own declarations*, the instant a Negro sets his foot in America, he is as free as if he had landed in England."

Read in light of *Somerset*, several of Wheatley's poems demonstrate a nuanced treatment of slavery. For example, written in October 1772 to celebrate Dartmouth's appointment the previous August, "To the Right Honourable WILLIAM, Earl of Dartmouth, His Majesty's Principal Secretary of State for North America, &c." is one of the most carefully crafted poems in the 1773 volume. In it Wheatley re-appropriates the concept of *slavery* from its common metaphorical use in the colonial rhetoric of discontent, which described any perceived limitation on colonial rights and liberty as an attempt by England to "enslave" (white) Americans. Wheatley appears to use *slavery* in this conventional sense in the poem:

> No more, *America,* in mournful strain
> Of wrongs, and grievance unredress'd complain,
> No longer shall thou dread the iron chain,
> Which wanton *Tyranny* with lawless hand
> Had made, and with it meant t'enslave the land.

But Wheatley's reference to her authority to speak against this conventionally metaphorical slavery reminds her readers of the reality of chattel slavery trivialized by the political metaphor:

> Should you, my lord, while you peruse my song,
> Wonder from whence my love of *Freedom* sprung,
> Whence flow these wishes for the common good,
> By feeling hearts alone best understood,
> I, young in life, by seeming cruel fate
> Was snatch'd from *Afric's* fancy'd happy seat
> . . . .
> Such, such my case. And can I then but pray
> Others may never feel tyrannic sway?

Anticipation of the application of *Somerset* to the colonies would have enabled Wheatley to condemn both metaphorical and real slavery and to see herself as partaking of "the common good." She subtly reminds her readers that physical enslavement has already led to *"Freedom"* in America on the spiritual level. In retrospect, her kidnapping in Africa was an act of only "seeming cruel fate" because she has since discovered that it was a fortunate fall into religious liberation. Thus, *"Afric's* fancy'd happy seat" is "fancy'd" (alive in her imagination) in two senses: *now* (at the time of writing the poem) because *"Afric"* can only be recalled; but also *then* (at the time when she was kidnapped) because she mistook her pagan condition for a state of happiness. Complete *"Freedom"*—political, social, and religious—may be realized and restored by the new political order represented by Dartmouth and the new judicial order represented by *Somerset.*

The doubts Wheatley probably had about the applicability of *Somerset* outside of England may account for the Janus-like ambivalence found in the various versions of "A Farewel to America. To Mrs. S.W.," dated *"May* 7, 1773," and first published in Boston newspapers on May 10, 1773, as Wheatley sailed with her master's son to London. "A Farewel" is prospective as well as retrospective: the first half looks back at her separation from America and her mistress; the second half looks ahead, anticipating the speaker's arrival in England, the restoration of her health, and, I believe, the possibility of the restoration of her freedom. Stanzas VIII–XI express the speaker's increasingly impatient desire to reach London and "Give us the famous town to view."

In the course of the poem, *"Health,"* "Celestial maid of rosy hue" (stanza III), transforms into the image of *"Aurora"*—a figure of resurrection and restoration: her "thousand dyes" are both her colors and her repeated nocturnal deaths—associated in stanza IX with *"London"* and *"Health."* Wheatley's association of England with the recovery and restoration of physical health appears elsewhere in *Poems*: in "To a Gentleman on His Voyage to Great-Britain for the Recovery of His Health" and "Ode to Neptune. On Mrs. W—'s Voyage to England." We do not, however, find in Wheatley's poems a simple dichotomy in which America equals illness and England health: as her poem "To a Lady on her coming to North-America with her Son, for the Recovery of her Health" demonstrates, Philadelphia and Boston are healthier than the West Indies, the diseased heart of the empire and of course the area most dependent upon and associated with slavery, the part of the empire that Equiano calls "this land of bondage." In "To a Lady," Wheatley's "ideal [imagined] view" of "*Jamaica's* fervid shore," where "Each branch, wide-spreading to the ambient sky, / Forgets its verdure, and submits to die," is the negative equivalent to the image of "*Afric's* fancy'd happy seat" found in her poem to Dartmouth.

Read in light of the *Somerset* ruling, the health Wheatley locates in England in "A Farewel to America" becomes social and political as well as physical because in England she will face the opportunity to resurrect herself from the social death of slavery. Legally as well as geographically, England is even further than New England from "*Jamaica's* fervid shore." The speaker in "A Farewel" sees herself as choosing between "*Britannia*" and "*New-England*" in stanza XI, and in the version of "A Farewel" published in *Poems* she expresses a seemingly clear desire to return to America: "To View again her charms divine, / What joy the prospect yields!" But the stanzas that follow indicate possible ambivalence about the attractiveness of America. At the end of the first stanza of the poem, Wheatley slyly plays on the equivocal contemporaneous meanings of the word *tempt* as both *to attempt* and *to lure or solicit to ill* to introduce a tone of ambiguity into the poem:

> ADIEU, *New-England's* smiling meads,
>   Adieu, the flow'ry plain:
> I leave thine op'ning charms, O spring,
>   And tempt the roaring main.

What is the "*Temptation*" that threatens her later in the poem? Is the "thou" addressed in stanza XII "*New-England*?" Does the speaker consider returning to America the equivalent of returning to slavery rather than choosing the self-emancipation available to her in England and thus a temptation to be resisted? As she says in stanza XIII, the choice before her requires a different kind of heroism than that displayed in battle.

Or might the "*Temptation*" be "*Britannia*" and freedom? Was the version of "A Farewel" published "by request" in *The Mas-*

sachusetts Gazette and Boston Post-Boy and Advertiser intended to warn Wheatley's owners that she was aware of the possibility for freedom that would, from her owners' point of view, tempt her not to return to America? Certainly, the speaker's desire to see America again is less enthusiastic in the newspaper version than in the one that appears in *Poems:* "To view again her Charms divine, / One short reluctant Space." Is she regretting the separation itself or its shortness? I do not think that the poem is confused but rather that Wheatley demonstrates her ability to exploit the rhetorical possibilities that ambivalence and ambiguity offered her: to a colonial audience of slave owners, post-*Somerset* England represented temptation to a slave, and "Virtue" (line 52 in the newspaper version) was returning to one's condition as slave; to an enslaved audience and to Wheatley herself, the temptation to be resisted was returning to America, the chance for freedom in England unseized.

Other Wheatley poems also profit from what might be called post-*Somerset* readings. For example, consider the line "Once I redemption neither sought nor knew" from the often discussed religious poem "On Being Brought from AFRICA to AMERICA," probably written in 1768. A post-*Somerset* reading of this line invests it with a previously unrecognized conscious level of authorial agency because, in light of the Mansfield decision, Wheatley's use of "redemption" appears in 1773 to play on the religious and slavery contexts of the word: England promises the possibility of social and physical as well as spiritual redemption. The association of England with the lost freedom of Africa reappears in "Phillis's Reply to the Answer," first published in Boston on December 5, 1774, in the *Royal American Magazine*:

> And pleasing Gambia on my soul returns,
> With native grace in spring's luxuriant reign,
> Smiles the gay mead, and Eden blooms again
>
> . . .
>
>   There, as in Britain's favour'd isle, behold
> The bending harvest ripens into gold!
> Just are thy views of Afric's blissful plain,
> On the warm limits of the land and main.

Wheatley's likely ambivalence about choosing between Boston and London as the site of her anticipated emancipation is understandable. The London alternative must have appeared pretty certain; and in light of recent events, the abolition of slavery in Massachusetts may have seemed imminent, even though it did not actually happen until sometime later (historians disagree about exactly when slavery legally ended in the state). Like England, Wheatley's Massachusetts was a *slave-owning* society, where some slaves could be found, rather than a *slave society*, where slavery was the basis of the economy and social structure, as in the deep South and the West Indies. The Mansfield ruling energized the abolitionist movement in New England that had been developing since the 1760s. While Wheatley was in London, the abolition of slavery was the subject debated at Harvard's commencement, an annual event that in 1767 may have occasioned one of her earliest poems, and slaves in Massachusetts began to petition for their freedom and wages. Moreover, all available evidence indicates that Wheatley's yoke as a favored domestic slave was a light one, virtually that of a free servant. She seems to have had an intimate, nearly familial relationship with her owners. In a letter to her black friend Miss Obour Tanner on March 21, 1774, Wheatley compares the death of her mistress to "the loss of a parent, sister, or brother." To Wheatley, freedom in America among her friends and surrogate family in 1773 probably seemed easily within reach. Ambivalence and caution, however, would explain why Wheatley did not share her hopes with the Countess of Huntingdon in the farewell letter of July 17, 1773, Wheatley wrote her on the eve of her departure for America. Like most people during the period, Huntingdon, who had inherited slaves in Georgia in 1770, did not see slavery and Christianity as necessarily incompatible.

Wheatley was also artful enough to take out an extra insurance policy by sending a copy of her manumission papers to Israel Mauduit, the London agent representing the interests of Massachusetts since 1763, and she is clear in her letter to Wooster about her motives for having done so: "The Instrument is drawn, so as to secure me and my property from the hands of the Execturs [executors], administrators, &c. of my master, & secure whatsoever should be given me as my Own [in case, at the death of her master, any of his heirs tried to claim Wheatley or her possessions as part of his estate, as if she were still a slave]. A Copy is sent to Isra. Mauduit Esq. F.R.S. [Fellow of the Royal Society]." A decade before Wheatley gained her freedom, Equiano had recognized that "[h]itherto I had thought only slavery dreadful; but the state of a free negro appeared to me now equally so at least, and in some respects even worse, for they live in constant alarm for their liberty, which is but nominal. . . ." Wheatley chose the method of emancipation that appeared to grant her the most freedom of movement. She used Mauduit as the equivalent of a safe deposit box for her manumission papers so that she could live legally free as either an African Briton or an African American.

Wheatley returned to America on September 13, 1773, was granted her freedom by October 18, and received the first copies of her book to sell in early January 1774. Having gone to England as an enslaved African Briton, Wheatley returned to the colonies prepared to embrace the free African-American identity the American Revolution would make available to her. As her letter to Occom denouncing slavery indicates, once back in Boston, Wheatley increasingly came to believe that the colonial struggle for freedom from Britain would lead to the end of slavery in the former colonies. Her anti-slavery stance became more overt than in her poems published while she had been enslaved. For example, in the poem "On the Death of General Wooster," included in a letter to Wooster's widow, Mary, on July 15, 1778, Wheatley exclaims, "But how, presumptuous shall we hope to find/Divine acceptance with th'Almighty mind—/While yet (O deed ungenerous!) they disgrace/And hold in bondage Afric's blameless race?" In retrospect, however, subsequent events would render her trip to London and its immediate aftermath the most fortunate period of her life.

Susanna Wheatley died on March 3, 1774. At the end of October 1774, Phillis declined the invitation by the English philanthropist John Thornton to join the African-born men Bristol Yamma and John Quamine as missionaries to Africa. Phillis continued to live in John Wheatley's house until growing hostilities with Britain forced her Loyalist master to leave the city. Phillis apparently moved to Providence, Rhode Island, to live with the former Mary Wheatley, now married to John Lathrop, a minister. The Lathrops had fled Boston some time before May 1775. From Providence, Wheatley sent her panegyrical poem and covering letter dated October 26, 1775, to General George Washington in Cambridge, Massachusetts. Publication of the poem by others in periodicals the following spring kept her name before the public. Before the British evacuated Boston in March 1776, Wheatley may have accepted Washington's invitation to visit him: "[i]f you should ever come to Cambridge, or near Head Quarters, I shall be happy to see a person so favoured by the Muses, and to whom Nature has been so liberal and beneficent in her dispensations." By December 1776 she was back in Boston, where she composed another patriotic panegyric, to General Charles Lee, but the poem remained unpublished until 1863. Wheatley published no more poems between December 1774 and January 1784, when she celebrated the formal end of the American Revolution with *Liberty and Peace, A Poem*.

But events in Wheatley's personal life gave her little reason for celebration. By 1778 nearly half of the dignitaries who had signed the "Attestation" to her *Poems* were dead. In March 1778 John Wheatley died, leaving Phillis nothing in his estate; Mary Wheatley Lathrop died in September 1778; Nathaniel Wheatley was still in London, where he would die in 1783. Struggling to make a living on her own by selling copies of *Poems*, Phillis married John Peters, a free black, on April 1, 1778, and used his surname thereafter. Each week between October 30 and December 18, 1779, she published proposals for a second volume of poems, with letters, in the *Boston Evening Post and General Advertiser*, without success. Although probably written before her marriage, her last known published poem appeared in the September 1784 issue of *The Boston Magazine*, with her final unsuccessful attempt to find support for a second volume. What appears to have been an initially financially sound marriage soon deteriorated for reasons that remain somewhat mysterious. All we know about Peters is that he changed occupations frequently, was often in debt, and seems to have been rather conceited. John and Phillis had three children, all of whom died very early, the last dying with Phillis on Sunday, December 5, 1784. On December 8, mother and daughter were buried together in an unmarked grave. John sold his late wife's manuscripts and books to cover his debts. The first American edition of her *Poems* was not published until 1786, in Philadelphia.

Had she remained in London in 1773, Wheatley very probably would have found a publisher for her second volume. Interest in her work and her status as a woman writer of color certainly continued after her departure. The celebrity she maintained in England gave her what we today might call cultural capital. For example, an anonymous satirist in the London newspaper *The Public Advertiser* during the summer of 1777 includes her in (presumably) his attacks on contemporaneous literary women such as Hannah More and Catherine Macaulay. The satirist assumes that Wheatley is as familiar to his readers as the English members of the so-called Blue Stocking Circle of literary ladies. In the July 14 issue, a fictional "Phillis Wheatley" responds to this "*white-faced* (I might have added *white-livered*) Enemy of modern *Poetesses*" on behalf of her fellow writers. She threatens, "It will . . . be a *black Affair* for him if (to use a Sea Phrase) he comes under my Lee; for I will have no Mercy on a Man who *stands up* against me on that Score." She assures him "that I am a Match for any Literary Male in the Kingdom." The sexual subtext becomes even more explicit in his July 23 ironic "Palinode to *Phillis Wheatley*," in which he addresses her as the "Poetic Queen of parch'd WHIDAW [an area on the slave coast of Africa]!" Repeatedly during the 1780s, her poetry was reprinted in London in John Wesley's *Arminian Magazine*, and "An Elegy on Leaving—," perhaps the last poem she composed, first appeared in the July 1784 issue of that periodical.

The literary quality of Wheatley's poetry, usually in combination with that of Sancho's *Letters*, was frequently cited by opponents of slavery and the slave trade, especially in Britain, as evidence of the humanity and inherent equality of Africans. Such citations began the development of the canon of authors of African descent writing in the English language. For example, in his *Essays Historical and Moral* (London, 1785), George Gregory sees Wheatley's poems and Sancho's letters as "striking instances of genius contending against every disadvantage, resulting from want of encouragement, and of early cultivation." Thomas Clarkson, a leading abolitionist, says of Wheatley, in *An Essay on the Slavery and Commerce of the Human Species, Particularly the African* (London, 1786), "if the authoress *was designed for slavery,* . . . the greater part of the inhabitants of Britain must lose their claim to freedom." In support of his position, Clarkson quotes liberally from her *Poems.* Not only abolitionists acknowledged the merit of some black writers, as John Gabriel Stedman demonstrates in his *Narrative of a Five Years Expedition against the Revolted Negroes of Surinam* (London, 1796):

> That these people are neither divested of a good ear, nor poetical genius, has been frequently proved, when they had the advantage of a good education. Amongst others, *Phillis Wheatley,* who was a slave at *Boston* in New England, learned the Latin language, and wrote thirty-eight elegant pieces of poetry on different subjects, which were published in 1773.

Even those who denied the achievement of black writers implicitly acknowledged the developing black canon by disputing the quality of the authors' literary productions. This sort of negative recognition is most notoriously expressed by Thomas Jefferson in his *Notes on the State of Virginia* (London, 1787), Query XIV:

> Among the blacks is misery enough, God knows, but no poetry. Love is the peculiar oestrum [inspiration] of the poet. Their love is ardent, but it kindles the senses only, not the imagination. Religion indeed has produced a Phillis Whately [*sic*]; but it could not produce a poet. The compositions composed under her name are below the dignity of criticism. The heroes of the Dunciad are to her, as Hercules to the author of that poem. [Rather than intentionally misspelling Wheatley's name, Jefferson was probably correctly spelling it phonetically from memory: during the eighteenth century the words *eat* and *ate* were both pronounced as we now pronounce *ate*, and when Jefferson was writing *Notes* in

France, he most likely did not have with him his copy of Wheatley's *Poems*, now in the Library of Congress. The "heroes" of Alexander Pope's satiric mock-epic *Dunciad*, published in London initially in 1728 and expanded in 1743, are the bad writers he targets. Unlike Hercules, Pope was hunch-backed, very thin, and less than five feet tall.]

The American Gilbert Imlay was one of the first to answer Jefferson's attack on Wheatley in his *A Topographical Description of the Western Territory of North America* (New York, 1793):

> I will transcribe part of her Poem on Imagination, and leave you to judge whether it is poetical or not. It will afford you an opportunity, if you have never met with it, of estimating her genius and Mr. Jefferson's judgment; and I think, without any disparagement to him, that by comparison, Phillis appears much the superior. Indeed, I should be glad to be informed what white upon this continent has written more beautiful lines.

Wheatley's poetry continued to be used by ante-bellum American abolitionists as evidence for the humanity, equality, and literary talents of African Americans. At the beginning of the twenty-first century, her place in the developing tradition of early transatlantic literature by people of African descent, and her role as the mother of African-American literature are secure. The prophecy the pseudonymous "Matilda" offered in "On Reading the Poems of Phillis Wheatley, the African Poetess" (*New York Magazine*, October 1796) has been realized:

> A PHILLIS rises, and the world no more
> Denies the sacred right to mental pow'r;
> While, Heav'n-inspir'd, she proves *her Country's* claim
> To Freedom, and *her own* to deathless Fame.

SUGGESTIONS FOR FURTHER READING

EDITIONS

Mason, Julian D., Jr., ed. *The Poems of Phillis Wheatley*. Chapel Hill: University of North Carolina Press, 1966. Revised and enlarged, 1989. Includes Wheatley's prose works.

Robinson, William H. *Phillis Wheatley and Her Writings*. New York: Garland, 1984.

Shields, John C. *The Collected Works of Phillis Wheatley*. New York: Oxford University Press, 1988.

CRITICISM AND SCHOLARSHIP

Akers, Charles. " 'Our Modern Egyptians': Phillis Wheatley and the Whig Campaign Against Slavery in Revolutionary Boston." *Journal of Negro History* 60, 1975.

Baker, Houston A., Jr. *The Journey Back: Issues in Black Literature and Criticism*. Chicago: University of Chicago Press, 1980.

———. *Workings of the Spirit: The Poetics of Afro-American Women's Writing*. Chicago: University of Chicago Press, 1991.

Connor, Kimberly Rae. *Conversions and Visions in the Writings of African-American Women*. Knoxville: University of Tennessee Press, 1994.

Erkkila, Betsy. "Phillis Wheatley and the Black American Revolution," in *A Mixed Race: Ethnicity in Early America*, edited by Frank Shuffleton. New York: Oxford University Press, 1993.

Foster, Frances Smith. *Written by Herself: Literary Production by African-American Women, 1746–1892*. Bloomington: Indiana University Press, 1993.

Gates, Henry Louis, Jr. *Figures in Black: Words, Signs, and the "Racial" Self*. New York: Oxford University Press, 1987.

———. *The Signifying Monkey: A Theory of African-American Literary Criticism*. New York: Oxford University Press, 1988.

Grimsted, David. "Anglo-American Racism and Phillis Wheatley's 'Sable Veil,' 'Length'ned Chain,' and 'Knitted Heart,' " in *Women in the Age of the American Revolution*, edited by Ronald Hoffman and Peter J. Albert. Charlottesville: University of Virginia Press, 1989.

Isani, Mukhtar Ali. " 'Gambia on My Soul': Africa and the African in the Writings of Phillis Wheatley." *MELUS* 6 (1979).

Johnson, Barbara E. "Euphemism, Understatement, and the Passive Voice: A Genealogy of Afro-American Poetry," in *Reading Black, Reading Feminist: A Critical Anthology*, edited by Henry Louis Gates, Jr. New York: Meridian, 1990.

Kendrick, Robert. "Other Questions: Phillis Wheatley and the Ethics of Interpretation." *Cultural Critique* 38 (1998).

Mason, Julian. " 'Ocean': A New Poem by Phillis Wheatley." *Early American Literature* 34, 1999.

Nott, Walt. "From 'Uncultivated Barbarian' to 'Poetical Genius': The Public Presence of Phillis Wheatley." *MELUS* 18 (1993).

O'Neale, Sondra. "A Slave's Subtle War: Phillis Wheatley's Use of Biblical Myth and Symbol." *Early American Literature* 21 (1986).

Richards, Phillip M. "Phillis Wheatley and Literary Americanization." *American Quarterly* 44 (1992).

Richmond, Merle. *Bid the Vassal Soar*. Washington, D.C.: Howard University Press, 1974.

Robinson, William H. *Critical Essays on Phillis Wheatley*. Boston: Hall, 1982.

Scheick, William J. "Subjection and Prophecy in Phillis Wheatley's Verse Paraphrases of Scripture." *College Literature* 22 (1995).

Shuffleton, Frank. "Phillis Wheatley, the Aesthetic, and the Form of Life," in *Studies in Eighteenth-Century Culture* 26, edited by Syndy M. Conger and Julie C. Hayes. Baltimore: Johns Hopkins University Press, 1998.

————. "On Her Own Footing: Phillis Wheatley in Freedom," in *"Genius in Bondage": A Critical Anthology of the Literature of the Early Black Atlantic*, edited by Vincent Carretta and Philip Gould. Lexington: University Press of Kentucky, 2001.

Smith, Cynthia J. " 'To Maecenas': Phillis Wheatley's Invocation of an Idealized Reader." *Black American Literature Forum* 23, 1989.

Watson, Marcia. "A Classic Case: Phillis Wheatley and Her Poetry." *Early American Literature* 31, 1996.

Wilcox, Kirstin. "The Body into Print: Marketing Phillis Wheatley." *American Literature* 71, 1999.

Willard, Carla. "Wheatley's Turns of Praise: Heroic Entrapment and the Paradox of Revolution." *American Literature* 67, 1995.

A NOTE ON MONEY

Before 1971, when the British monetary system was decimalized, British money was counted in pounds sterling (£), shillings (s.), pence, or pennies (d.), and farthings. One pound sterling = 20 shillings; 5 shillings = 1 crown; 1 shilling = 12 pennies; 1 farthing = ¼ pence. One guinea = 21 shillings. (The coin was so named because the gold from which it was made came from the Gold Coast of Africa and because the coin was first struck to celebrate the founding in 1663 of the slave-trading monopoly the Royal Adventurers into Africa.

Each colony issued its own local paper currency, and a colonial pound was worth less than a pound sterling, with the conversion rates for the currencies of the various colonies fluctuating throughout the eighteenth century. The price of Wheatley's 1772 volume was advertized in pounds sterling. In 1774, 135 Massachusetts pounds equalled 100 pounds sterling in value. After the onset of hostilities the value of a Massachusetts pound depreciated rapidly. Between January 1777 and December 1779, when Wheatley sought subscribers for her proposed second volume of works, the value of a Massachusetts pound depreciated nearly thirtyfold. But even at that rate of depreciation, adjusted for inflation, the price in Massachusetts pounds asked by John Peters for Phillis's proposed second volume was still approximately three times the value in pounds sterling asked for her 1772 volume.

ACKNOWLEDGMENTS

My greatest debts are to the textual work and research of the excellent editors of Phillis Wheatley's works who have gone before me: William H. Robinson, John C. Shields, and Julian D. Mason, Jr. I am especially grateful to Professor Mason for his generous advice and encouragement and for bringing to my attention the newly discovered "Hymn to Humanity" variant at Emory University; to Joseph F. Marcy, Jr., for telling me of the new Wheatley variant poems at Dartmouth College; to William W. Cook for information on and photocopies of the Dartmouth variants; to Randall K. Burkett and Philip N. Cronenwett for conversations and correspondence regarding Wheatley variants at, respectively, Emory University and Dartmouth College; to Ruth Holmes Whitehead and Garry Shutak for, respectively, making known to me and making available to me the references to Phillis Wheatley in the *Nova Scotia Gazette* and the *Weekly Chronicle* in the collections of the Nova Scotia Archives and Records Management.

I am also very grateful to the following people and institutions for permission to reproduce transcriptions of Phillis Wheatley's manuscripts and published poems used in this edition:

"To the University of Cambridge, Wrote in 1767" and "On the Death of the Rev'd Dr. Sewall. 1769," reproduced courtesy, American Antiquarian Society.

Wheatley's May 6, 1774 letter to Samuel Hopkins (Ch A.6.20), reproduced by courtesy of the Trustees of the Boston Public Library.

"[On the Capture of General Lee]." Miscellaneous Manuscripts [M194]. Special Collections and Archives, Bowdoin College Library.

"On the Decease of the Rev'd Dr. Sewell"; Wheatley's October 25, 1770, June 27, 1773, and July 17, 1773 letters to the Countess of Huntingdon. Reproduced by permission from the Papers of the Countess of Huntingdon, the Cheshunt Foundation, Westminster College, Cambridge, United Kingdom.

"To the Rev. Mr. Pitkin, on the Death of his Lady" and "On the Death of Dr. Samuel Marshall." The Connecticut Historical Society.

"On the Decease of the Revd Doctr Sewall" and "A Poem on the death of Charles Eliot aged 12 months," by permission of the Dartmouth College Library.

"Hymn to Humanity To S.P. Galloway Esq: who corrected some Poetic Essays of the Authoress" and "The Voice of Freedom," by permission of the Special Collections Department, Robert W. Woodruff Library, Emory University.

Wheatley's May 19, 1772 manuscript letter to Arbour Tanner, reproduced from the Charles Roberts Autograph Collection, Haverford College Library.

Wheatley's manuscript February 9, 1774 letter to Samuel Hopkins, and Wheatley's manuscript poem "To the King's Most Excellent Majesty," by permission of The Historical Society of Pennsylvania.

"A Poem on the Death of Charles Eliot," by permission of the Houghton Library, Harvard University.

Wheatley's broadside poem *An Ode of Verses on the Death of George Whitefield* (RB 41245), by permission of The Huntington Library.

Poems on Various Subjects, Religious and Moral (London, 1773), courtesy, Library of Congress.

"Atheism," "Deism," "America," "To the Hon.ble Commodore Hood," "On the Death of Mr. Snider," and "On Atheism," by permission of The Library Company of Philadelphia.

"An Address to the Atheist" (1767, Ms. N-25, Phillis Wheatley Papers), "An Address to the Deist" (1767, Ms. N-25, Phillis Wheatley Papers), "Atheism" (July 1769, Ms. N-25, Phillis Wheatley Papers), "A Poem on the Death of Charles Eliot" (1772, Ms. N-25, Phillis Wheatley Papers), and "An Elegy Sacred to the Memory of the Revd. Samuel Cooper D.D." (1784, Smith-Carter Papers); as well as Wheatley's manuscript October 18,

1773 letter to David Worcester [Wooster] (Ms. N-25, Phillis Wheatley Papers), her July 15 letter to Mary Wooster (Ms. N-25, Phillis Wheatley Papers), and Wheatley's July 19, 1772, October 30, 1773, March 21, 1774, May 6, 1774, May 29, 1778, and May 10, 1779 letters to Obour (Arbour) Tanner (Miscellaneous Bound Collection); and Wheatley's published *An Elegy to Miss. Mary Moorhead* and *An Elegy Sacred to the Memory of . . . Dr. Samuel Cooper*, by permission of the Massachusetts Historical Society.

"Ocean," Courtesy of The Mark E. Mitchell Collection of African-American History.

Wheatley's April 21, 1772, December 1, 1773, March 29, 1774, and October 30, 1770 [1774] letters to John Thornton, in the Scottish Record Office (GD26/13/663), Edinburgh, are reproduced by permission of their owner, the Earl of Leven and Melville.

"To the Right Honl. William Earl of Dartmouth," and Wheatley's October 10, 1772 letter to Lord Dartmouth. Staffordshire & Stoke on Trent Archive Service, Staffordshire Record Office, Stafford, United Kingdom.

POEMS ON VARIOUS SUBJECTS,
RELIGIOUS AND MORAL

Entered at Stationer's Hall

DEDICATION.

To the Right Honourable the

COUNTESS OF HUNTINGDON,

THE FOLLOWING

POEMS

Are most respectfully

Inscribed,

By her much obliged,

Very humble,

And devoted Servant,

Phillis Wheatley.

Boston, June 12,
1773.

PREFACE

THE following Poems were written originally for the Amusement of the Author, as they were the Products of her leisure Moments. She had no Intention ever to have published them; nor would they now have made their Appearance, but at the Importunity of many of her best, and most generous Friends; to whom she considers herself, as under the greatest Obligations.

As her Attempts in Poetry are now sent into the World, it is hoped the Critic will not severely censure their Defects; and we presume they will have too much Merit to be cast aside with Contempt, as worthless and trifling Effusions.

As to the Disadvantages she has laboured under, with Regard to Learning, nothing needs to be offered, as her Master's Letter in the following Page will sufficiently shew the Difficulties in this Respect she had to encounter.

With all their Imperfections, the Poems are now humbly submitted to the Perusal of the Public.

The following is a Copy of a LETTER sent by
the Author's Master to the Publisher.

PHILLIS was brought from *Africa* to *America*, in the Year
1761, between Seven and Eight Years of age. Without any Assistance from School Education, and by only what she was taught
in the Family, she, in sixteen Months Time from her arrival, attained the English Language, to which she was an utter Stranger
before, to such a Degree, as to read any, the most difficult Parts
of the Sacred Writings, to the great Astonishment of all who
heard her.

As to her WRITING, her own curiosity led her to it; and this
she learnt in so short a Time, that in the Year 1765, she wrote a
Letter to the Rev. Mr. OCCOM, the *Indian* Minister, while in
England.

She has a great Inclination to learn the Latin Tongue, and has
made some Progress in it. This Relation is given by her Master
who bought her, and with whom she now lives.

JOHN WHEATLEY.
Boston, Nov. 14, 1772.

To the PUBLICK.

AS it has been repeatedly suggested to the Publisher, by Persons, who have seen the Manuscript, that Numbers would be ready to suspect they were not really the Writings of PHILLIS, he has procured the following Attestation, from the most respectable Characters in *Boston*, that none might have the least Ground for disputing their *Original*.

WE whose Names are under-written, do assure the World, that the POEMS specified in the following Page,* were (as we verily believe) written by PHILLIS, a young Negro Girl, who was but a few Years since, brought an uncultivated Barbarian from *Africa*, and has ever since been, and now is, under the Disadvantage of serving as a Slave in a Family in this Town. She has been examined by some of the best Judges, and is thought qualified to write them.

His Excellency THOMAS HUTCHINSON, *Governor*,
The Hon. ANDREW OLIVER, *Lieutenant-Governor*.

The Hon. Thomas Hubbard,	*The Rev.* Charles Cheuney, *D.D.*
The Hon. John Erving,	*The Rev.* Mather Byles, *D.D.*
The Hon. James Pitts,	*The Rev.* Ed. Pemberton, *D.D.*
The Hon. Harrison Gray,	*The Rev.* Andrew Elliot, *D.D.*
The Hon. James Bowdoin,	*The Rev.* Samuel Cooper, *D.D.*
John Hancock, *Esq*;	*The Rev.* Samuel Mather, *D.D.*
Joseph Green, *Esq*;	*The Rev.* Mr. John Moorhead, *D.D.*
Richard Carey, *Esq*;	Mr. John Wheatley, *her Master.*

N.B. The original Attestation, signed by the above Gentlemen, may be seen by applying to *Archibald Bell* Bookseller, No. 8, *Aldgate-Street.*

*The Words *"following Page"* allude to the Contents of the Manuscript Copy, which are wrote at the Back of the above Attestation.

POEMS

ON

VARIOUS SUBJECTS.

To MAECENAS.

MAECENAS, you, beneath the myrtle shade,
Read o'er what poets sung, and shepherds play'd.
What felt those poets but you feel the same?
Does not your soul possess the sacred flame?
5   Their noble strains your equal genius shares
In softer language, and diviner airs.

While *Homer* paints lo! circumfus'd in air,
Celestial Gods in mortal forms appear;
Swift as they move hear each recess rebound,
10   Heav'n quakes, earth trembles, and the shores resound.
Great Sire of verse, before my mortal eyes,
The lightnings blaze across the vaulted skies,
And, as the thunder shakes the heav'nly plains,
A deep-felt horror thrills through all my veins.
15   When gentler strains demand thy graceful song,
The length'ning line moves languishing along.
When great *Patroclus* courts *Achilles'* aid,
The grateful tribute of my tears is paid;
Prone on the shore he feels the pangs of love,
20   And stern *Pelides* tend'rest passions move.

Great *Maro*'s strain in heav'nly numbers flows,
The *Nine* inspire, and all the bosom glows.
O could I rival thine and *Virgil*'s page,

9

Or claim the *Muses* with the *Mantuan* Sage;
25 Soon the same beauties should my mind adorn,
And the same ardors in my soul should burn:
Then should my song in bolder notes arise,
And all my numbers pleasingly surprize;
But here I sit, and mourn a grov'ling mind
30 That fain would mount, and ride upon the wind.

Not you, my friend, these plaintive strains become,
Not you, whose bosom is the *Muses* home;
When they from tow'ring *Helicon* retire,
They fan in you the bright immortal fire,
35 But I less happy, cannot raise the song,
The fault'ring music dies upon my tongue.

The happier *Terence** all the choir inspir'd,
His soul replenish'd, and his bosom fir'd;
But say, ye *Muses*, why this partial grace,
40 To one alone of *Afric*'s sable race;
From age to age transmitting thus his name
With the first glory in the rolls of fame?

Thy virtues, great *Maecenas*! shall be sung
In praise of him, from whom those virtues sprung:
45 While blooming wreaths around thy temples spread,
I'll snatch a laurel from thine honour'd head,
While you indulgent smile upon the deed.

As long as *Thames* in streams majestic flows,
Or *Naiads* in their oozy beds repose,
50 While *Phoebus* reigns above the starry train,
While bright *Aurora* purples o'er the main,
So long, great Sir, the muse thy praise shall sing,
So long thy praise shall make *Parnassus* ring:
Then grant, *Maecenas*, thy paternal rays,
55 Hear me propitious, and defend my lays.

*He was *African* by birth.

On VIRTUE.

O Thou bright jewel in my aim I strive
To comprehend thee. Thine own words declare
Wisdom is higher than a fool can reach.
I cease to wonder, and no more attempt
5   Thine height t'explore, or fathom thy profound.
But, O my soul, sink not into despair,
Virtue is near thee, and with gentle hand
Would now embrace thee, hovers o'er thine head.
Fain would the heav'n-born soul with her converse,
10 Then seek, then court her for her promis'd bliss.

Auspicious queen, thine heav'nly pinions spread,
And lead celestial *Chastity* along;
Lo! now her sacred retinue descends,
Array'd in glory from the orbs above.
15 Attend me, *Virtue*, thro' my youthful years!
O leave me not to the false joys of time!
But guide my steps to endless life and bliss.
Greatness, or *Goodness*, say what I shall call thee,
To give an higher appellation still,
20 Teach me a better strain, a nobler lay,
O Thou, enthron'd with Cherubs in the realms of day!

To the University of CAMBRIDGE, in NEW-ENGLAND.

WHILE an intrinsic ardor prompts to write,
The muses promise to assist my pen;
'Twas not long since I left my native shore
The land of errors, and *Egyptian* gloom:
5 Father of mercy, 'twas thy gracious hand
Brought me in safety from those dark abodes.

Students, to you 'tis giv'n to scan the heights
Above, to traverse the ethereal space,

And mark the systems of revolving worlds.
10 Still more, ye sons of science ye receive
The blissful news by messengers from heav'n,
How *Jesus'* blood for your redemption flows.
See him with hands out-stretcht upon the cross;
Immense compassion in his bosom glows;
15 He hears revilers, nor resents their scorn:
What matchless mercy in the Son of God!
When the whole human race by sin had fall'n,
He deign'd to die that they might rise again,
And share with him in the sublimest skies,
20 Life without death, and glory without end.

Improve your privileges while they stay,
Ye pupils, and each hour redeem, that bears
Or good or bad report of you to heav'n.
Let sin, that baneful evil to the soul,
25 By you be shunn'd, nor once remit your guard;
Suppress the deadly serpent in its egg.
Ye blooming plants of human race divine,
An *Ethiop* tells you 'tis your greatest foe;
Its transient sweetness turns to endless pain,
30 And in immense perdition sinks the soul.

To the KING's Most Excellent Majesty. 1768.

YOUR subjects hope, dread Sire—
The crown upon your brows may flourish long,
And that your arm may in your God be strong!
O may your sceptre num'rous nations sway,
5   And all with love and readiness obey!

But how shall we the *British* king reward!
Rule thou in peace, our father, and our lord!
Midst the remembrance of thy favours past,
The meanest peasants most admire the last.*

10   May *George*, belov'd by all the nations round,
      Live with heav'ns choicest constant blessings crown'd!
      Great God, direct, and guard him from on high,
      And from his head let ev'ry evil fly!
      And may each clime with equal gladness see
15   A monarch's smile can set his subjects free!

*The Repeal of the Stamp Act.

On being brought from AFRICA to AMERICA.

            'TWAS mercy brought me from my *Pagan* land,
      Taught my benighted soul to understand
      That there's a God, that there's a *Saviour* too:
      Once I redemption neither sought nor knew.
5   Some view our sable race with scornful eye,
      "Their colour is a diabolic die."
      Remember, *Christians*, *Negros*, black as *Cain*,
      May be refin'd, and join th' angelic train.

On the Death of the Rev. Dr. SEWELL. 1769.

            ERE yet the morn its lovely blushes spread,
      See *Sewell* number'd with the happy dead.
      Hail, holy man, arriv'd th' immortal shore,
      Though we shall hear thy warning voice no more.
5   Come, let us all behold with wishful eyes
      The saint ascending to his native skies;
      From hence the prophet wing'd his rapt'rous way
      To the blest mansions in eternal day.
      Then begging for the Spirit of our God,
10   And panting eager for the same abode,
      Come, let us all with the same vigour rise,
      And take a prospect of the blissful skies;

While on our minds *Christ's* image is imprest,
And the dear Saviour glows in ev'ry breast,
Thrice happy saint! to find thy heav'n at last,
What compensation for the evils past!

    Great God, incomprehensible, unknown
By sense, we bow at thine exalted throne.
O, while we beg thine excellence to feel,
Thy sacred Spirit to our hearts reveal,
And give us of that mercy to partake,
Which thou hast promis'd for the *Saviour's* sake!

    "*Sewell* is dead." Swift-pinion'd *Fame* thus cry'd.
"Is *Sewell* dead," my trembling tongue reply'd,
O what a blessing in his flight deny'd!
How oft for us the holy prophet pray'd!
How oft to us the Word of Life convey'd!
By duty urg'd my mournful verse to close,
I for his tomb this epitaph compose.

    "Lo, here a Man, redeem'd by *Jesus'* blood,
A sinner once, but now a saint with God;
Behold ye rich, ye poor, ye fools, ye wise,
Nor let his monument your heart surprize;
'Twill tell you what this holy man has done,
Which gives him brighter lustre than the sun.
Listen, ye happy, from your seats above.
I speak sincerely, while I speak and love,
He sought the paths of piety and truth,
By these made happy from his early youth!
In blooming years that grace divine he felt,
Which rescues sinners from the chains of guilt.
Mourn him, ye indigent, whom he has fed,
And henceforth seek, like him, for living bread;
Ev'n *Christ*, the bread descending from above,
And ask an int'rest in his saving love.
Mourn him, ye youth, to whom he oft has told
God's gracious wonders from the times of old.
I, too have cause this mighty loss to mourn,

15

20

25

30

35

40

45

For he my monitor will not return.
50   O when shall we to his blest state arrive?
When the same graces in our bosoms thrive."

On the Death of the Rev. Mr. GEORGE WHITEFIELD. 1770.

    HAIL, happy saint, on thine immortal throne,
Possest of glory, life, and bliss unknown;
We hear no more the music of thy tongue,
Thy wonted auditories cease to throng.
5   Thy sermons in unequall'd accents flow'd,
And ev'ry bosom with devotion glow'd;
Thou didst in strains of eloquence refin'd
Inflame the heart, and captivate the mind.
Unhappy we the setting sun deplore,
10   So glorious once, but ah! it shines no more.

    Behold the prophet in his tow'ring flight!
He leaves the earth for heav'n's unmeasur'd height,
And worlds unknown receive him from our sight.
There *Whitefield* wings with rapid course his way,
15   And sails to *Zion* through vast seas of day.
Thy pray'rs, great saint, and thine incessant cries
Have pierc'd the bosom of thy native skies.
Thou moon hast seen, and all the stars of light,
How he has wrestled with his God by night.
20   He pray'd that grace in ev'ry heart might dwell,
He long'd to see *America* excel;
He charg'd its youth that ev'ry grace divine
Should with full lustre in their conduct shine;
That Saviour, which his soul did first receive,
25   The greatest gift that ev'n a God can give,
He freely offer'd to the num'rous throng,
That on his lips with list'ning pleasure hung.

    "Take him, ye wretched, for your only good,
Take him ye starving sinners, for your food;

30   Ye thirsty, come to this life-giving stream,
      Ye preachers, take him for your joyful theme;
      Take him my dear *Americans*, he said,
      Be your complaints on his kind bosom laid:
      Take him, ye *Africans*, he longs for you,
35   *Impartial Saviour* is his title due:
      Wash'd in the fountain of redeeming blood,
      You shall be sons, and kings, and priests to God."

           Great *Countess*,* we *Americans* revere
      Thy name, and mingle in thy grief sincere;
40   *New England* deeply feels, the *Orphans* mourn,
      Their more than father will no more return.

           But, though arrested by the hand of death,
      Whitefield no more exerts his lab'ring breath,
      Yet let us view him in th' eternal skies,
45   Let ev'ry heart to this bright vision rise;
      While the tomb safe retains its sacred trust,
      Till life divine re-animates his dust.

*The Countess of *Huntingdon*, to whom Mr. *Whitefield* was Chaplain.

On the Death of a young Lady of Five Years of Age.

           FROM dark abodes to fair etherial light
      Th' enraptur'd innocent has wing'd her flight;
      On the kind bosom of eternal love
      She finds unknown beatitude above.
5   This know, ye parents, nor her loss deplore,
      She feels the iron hand of pain no more;
      The dispensations of unerring grace,
      Should turn your sorrows into grateful praise;
      Let then no tears for her henceforward flow,
10   No more distress'd in our dark vale below.

Her morning sun, which rose divinely bright,
Was quickly mantled with the gloom of night;
But hear in heav'n's blest bow'rs your *Nancy* fair,
And learn to imitate her language there.
15   "Thou, Lord, whom I behold with glory crown'd,
By what sweet name, and in what tuneful sound
Wilt thou be prais'd? Seraphic pow'rs are faint
Infinite love and majesty to paint.
To thee let all their grateful voices raise,
20   And saints and angels join their songs of praise."

Perfect in bliss she from her heav'nly home
Looks down, and smiling beckons you to come;
Why then, fond parents, why these fruitless groans?
Restrain your tears, and cease your plaintive moans.
25   Freed from a world of sin, and snares, and pain,
Why would you wish your daughter back again?
No—bow resign'd. Let hope your grief control,
And check the rising tumult of the soul.
Calm in the prosperous, and adverse day,
30   Adore the God who gives and takes away;
Eye him in all, his holy name revere,
Upright your actions, and your hearts sincere,
Till having sail'd through life's tempestuous sea,
And from its rocks, and boist'rous billows free,
35   Yourselves, safe landed on the blissful shore,
Shall join your happy babe to part no more.

On the Death of a young Gentleman.

WHO taught thee conflict with the pow'rs of night,
To vanquish Satan in the fields of fight?
Who strung thy feeble arms with might unknown,
How great thy conquest, and how bright thy crown!
5   War with each princedom, throne, and pow'r is o'er.
The scene is ended to return no more.

O could my muse thy seat on high behold,
How deckt with laurel, how enrich'd with gold!
O could she hear what praise thine harp employs,
How sweet thine anthems, how divine thy joys!
What heav'nly grandeur should exalt her strain!
What holy raptures in her numbers reign!
To sooth the troubles of the mind to peace,
To still the tumult of life's tossing seas,
To ease the anguish of the parents heart,
What shall my sympathizing verse impart?
Where is the balm to heal so deep a wound?
Where shall a sov'reign remedy be found?
Look, gracious Spirit, from thine heav'nly bow'r,
And thy full joys into their bosoms pour;
The raging tempest of their grief control,
And spread the dawn of glory through the soul,
To eye the path the saint departed trod,
And trace him to the bosom of his God.

To a Lady on the Death of her Husband.

GRIM monarch! see, depriv'd of vital breath,
A young physician in the dust of death:
Dost thou go on incessant to destroy,
Our griefs to double, and lay waste our joy?
Enough thou never yet wast known to say,
Though millions die, the vassals of thy sway:
Nor youth, nor science, nor the ties of love,
Nor aught on earth thy flinty heart can move.
The friend, the spouse from his dire dart to save,
In vain we ask the sovereign of the grave.
Fair mourner, there see thy lov'd *Leonard* laid,
And o'er him spread the deep impervious shade;
Clos'd are his eyes, and heavy fetters keep
His senses bound in never-waking sleep,
Till time shall cease, till many a starry world

Shall fall from heav'n, in dire confusion hurl'd,
Till nature in her final wreck shall lie,
And her last groan shall rend the azure sky:
Not, not till then his active soul shall claim
20   His body, a divine immortal frame.

But see the softly-stealing tears apace
Pursue each other down the mourner's face;
But cease thy tears, bid ev'ry sigh depart,
And cast the load of anguish from thine heart:
25   From the cold shell of his great soul arise,
And look beyond, thou native of the skies;
There fix thy view, where fleeter than the wind
Thy *Leonard* mounts, and leaves the earth behind.
Thyself prepare to pass the vale of night
30   To join for ever on the hills of light:
To thine embrace his joyful spirit moves
To thee, the partner of his earthly loves;
He welcomes thee to pleasures more refin'd,
And better suited to th' immortal mind.

GOLIATH of GATH.
1 Sam. Chap. xvii.

YE martial pow'rs, and all ye tuneful nine,
Inspire my song, and aid my high design.
The dreadful scenes and toils of war I write,
The ardent warriors, and the fields of fight:
5   You best remember, and you best can sing
The acts of heroes to the vocal string:
Resume the lays with which your sacred lyre,
Did then the poet and the sage inspire.

Now front to front the armies were display'd,
10   Here *Israel* rang'd, and there the foes array'd;
The hosts on two opposing mountains stood,

Thick as the foliage of the waving wood;
Between them an extensive valley lay,
O'er which the gleaming armour pour'd the day,
15   When from the camp of the *Philistine* foes,
Dreadful to view, a mighty warrior rose;
In the dire deeds of bleeding battle skill'd,
The monster stalks the terror of the field.
From *Gath* he sprung, *Goliath* was his name,
20   Of fierce deportment, and gigantic frame:
A brazen helmet on his head was plac'd,
A coat of mail his form terrific grac'd,
The greaves his legs, the targe his shoulders prest:
Dreadful in arms high-tow'ring o'er the rest
25   A spear he proudly wav'd, whose iron head,
Strange to relate, six hundred shekels weigh'd;
He strode along, and shook the ample field,
While *Phoebus* blaz'd refulgent on his shield:
Through *Jacob's* race a chilling horror ran,
30   When thus the huge, enormous chief began:

"Say, what the cause that in this proud array
You set your battle in the face of day?
One hero find in all your vaunting train,
Then see who loses, and who wins the plain;
35   For he who wins, in triumph may demand
Perpetual service from the vanquish'd land:
Your armies I defy, your force despise,
By far inferior in *Philistia's* eyes:
Produce a man, and let us try the fight,
40   Decide the contest, and the victor's right."

Thus challeng'd he: all *Israel* stood amaz'd,
And ev'ry chief in consternation gaz'd;
But *Jesse's* son in youthful bloom appears,
And warlike courage far beyond his years:
45   He left the folds, he left the flow'ry meads,
And soft recesses of the sylvan shades.
Now *Israel's* monarch, and his troops arise,

With peals of shouts ascending to the skies;
In *Elah's* vale the scene of combat lies.

50   When the fair morning blush'd with orient red,
What *David's* sire enjoin'd the son obey'd,
And swift of foot towards the trench he came,
Where glow'd each bosom with the martial flame.
He leaves his carriage to another's care,
55   And runs to greet his brethren of the war.
While yet they spake the giant-chief arose,
Repeats the challenge, and insults his foes:
Struck with the sound, and trembling at the view,
Affrighted *Israel* from its post withdrew.
60   "Observe ye this tremendous foe, they cry'd,
Who in proud vaunts our armies hath defy'd:
Whoever lays him prostrate on the plain,
Freedom in *Israel* for his house shall gain;
And on him wealth unknown the king will pour,
65   And give his royal daughter for his dow'r."

Then *Jesse's* youngest hope: "My brethren say,
What shall be done for him who takes away
Reproach from *Jacob*, who destroys the chief,
And puts a period to his country's grief.
70   He vaunts the honours of his arms abroad,
And scorns the armies of the living God."

Thus spoke the youth, th' attentive people ey'd
The wond'rous hero, and again reply'd:
"Such the rewards our monarch will bestow,
75   On him who conquers, and destroys his foe."

Eliab heard, and kindled into ire
To hear his shepherd-brother thus inquire,
And thus begun? [*sic*] "What errand brought thee? say
Who keeps thy flock? or does it go astray?
80   I know the base ambition of thine heart,
But back in safety from the field depart."

Eliab thus to *Jesse's* youngest heir,
Express'd his wrath in accents most severe.
When to his brother mildly he reply'd,
85 "What have I done? or what the cause to chide?"

  The words were told before the king, who sent
For the young hero to his royal tent:
Before the monarch dauntless he began,
"For this *Philistine* fail no heart of man:
90 I'll take the vale, and with the giant fight:
I dread not all his boasts, nor all his might."
When thus the king: "Dar'st thou a stripling go,
And venture combat with so great a foe?
Who all his days has been inur'd to fight,
95 And made its deeds his study and delight:
Battles and bloodshed brought the monster forth,
And clouds and whirlwinds usher'd in his birth."
When *David* thus: "I kept the fleecy care,
And out there rush'd a lion and a bear;
100 A tender lamb the hungry lion took,
And with no other weapon than my crook
Bold I pursu'd, and chas'd him o'er the field,
The prey deliver'd, and the felon kill'd:
As thus the lion and the bear I slew,
105 So shall *Goliath* fall, and all his crew:
The God, who sav'd me from these beasts of prey,
By me this monster in the dust shall lay."
So *David* spoke. The wond'ring king reply'd;
"Go thou with heav'n and victory on thy side:
110 This coat of mail, this sword gird on," he said,
And plac'd a mighty helmet on his head:
The coat, the sword, the helm he laid aside,
Nor chose to venture with those arms untry'd,
Then took his staff, and to the neighb'ring brook
115 Instant he ran, and thence five pebbles took.
Mean time descended to *Philistia's* son
A radiant cherub, and he thus begun:
"Goliath, well thou know'st thou hast defy'd

Yon Hebrew armies, and their God deny'd:
120   Rebellious wretch! audacious worm! forbear,
Nor tempt the vengeance of their God too far:
Them, who with his omnipotence contend,
No eye shall pity, and no arm defend:
Proud as thou art, in short liv'd glory great,
125   I come to tell thee thine approaching fate.
Regard my words. The judge of all the gods,
Beneath whose steps the tow'ring mountain nods,
Will give thine armies to the savage brood,
That cut the liquid air, or range the wood.
130   Thee too a well-aim'd pebble shall destroy,
And thou shalt perish by a beardless boy:
Such is the mandate from the realms above,
And should I try the vengeance to remove,
Myself a rebel to my king would prove.
135   *Goliath* say, shall grace to him be shown,
Who dares heav'ns monarch, and insults his throne?"

"Your words are lost on me," the giant cries,
While fear and wrath contended in his eyes,
When thus the messenger from heav'n replies:
140   "Provoke no more *Jehovah's* awful hand
To hurl its vengeance on thy guilty land:
He grasps the thunder, and, he wings the storm,
Servants their sov'reign's orders to perform."

The angel spoke, and turn'd his eyes away,
145   Adding new radiance to the rising day.

Now *David* comes: the fatal stones demand
His left, the staff engag'd his better hand:
The giant mov'd, and from his tow'ring height
Survey'd the stripling, and disdain'd the sight,
150   And thus began: "Am I a dog with thee?
Bring'st thou no armour, but a staff to me?
The gods on thee their vollied curses pour,
And beasts and birds of prey thy flesh devour."

      David undaunted thus, "Thy spear and shield
155   Shall no protection to thy body yield:
Jehovah's name—no other arms I bear,
I ask no other in this glorious war.
To-day the Lord of Hosts to me will give
Vict'ry, to-day thy doom thou shalt receive;
160   The fate you threaten shall your own become,
And beasts shall be your animated tomb,
That all the earth's inhabitants may know
That there's a God, who governs all below:
This great assembly too shall witness stand,
165   That needs nor sword, nor spear, th' Almighty's hand:
The battle his, the conquest he bestows,
And to our pow'r consigns our hated foes."

      Thus *David* spoke; *Goliath* heard and came
To meet the hero in the field of fame.
170   Ah! fatal meeting to thy troops and thee,
But thou wast deaf to the divine decree;
Young *David* meets thee, meets thee not in vain;
'Tis thine to perish on th' ensanguin'd plain.

      And now the youth the forceful pebble flung,
175   *Philistia* trembled as it whizz'd along:
In his dread forehead, where the helmet ends,
Just o'er the brows the well-aim'd stone descends,
It pierc'd the skull, and shatter'd all the brain,
Prone on his face he tumbled to the plain:
180   *Goliath's* fall no smaller terror yields
Than riving thunders in aerial fields:
The soul still ling'red in its lov'd abode,
Till conq'ring *David* o'er the giant strode:
Goliath's sword then laid its master dead,
185   And from the body hew'd the ghastly head;
The blood in gushing torrents drench'd the plains,
The soul found passage through the spouting veins.

And now aloud th' illustrious victor said,
"Where are your boastings now your champion's dead?"
190 Scarce had he spoke, when the *Philistines* fled:
But fled in vain; the conqu'ror swift pursu'd:
What scenes of slaughter! and what seas of blood!
There *Saul* thy thousands grasp'd th' impurpled sand
In pangs of death the conquest of thine hand;
195 And *David* there were thy ten thousands laid:
Thus *Israel's* damsels musically play'd.

Near *Gath* and *Ekron* many an hero lay,
Breath'd out their souls, and curs'd the light of day:
Their fury, quench'd by death, no longer burns,
200 And *David* with *Goliath's* head returns,
To *Salem* brought, but in his tent he plac'd
The load of armour which the giant grac'd.
His monarch saw him coming from the war,
And thus demanded of the son of *Ner.*
205 "Say, who is this amazing youth?" he cry'd,
When thus the leader of the host reply'd;
"As lives thy soul I know not whence he sprung,
So great in prowess though in years so young:"
"Inquire whose son is he," the sov'reign said,
210 "Before whose conq'ring arm *Philistia* fled."
Before the king behold the stripling stand,
Goliath's head depending from his hand:
To him the king: "Say of what martial line
Art thou, young hero, and what sire was thine?"
215 He humbly thus; "the son of *Jesse* I:
I came the glories of the field to try.
Small is my tribe, but valiant in the fight;
Small is my city, but thy royal right."
"Then take the promis'd gifts," the monarch cry'd,
220 Conferring riches and the royal bride:
"Knit to my soul for ever thou remain
With me, nor quit my regal roof again."

Thoughts on the WORKS of PROVIDENCE.

> ARISE, my soul, on wings enraptur'd, rise
> To praise the monarch of the earth and skies,
> Whose goodness and beneficence appear
> As round its centre moves the rolling year,
> 5   Or when the morning glows with rosy charms,
> Or the sun slumbers in the ocean's arms:
> Of light divine be a rich portion lent
> To guide my soul, and favour my intent.
> Celestial muse, my arduous flight sustain,
> 10   And raise my mind to a seraphic strain!
>
> Ador'd for ever be the God unseen,
> Which round the sun revolves this vast machine,
> Though to his eye its mass a point appears:
> Ador'd the God that whirls surrounding spheres,
> 15   Which first ordain'd that mighty *Sol* should reign
> The peerless monarch of th' ethereal train:
> Of miles twice forty millions is his height,
> And yet his radiance dazzles mortal sight
> So far beneath—from him th' extended earth
> 20   Vigour derives, and ev'ry flow'ry birth:
> Vast through her orb she moves with easy grace
> Around her *Phoebus* in unbounded space;
> True to her course th' impetuous storm derides,
> Triumphant o'er the winds, and surging tides.
>
> 25   Almighty, in these wond'rous works of thine,
> What *Pow'r,* what *Wisdom,* and what *Goodness* shine?
> And are thy wonders, Lord, by men explor'd,
> And yet creating glory unador'd!
>
> Creation smiles in various beauty gay,
> 30   While day to night, and night succeeds to day:
> That *Wisdom,* which attends *Jehovah's* ways,
> Shines most conspicuous in the solar rays:

Without them, destitute of heat and light,
This world would be the reign of endless night:
35 In their excess how would our race complain,
Abhorring life! how hate its length'ned chain!
From air adust what num'rous ills would rise?
What dire contagion taint the burning skies?
What pestilential vapours, fraught with death,
40 Would rise, and overspread the lands beneath?

Hail, smiling morn, that from the orient main
Ascending dost adorn the heav'nly plain!
So rich, so various are thy beauteous dies,
That spread through all the circuit of the skies,
45 That, full of thee, my soul in rapture soars,
And thy great God, the cause of all adores.
O'er beings infinite his love extends,
His *Wisdom* rules them, and his *Pow'r* defends.
When tasks diurnal tire the human frame,
50 The spirits faint, and dim the vital flame,
Then too that ever active bounty shines,
Which not infinity of space confines.
The sable veil, that *Night* in silence draws,
Conceals effects, but shews th' *Almighty Cause;*
55 Night seals in sleep the wide creation fair,
And all is peaceful but the brow of care.
Again, gay *Phoebus*, as the day before,
Wakes ev'ry eye, but what shall wake no more;
Again the face of nature is renew'd,
60 Which still appears harmonious, fair, and good.
May grateful strains salute the smiling morn,
Before its beams the eastern hills adorn!

Shall day to day, and night to night conspire
To show the goodness of the Almighty Sire?
65 This mental voice shall man regardless hear,
And never, never raise the filial pray'r?
To-day, O hearken, nor your folly mourn
For time mispent, that never will return.

But see the sons of vegetation rise,
70 And spread their leafy banners to the skies.
All-wise Almighty providence we trace
In trees, and plants, and all the flow'ry race;
As clear as in the nobler frame of man,
All lovely copies of the Maker's plan.
75 The pow'r the same that forms a ray of light,
That call'd creation from eternal night.
"Let there be light," he said: from his profound
Old *Chaos* heard, and trembled at the sound:
Swift as the word, inspir'd by pow'r divine,
80 Behold the light around its maker shine,
The first fair product of th' omnific God,
And now through all his works diffus'd abroad.

As reason's pow'rs by day our God disclose,
So we may trace him in the night's repose:
85 Say what is sleep? and dreams how passing strange!
When action ceases, and ideas range
Licentious and unbounded o'er the plains,
Where *Fancy*'s queen in giddy triumph reigns.
Hear in soft strains the dreaming lover sigh
90 To a kind fair, or rave in jealousy;
On pleasure now, and now on vengeance bent,
The lab'ring passions struggle for a vent.
What pow'r, O man! thy *reason* then restores,
So long suspended in nocturnal hours?
95 What secret hand returns the mental train,
And gives improv'd thine active pow'rs again?
From thee, O man, what gratitude should rise!
And, when from balmy sleep thou op'st thine eyes,
Let thy first thoughts be praises to the skies.
100 How merciful our God who thus imparts
O'erflowing tides of joy to human hearts,
When wants and woes might be our righteous lot,
Our God forgetting, by our God forgot!

Among the mental pow'rs a question rose,
105 "What most the image of th' Eternal shows?"

When thus to *Reason* (so let *Fancy* rove)
Her great companion spoke immortal *Love*.

"Say, mighty pow'r, how long shall strife prevail,
And with its murmurs load the whisp'ring gale?
110 Refer the cause to *Recollection's* shrine,
Who loud proclaims my origin divine,
The cause whence heav'n and earth began to be,
And is not man immortaliz'd by me?
Reason let this most causeless strife subside."
115 Thus *Love* pronounc'd, and *Reason* thus reply'd.

"Thy birth, celestial queen! 'tis mine to own,
In thee resplendent is the Godhead shown;
Thy words persuade, my soul enraptur'd feels
Resistless beauty which thy smile reveals."
120 Ardent she spoke, and, kindling at her charms,
She clasp'd the blooming goddess in her arms.

Infinite *Love* wher'er we turn our eyes
Appears: this ev'ry creature's wants supplies;
This most is heard in *Nature's* constant voice,
125 This makes the morn, and this the eve rejoice;
This bids the fost'ring rains and dews descend
To nourish all, to serve one gen'ral end,
The good of man: yet man ungrateful pays
But little homage, and but little praise.
130 To him, whose works array'd with mercy shine,
What songs should rise, how constant, how divine!

To a Lady on the Death of Three Relations.

WE trace the pow'r of Death from tomb to tomb,
And his are all the ages yet to come.
'Tis his to call the planets from on high,
To blacken *Phoebus*, and dissolve the sky;
5 His too, when all in his dark realms are hurl'd,

From its firm base to shake the solid world;
His fatal sceptre rules the spacious whole,
And trembling nature rocks from pole to pole.

Awful he moves, and wide his wings are spread:
10   Behold thy brother number'd with the dead!
From bondage freed, the exulting spirit flies
Beyond *Olympus,* and these starry skies.
Lost in our woe for thee, blest shade, we mourn
In vain; to earth thou never must return.
15   Thy sisters too, fair mourner, feel the dart
Of Death, and with fresh torture rend thine heart.
Weep not for them, who wish thine happy mind
To rise with them, and leave the world behind.

As a young plant by hurricanes up torn,
20   So near its parent lies the newly born—
But 'midst the bright ethereal train behold
It shines superior on a throne of gold:
Then, mourner, cease; let hope thy tears restrain,
Smile on the tomb, and sooth the raging pain.
25   On yon blest regions fix thy longing view,
Mindless of sublunary scenes below;
Ascend the sacred mount, in thought arise,
And seek substantial and immortal joys;
Where hope receives, where faith to vision springs,
30   And raptur'd seraphs tune th' immortal strings
To strains extatic. Thou the chorus join,
And to thy father tune the praise divine.

To a Clergyman on the Death of his Lady.

WHERE contemplation finds her sacred spring,
Where heav'nly music makes the arches ring,
Where virtue reigns unsully'd and divine,
Where wisdom thron'd, and all the graces shine,

5   There sits thy spouse amidst the radiant throng,
     While praise eternal warbles from her tongue;
     There choirs angelic shout her welcome round,
     With perfect bliss, and peerless glory crown'd.

          While thy dear mate, to flesh no more confin'd,
10. Exults a blest, an heav'n-ascended mind,
     Say in thy breast shall floods of sorrow rise?
     Say shall its torrents overwhelm thine eyes?
     Amid the seats of heav'n a place is free,
     And angels ope their bright ranks for thee;
15   For thee they wait, and with expectant eye
     Thy spouse leans downward from th' empyreal sky:
     "O come away, her longing spirit cries,
     And share with me the raptures of the skies.
     Our bliss divine to mortals is unknown;
20   Immortal life and glory are our own.
     There too may the dear pledges of our love
     Arrive, and taste with us the joys above;
     Attune the harp to more than mortal lays,
     And join with us the tribute of their praise
25   To him, who dy'd stern justice to atone,
     And make eternal glory all our own.
     He in his death slew ours, and, as he rose,
     He crush'd the dire dominion of our foes;
     Vain were their hopes to put the God to flight,
30   Chain us to hell, and bar the gates of light."

          She spoke, and turn'd from mortal scenes her eyes,
     Which beam'd celestial radiance o'er the skies.

          Then thou, dear man, no more with grief retire,
     Let grief no longer damp devotion's fire,
35   But rise sublime, to equal bliss aspire.
     Thy sighs no more be wafted by the wind,
     No more complain, but be to heav'n resign'd.
     'Twas thine t' unfold the oracles divine,
     To sooth our woes the task was also thine;

40　　　Now sorrow is incumbent on thy heart,
　　　　Permit the muse a cordial to impart;
　　　　Who can to thee their tend'rest aid refuse?
　　　　To dry thy tears how longs the heav'nly muse!

An HYMN to the MORNING.

　　　　　ATTEND my lays, ye ever honour'd nine,
　　　　Assist my labours, and my strains refine;
　　　　In smoothest numbers pour the notes along,
　　　　For bright *Aurora* now demands my song.

5　　　　　*Aurora* hail, and all the thousand dies,
　　　　Which deck thy progress through the vaulted skies:
　　　　The morn awakes, and wide extends her rays,
　　　　On ev'ry leaf the gentle zephyr plays;
　　　　Harmonious lays the feather'd race resume,
10　　　Dart the bright eye, and shake the painted plume.

　　　　　Ye shady groves, your verdant gloom display
　　　　To shield your poet from the burning day:
　　　　Calliope awake the sacred lyre,
　　　　While thy fair sisters fan the pleasing fire:
15　　　The bow'rs, the gales, the variegated skies
　　　　In all their pleasures in my bosom rise.

　　　　　See in the east th' illustrious king of day!
　　　　His rising radiance drives the shades away—
　　　　But Oh! I feel his fervid beams too strong,
20　　　And scarce begun, concludes th' abortive song.

An HYMN to the EVENING.

　　　　　SOON as the sun forsook the eastern main
　　　　The pealing thunder shook the heav'nly plain;

Majestic grandeur! From the zephyr's wing,
Exhales the incense of the blooming spring.
5   Soft purl the streams, the birds renew their notes,
And through the air their mingled music floats.

     Through all the heav'ns what beauteous dies are
         spread!
But the west glories in the deepest red:
So may our breasts with ev'ry virtue glow,
10   The living temples of our God below!

     Fill'd with the praise of him who gives the light,
And draws the sable curtains of the night,
Let placid slumbers sooth each weary mind,
At morn to wake more heav'nly, more refin'd;
15   So shall the labours of the day begin
More pure, more guarded from the snares of sin.

     Night's leaden sceptre seals my drowsy eyes,
Then cease, my song, till fair *Aurora* rise.

Isaiah lxiii. 1–8.

     SAY, heav'nly muse, what king, or mighty God,
That moves sublime from *Idumea's* road?
In *Bozrah's* dies, with martial glories join'd,
His purple vesture waves upon the wind.
5   Why thus enrob'd delights he to appear
In the dread image of the *Pow'r* of war?

     Compress'd in wrath the swelling wine-press
         groan'd,
It bled, and pour'd the gushing purple round.

     "Mine was the act," th' Almighty Saviour said,
10   And shook the dazzling glories of his head,

"When all forsook I trod the press alone,
And conquer'd by omnipotence my own;
For man's release sustain'd the pond'rous load,
For man the wrath of an immortal God:
15   To execute th' Eternal's dread command
My soul I sacrific'd with willing hand;
Sinless I stood before the avenging frown,
Atoning thus for vices not my own."

His eye the ample field of battle round
20   Survey'd, but no created succours found;
His own omnipotence sustain'd the fight,
His vengeance sunk the haughty foes in night;
Beneath his feet the prostrate troops were spread,
And round him lay the dying, and the dead.

25   Great God, what light'ning flashes from thine eyes?
What pow'r withstands if thou indignant rise?

Against thy *Zion* though her foes may rage,
And all their cunning, all their strength engage,
Yet she serenely on thy bosom lies,
30   Smiles at their arts, and all their force defies.

On RECOLLECTION.

MNEME begin. Inspire, ye sacred nine,
Your vent'rous *Afric* in her great design.
Mneme, immortal pow'r, I trace thy spring:
Assist my strains, while I thy glories sing:
5   The acts of long departed years, by thee
Recover'd, in due order rang'd we see:
Thy pow'r the long-forgotten calls from night,
That sweetly plays before the *fancy's* sight.

Mneme in our nocturnal visions pours
10   The ample treasure of her secret stores;

Swift from above she wings her silent flight
Through *Phoebe's* realms, fair regent of the night;
And, in her pomp of images display'd,
To the high-raptur'd poet gives her aid,
15   Through the unbounded regions of the mind,
Diffusing light celestial and refin'd.
The heav'nly *phantom* paints the actions done
By ev'ry tribe beneath the rolling sun.

Mneme, enthron'd within the human breast,
20   Has vice condemn'd, and ev'ry virtue blest.
How sweet the sound when we her plaudit hear?
Sweeter than music to the ravish'd ear,
Sweeter than *Maro's* entertaining strains
Resounding through the groves, and hills, and plains.
25   But how is *Mneme* dreaded by the race,
Who scorn her warnings and despise her grace?
By her unveil'd each horrid crime appears,
Her awful hand a cup of wormwood bears.
Days, years mispent, O what a hell of woe!
30   Hers the worst tortures that our souls can know.

Now eighteen years their destin'd course have run,
In fast succession round the central sun.
How did the follies of that period pass
Unnotic'd, but behold them writ in brass!
35   In Recollection see them fresh return,
And sure 'tis mine to be asham'd, and mourn.

O *Virtue*, smiling in immortal green,
Do thou exert thy pow'r, and change the scene;
Be thine employ to guide my future days,
40   And mine to pay the tribute of my praise.

Of *Recollection* such the pow'r enthron'd
In ev'ry breast, and thus her pow'r is own'd.
The wretch, who dar'd the vengeance of the skies,
At last awakes in horror and surprize,
45   By her alarm'd, he sees impending fate,

He howls in anguish, and repents too late.
But O! what peace, what joys are hers t'impart
To ev'ry holy, ev'ry upright heart!
Thrice blest the man, who, in her sacred shrine,
50 Feels himself shelter'd from the wrath divine!

On IMAGINATION.

THY various works, imperial queen, we see,
How bright their forms! how deck'd with pomp by thee!
Thy wond'rous acts in beauteous order stand,
And all attest how potent is thine hand.

5   From *Helicon's* refulgent heights attend,
Ye sacred choir, and my attempts befriend:
To tell her glories with a faithful tongue,
Ye blooming graces, triumph in my song.

Now here, now there, the roving *Fancy* flies,
10 Till some lov'd object strikes her wand'ring eyes,
Whose silken fetters all the senses bind,
And soft captivity involves the mind.

Imagination! who can sing thy force?
Or who describe the swiftness of thy course?
15 Soaring through air to find the bright abode,
Th' empyreal palace of the thund'ring God,
We on thy pinions can surpass the wind,
And leave the rolling universe behind:
From star to star the mental optics rove,
20 Measure the skies, and range the realms above.
There in one view we grasp the mighty whole,
Or with new worlds amaze th' unbounded soul.

Though *Winter* frowns to *Fancy's* raptur'd eyes
The fields may flourish, and gay scenes arise;
25 The frozen deeps may break their iron bands,

And bid their waters murmur o'er the sands.
Fair *Flora* may resume her fragrant reign,
And with her flow'ry riches deck the plain;
Sylvanus may diffuse his honours round,
30 And all the forest may with leaves be crown'd:
Show'rs may descend, and dews their gems disclose,
And nectar sparkle on the blooming rose.

Such is thy pow'r, nor are thine orders vain,
O thou the leader of the mental train:
35 In full perfection all thy works are wrought,
And thine the sceptre o'er the realms of thought.
Before thy throne the subject-passions bow,
Of subject-passions sov'reign ruler Thou,
At thy command joy rushes on the heart,
40 And through the glowing veins the spirits dart.

Fancy might now her silken pinions try
To rise from earth, and sweep th' expanse on high;
From *Tithon's* bed now might *Aurora* rise,
Her cheeks all glowing with celestial dies,
45 While a pure stream of light o'erflows the skies.
The monarch of the day I might behold,
And all the mountains tipt with radiant gold,
But I reluctant leave the pleasing views,
Which *Fancy* dresses to delight the *Muse;*
50 *Winter* austere forbids me to aspire,
And northern tempests damp the rising fire;
They chill the tides of *Fancy's* flowing sea,
Cease then, my song, cease the unequal lay.

A Funeral POEM on the Death of C. E.
an Infant of Twelve Months.

THROUGH airy roads he wings his instant flight
To purer regions of celestial light;
Enlarg'd he sees unnumber'd systems roll,

Beneath him sees the universal whole,
Planets on planets run their destin'd round,
And circling wonders fill the vast profound.
Th' ethereal now, and now th' empyreal skies
With growing splendors strike his wond'ring eyes:
The angels view him with delight unknown,
Press his soft hand, and seat him on his throne;
Then smiling thus. "To this divine abode,
The seat of saints, of seraphs, and of God,
Thrice welcome thou." The raptur'd babe replies,
"Thanks to my God, who snatch'd me to the skies,
E'er vice triumphant had possess'd my heart,
E'er yet the tempter had beguil'd my heart,
E'er yet on sin's base actions I was bent,
E'er yet I knew temptation's dire intent;
E'er yet the lash for horrid crimes I felt,
E'er vanity had led my way to guilt,
But, soon arriv'd at my celestial goal,
Full glories rush on my expanding soul."
Joyful he spoke: exulting cherubs round
Clapt their glad wings, the heav'nly vaults resound.

Say, parents, why this unavailing moan?
Why heave your pensive bosoms with the groan?
To *Charles,* the happy subject of my song,
A brighter world, and nobler strains belong.
Say would you tear him from the realms above
By thoughtless wishes, and prepost'rous love?
Doth his felicity increase your pain?
Or could you welcome to this world again
The heir of bliss? with a superior air
Methinks he answers with a smile severe,
"Thrones and dominions cannot tempt me there."
But still you cry, "Can we the sigh forbear,
And still and still must we not pour the tear?
Our only hope, more dear than vital breath,
Twelve moons revolv'd, becomes the prey of death;
Delightful infant, nightly visions give

Thee to our arms, and we with joy receive,
We fain would clasp the *Phantom* to our breast,
The *Phantom* flies, and leaves the soul unblest."

To yon bright regions let your faith ascend,
45   Prepare to join your dearest infant friend
In pleasures without measure, without end.

To Captain H—D, of the 65th Regiment.

SAY, muse divine, can hostile scenes delight
The warrior's bosom in the fields of fight?
Lo! here the christian, and the hero join
With mutual grace to form the man divine.
5   In H—d see with pleasure and surprize,
Where *valour* kindles, and where *virtue* lies:
Go, hero brave, still grace the post of fame,
And add new glories to thine honour'd name,
Still to the field, and still to virtue true:
10   *Britannia* glories in no son like you.

To the Right Honourable WILLIAM, Earl of DARTMOUTH, His Majesty's Principal Secretary of State for North-America, &c.

HAIL, happy day, when, smiling like the morn,
Fair *Freedom* rose *New-England* to adorn:
The northern clime beneath her genial ray,
Dartmouth, congratulates thy blissful sway:
5   Elate with hope her race no longer mourns,
Each soul expands, each grateful bosom burns,
While in thine hand with pleasure we behold
The silken reins, and *Freedom's* charms unfold.
Long lost to realms beneath the northern skies

10 She shines supreme, while hated *faction* dies:
Soon as appear'd the *Goddess* long desir'd,
Sick at the view, she lanquish'd and expir'd;
Thus from the splendors of the morning light
The owl in sadness seeks the caves of night.

15   No more, *America*, in mournful strain
Of wrongs, and grievance unredress'd complain,
No longer shalt thou dread the iron chain,
Which wanton *Tyranny* with lawless hand
Had made, and with it meant t'enslave the land.

20   Should you, my lord, while you peruse my song,
Wonder from whence my love of *Freedom* sprung,
Whence flow these wishes for the common good,
By feeling hearts alone best understood,
I, young in life, by seeming cruel fate
25 Was snatch'd from *Afric's* fancy'd happy seat:
What pangs excruciating must molest,
What sorrows labour in my parent's breast?
Steel'd was that soul and by no misery mov'd
That from a father seiz'd his babe belov'd:
30 Such, such my case. And can I then but pray
Others may never feel tyrannic sway?

    For favours past, great Sir, our thanks are due,
And thee we ask thy favours to renew,
Since in thy pow'r, as in thy will before,
35 To sooth the griefs, which thou did'st once deplore.
May heav'nly grace the sacred sanction give
To all thy works, and thou for ever live
Not only on the wings of fleeting *Fame*,
Though praise immortal crowns the patriot's name,
40 But to conduct to heav'ns refulgent fane,
May fiery coursers sweep th' ethereal plain,
And bear thee upwards to that blest abode,
Where, like the prophet, thou shalt find thy God.

ODE to NEPTUNE.
On Mrs. W—'s Voyage to England.

I.

WHILE raging tempests shake the shore,
While *AE'lus'* thunders round us roar,
And sweep impetuous o'er the plain
Be still, O tyrant of the main;
5 Nor let thy brow contracted frowns betray,
While my *Susannah* skims the wat'ry way.

II.

The *Pow'r* propitious hears the lay,
The blue-ey'd daughters of the sea
With sweeter cadence glide along,
10 And *Thames* responsive joins the song.
Pleas'd with their notes *Sol* sheds benign his ray,
And double radiance decks the face of day.

III.

To court thee to *Britannia's* arms
      Serene the climes and mild the sky,
15 Her region boasts unnumber'd charms,
      Thy welcome smiles in ev'ry eye.
Thy promise, *Neptune* keep, record my pray'r,
Nor give my wishes to the empty air.

Boston, October 10, 1772.

To a LADY on her coming to North-America
with her Son, for the Recovery of her Health.

      INdulgent muse! my grov'ling mind inspire,
And fill my bosom with celestial fire.

     See from *Jamaica's* fervid shore she moves,
Like the fair mother of the blooming loves,
5   When from above the *Goddess* with her hand
Fans the soft breeze, and lights upon the land;
Thus she on *Neptune's* wat'ry realm reclin'd
Appear'd, and thus invites the ling'ring wind.

     "Arise, ye winds, *America* explore,
10   Waft me, ye gales, from this malignant shore;
The *Northern* milder climes I long to greet,
There hope that health will my arrival meet."
Soon as she spoke in my ideal view
The winds assented, and the vessel flew.

15   Madam, your spouse bereft of wife and son,
In the grove's dark recesses pours his moan;
Each branch, wide-spreading to the ambient sky,
Forgets its verdure, and submits to die.

     From thence I turn, and leave the sultry plain,
20   And swift pursue thy passage o'er the main:
The ship arrives before the fav'ring wind,
And makes the *Philadelphian* port assign'd,
Thence I attend you to *Bostonia's* arms,
Where gen'rous friendship ev'ry bosom warms:
25   Thrice welcome here! may health revive again,
Bloom on thy cheek, and bound in ev'ry vein!

     Then back return to gladden ev'ry heart,
And give your spouse his soul's far dearer part,
Receiv'd again with what a sweet surprize,
30   The tear in transport starting from his eyes!
While his attendant son with blooming grace
Springs to his father's ever dear embrace.
With shouts of joy *Jamaica's* rocks resound,
With shouts of joy the country rings around.

To a LADY on her remarkable Preservation
in an Hurricane in *North-Carolina*.

THOUGH thou did'st hear the tempest from afar,
And felt'st the horrors of the wat'ry war,
To me unknown, yet on this peaceful shore
Methinks I hear the storm tumultuous roar,
5   And how stern *Boreas* with impetuous hand
Compell'd the *Nereids* to usurp the land.
Reluctant rose the daughters of the main,
And slow ascending glided o'er the plain,
Till *AEolus* in his rapid chariot drove
10   In gloomy grandeur from the vault above:
Furious he comes. His winged sons obey
Their frantic sire, and madden all the sea.
The billows rave, the wind's fierce tyrant roars,
And with his thund'ring terrors shakes the shores:
15   Broken by waves the vessel's frame is rent,
And strows with planks the wat'ry element.

But thee, *Maria*, a kind *Nereid's* shield
Preserv'd from sinking, and thy form upheld:
And sure some heav'nly oracle design'd
20   At that dread crisis to instruct thy mind
Things of eternal consequence to weigh,
And to thine heart just feelings to convey
Of things above, and of the future doom,
And what the births of the dread world to come.

25   From tossing seas I welcome thee to land.
"Resign her, *Nereid*," 'twas thy God's command.
Thy spouse late buried, as thy fears conceiv'd,
Again returns, thy fears are all reliev'd:
Thy daughter blooming with superior grace
30   Again thou see'st, again thine arms embrace;
O come, and joyful show thy spouse his heir,
And what the blessings of maternal care!

To a LADY and her Children,
on the Death of her Son and their Brother.

   O'Erwhelming sorrow now demands my song:
  From death the overwhelming sorrow sprung.
  What flowing tears? What hearts with grief opprest?
  What sighs on sighs heave the fond parent's breast?
5 The brother weeps, the hapless sisters join
  Th' increasing woe, and swell the crystal brine;
  The poor, who once his gen'rous bounty fed,
  Droop, and bewail their benefactor dead.
  In death the friend, the kind companion lies,
10 And in one death what various comfort dies!

   Th' unhappy mother sees the sanguine rill
  Forget to flow, and nature's wheels stand still,
  But see from earth his spirit far remov'd,
  And know no grief recals your best-belov'd:
15 He, upon pinions swifter than the wind,
  Has left mortality's sad scenes behind
  For joys to this terrestrial state unknown,
  And glories richer than the monarch's crown.
  Of virtue's steady course the prize behold!
20 What blissful wonders to his mind unfold!
  But of celestial joys I sing in vain:
  Attempt not, muse, the too advent'rous strain.

   No more in briny show'rs, ye friends around,
  Or bathe his clay, or waste them on the ground:
25 Still do you weep, still wish for his return?
  How cruel thus to wish, and thus to mourn?
  No more for him the streams of sorrow pour,
  But haste to join him on the heav'nly shore,
  On harps of gold to tune immortal lays,
30 And to your God immortal anthems raise.

To a GENTLEMAN and LADY on the
Death of the Lady's Brother and Sister,
and a Child of the Name *Avis*,
aged one Year.

       ON *Death's* domain intent I fix my eyes,
    Where human nature in vast ruin lies:
    With pensive mind I search the drear abode,
    Where the great conqu'ror has his spoils bestow'd;
5   [W]here there the offspring of six thousand years
    In endless numbers to my view appears:
    Whole kingdoms in his gloomy den are thrust,
    And nations mix with their primeval dust:
    Insatiate still he gluts the ample tomb;
10   His is the present, his the age to come.
    See here a brother, here a sister spread,
    And a sweet daughter mingled with the dead.

       But, *Madam,* let your grief be laid aside,
    And let the fountain of your tears be dry'd,
15   In vain they flow to wet the dusty plain,
    Your sighs are wafted to the skies in vain,
    Your pains they witness, but they can no more,
    While *Death* reigns tyrant o'er this mortal shore.

       The glowing stars and silver queen of light
20   At last must perish in the gloom of night:
    Resign thy friends to that Almighty hand,
    Which gave them life, and bow to his command;
    Thine *Avis* give without a murm'ring heart,
    Though half thy soul be fated to depart.
25   To shining guards consign thine infant care
    To waft triumphant through the seas of air:
    Her soul enlarg'd to heav'nly pleasure springs,
    She feeds on truth and uncreated things.
    Methinks I hear her in the realms above,
30   And leaning forward with a filial love,

Invite you there to share immortal bliss
Unknown, untasted in a state like this.
With tow'ring hopes, and growing grace arise,
And seek beatitude beyond the skies.

On the Death of Dr. SAMUEL MARSHALL. 1771.

THROUGH thickest glooms look back, immortal
    shade,
On that confusion which thy death has made;
Or from *Olympus'* height look down, and see
A *Town* involv'd in grief bereft of thee.
5   Thy *Lucy* sees thee mingle with the dead,
And rends the graceful tresses from her head,
Wild in her woe, with grief unknown opprest
Sigh follows sigh deep heaving from her breast.

Too quickly fled, ah! whither art thou gone?
10 Ah! lost for ever to thy wife and son!
The hapless child, thine only hope and heir,
Clings round his mother's neck, and weeps his sorrows
    there.
The loss of thee on *Tyler's* soul returns,
And *Boston* for her dear physician mourns.

15   When sickness call'd for *Marshall's* healing hand,
With what compassion did his soul expand?
In him we found the father and the friend:
In life how lov'd! how honour'd in his end!

And must not then our *AEsculapius* stay
20 To bring his ling'ring infant into day?
The babe unborn in the dark womb is tost,
And seems in anguish for its father lost.

Gone is *Apollo* from his house of earth,
But leaves the sweet memorials of his worth:
25   The common parent, whom we all deplore,
From yonder world unseen must come no more,
Yet 'midst our woes immortal hopes attend
The spouse, the sire, the universal friend.

To a GENTLEMAN on his Voyage to
Great-Britain for the Recovery of his Health.

WHILE others chant of gay *Elysian* scenes,
Of balmy zephyrs, and of flow'ry plains,
My song more happy speaks a greater name,
Feels higher motives and a nobler flame.
5   For thee, O R—, the muse attunes her strings,
And mounts sublime above inferior things.

I sing not now of green embow'ring woods,
I sing not now the daughters of the floods,
I sing not of the storms o'er ocean driv'n,
10   And how they howl'd along the waste of heav'n,
But I to R— would paint the *British* shore,
And vast *Atlantic,* not untry'd before:
Thy life impair'd commands thee to arise,
Leave these bleak regions and inclement skies,
15   Where chilling winds return the winter past,
And nature shudders at the furious blast.

O thou stupendous, earth-enclosing main
Exert thy wonders to the world again!
If ere thy pow'r prolong'd the fleeting breath,
20   Turn'd back the shafts, and mock'd the gates of death,
If ere thine air dispens'd an healing pow'r,
Or snatch'd the victim from the fatal hour,
This equal case demands thine equal care,
And equal wonders may this patient share.

25   But unavailing, frantic is the dream
      To hope thine aid without the aid of him
      Who gave thee birth, and taught thee where to flow,
      And in thy waves his various blessings show.

      May R— return to view his native shore
30   Replete with vigour not his own before,
      Then shall we see with pleasure and surprize,
      And own thy work, great Ruler of the skies!

To the Rev. Dr. THOMAS AMORY on reading his
Sermons on DAILY DEVOTION, in which
that Duty is recommended and assisted.

      TO cultivate in ev'ry noble mind
      Habitual grace, and sentiments refin'd,
      Thus while you strive to mend the human heart,
      Thus while the heav'nly precepts you impart,
5   O may each bosom catch the sacred fire,
      And youthful minds to *Virtue's* throne aspire!

      When God's eternal ways you set in sight,
      And *Virtue* shines in all her native light,
      In vain would *Vice* her works in night conceal,
10   For *Wisdom's* eye pervades the sable veil.

      Artists may paint the sun's effulgent rays,
      But *Amory's* pen the brighter God displays:
      While his great works in *Amory's* pages shine,
      And while he proves his essence all divine,
15   The Atheist sure no more can boast aloud
      Of chance, or nature, and exclude the God;
      As if the clay without the potter's aid
      Should rise in various forms, and shapes self-made,
      Or worlds above with orb o'er orb profound
20   Self-mov'd could run the everlasting round.

It cannot be—unerring *Wisdom* guides
With eye propitious, and o'er all presides.

Still prosper, *Amory!* still may'st thou receive
The warmest blessings which a muse can give,
25 And when this transitory state is o'er,
When kingdoms fall, and fleeting *Fame's* no more,
May *Amory* triumph in immortal fame,
A noble title, and superior name!

On the Death of J. C. an Infant.

NO more the flow'ry scenes of pleasure rise,
Nor charming prospects greet the mental eyes,
No more with joy we view that lovely face
Smiling, disportive, flush'd with ev'ry grace.

5 The tear of sorrow flows from ev'ry eye,
Groans answer groans, and sighs to sighs reply;
What sudden pangs shot thro' each aching heart,
When, *Death*, thy messenger dispatch'd his dart?
Thy dread attendants, all-destroying *Pow'r*,
10 Hurried the infant to his mortal hour.
Could'st thou unpitying close those radiant eyes?
Or fail'd his artless beauties to surprize?
Could not his innocence thy stroke controul,
Thy purpose shake, and soften all thy soul?

15 The blooming babe, with shades of *Death* o'erspread,
No more shall smile, no more shall raise its head,
But, like a branch that from the tree is torn,
Falls prostrate, wither'd, languid, and forlorn.
"Where flies my *James?*" 'tis thus I seem to hear
20 The parent ask, "Some angel tell me where
He wings his passage thro' the yielding air?"
Methinks a cherub bending from the skies

Observes the question, and serene replies,
"In heav'ns high palaces your babe appears:
25 Prepare to meet him, and dismiss your tears."
Shall not th'intelligence your grief restrain,
And turn the mournful to the chearful strain?
Cease your complaints, suspend each rising sigh,
Cease to accuse the Ruler of the sky.
30 Parents, no more indulge the falling tear:
Let *Faith* to heav'n's refulgent domes repair,
There see your infant, like a seraph glow:
What charms celestial in his numbers flow
Melodious, while the soul-enchanting strain
35 Dwells on his tongue, and fills th'ethereal plain?
Enough—for ever cease your murm'ring breath;
Not as a foe, but friend converse with *Death*,
Since to the port of happiness unknown
He brought that treasure which you call your own.
40 The gift of heav'n intrusted to your hand
Chearful resign at the divine command:
Not at your bar must sov'reign *Wisdom* stand.

An HYMN to HUMANITY.
To S. P. G. Esq;

I.
LO! for this dark terrestrial ball
Forsakes his azure-paved hall
   A prince of heav'nly birth!
Divine *Humanity* behold.
5 What wonders rise, what charms unfold
   At his descent to earth!

II.
The bosoms of the great and good
With wonder and delight he view'd,
   And fix'd his empire there:

10   Him, close compressing to his breast,
      The sire of gods and men address'd,
             "My son, my heav'nly fair!

      III.
      Descend to earth, there place thy throne;
      To succour man's afflicted son
15   Each human heart inspire:
      To act in bounties unconfin'd
      Enlarge the close contracted mind,
             And fill it with thy fire."

      IV.
      Quick as the word, with swift career
20   He wings his course from star to star,
             And leaves the bright abode.
      The *Virtue* did his charms impart;
      Their G—y! then thy raptur'd heart
             Perceiv'd the rushing God:

      V.
25   For when thy pitying eye did see
      The languid muse in low degree,
             Then, then at thy desire
      Descended the celestial nine;
      O'er me methought they deign'd to shine,
30   And deign'd to string my lyre.

      VI.
      Can *Afric's* muse forgetful prove?
      Or can such friendship fail to move
             A tender human heart?
      Immortal *Friendship* laurel-crown'd
35   The smiling *Graces* all surround
             With ev'ry heav'nly *Art*.

To the Honourable T. H. Esq; on the Death of his Daughter.

WHILE deep you mourn beneath the cypress-shade
The hand of Death, and your dear daughter laid
In dust, whose absence gives your tears to flow,
And racks your bosom with incessant woe,
Let *Recollection* take a tender part,
Assuage the raging tortures of your heart,
Still the wild tempest of tumultuous grief,
And pour the heav'nly nectar of relief:
Suspend the sigh, dear Sir, and check the groan,
Divinely bright your daughter's *Virtues* shone:
How free from scornful pride her gentle mind,
Which ne'er its aid to indigence declin'd!
Expanding free, it sought the means to prove
Unfailing charity, unbounded love!

She unreluctant flies to see no more
Her dear-lov'd parents on earth's dusky shore:
Impatient heav'n's resplendent goal to gain,
She with swift progress cuts the azure plain,
Where grief subsides, where changes are no more,
And life's tumultuous billows cease to roar;
She leaves her earthly mansion for the skies,
Where new creations feast her wond'ring eyes.

To heav'n's high mandate chearfully resign'd
She mounts, and leaves the rolling globe behind;
She, who late wish'd that *Leonard* might return,
Has ceas'd to languish, and forgot to mourn;
To the same high empyreal mansions come,
She joins her spouse, and smiles upon the tomb:
And thus I hear her from the realms above:
"Lo! this the kingdom of celestial love!
Could ye, fond parents, see our present bliss,
How soon would you each sigh, each fear dismiss?
Amidst unutter'd pleasures whilst I play

In the fair sunshine of celestial day,
35   As far as grief affects an happy soul
So far doth grief my better mind controul,
To see on earth my aged parents mourn,
And secret wish for T——l to return:
Let brighter scenes your ev'ning-hours employ:
40   Converse with heav'n, and taste the promis'd joy."

NIOBE in Distress for her children slain by APOLLO,
from *Ovid's* Metamorphoses, Book VI. and from
a view of the Painting of Mr. *Richard Wilson.*

APOLLO'S wrath to man the dreadful spring
Of ills innum'rous, tuneful goddess, sing!
Thou who did'st first th' ideal pencil give,
And taught'st the painter in his works to live,
5   Inspire with glowing energy of thought,
What *Wilson* painted, and what *Ovid* wrote.
Muse! lend thy aid, nor let me sue in vain,
Tho' last and meanest of the rhyming train!
O guide my pen in lofty strains to show
10   The *Phrygian* queen, all beautiful in woe.

'Twas where *Maeonia* spreads her wide domain
Niobe dwelt, and held her potent reign:
See in her hand the regal sceptre shine,
The wealthy heir of *Tantalus* divine,
15   He most distinguish'd by *Dodonean Jove,*
To approach the tables of the gods above:
Her grandsire *Atlas,* who with mighty pains
Th' ethereal axis on his neck sustains:
Her other gran sire on the throne on high
20   Rolls the loud-pealing thunder thro' the sky.

Her spouse, *Amphion,* who from *Jove* too springs,
Divinely taught to sweep the sounding strings.

Seven sprightly sons the royal bed adorn,
Seven daughters beauteous as the op'ning morn,
25   As when *Aurora* fills the ravish'd sight,
And decks the orient realms with rosy light
From their bright eyes the living splendors play,
Nor can beholders bear the flashing ray.

Wherever, *Niobe,* thou turn'st thine eyes,
30   New beauties kindle, and new joys arise!
But thou had'st far the happier mother prov'd,
If this fair offspring had been less belov'd:
What if their charms exceed *Aurora's* teint,
No words could tell them, and no pencil paint,
35   Thy love too vehement hastens to destroy
Each blooming maid, and each celestial boy.

Now *Manto* comes, endu'd with mighty skill,
The past to explore, the future to reveal.
Thro' *Thebes'* wide streets *Tiresia's* daughter came,
40   Divine *Latona's* mandate to proclaim:
The *Theban* maids to hear the orders ran,
When thus *Moeonia's* prophetess began:

"Go *Thebans!* great *Latona's* will obey,
And pious tribute at her altars pay:
45   With rights divine, the goddess be implor'd,
Nor be her sacred offspring unador'd."
Thus *Manto* spoke. The *Theban* maids obey,
And pious tribute to the goddess pay.
The rich perfumes ascend in waving spires,
50   And altars blaze with consecrated fires;
The fair assembly moves with graceful air,
And leaves of laurel bind the flowing hair.

Niobe comes with all her royal race,
With charms unnumber'd, and superior grace:
55   Her *Phrygian* garments of delightful hue,
Inwove with gold, refulgent to the view,

Beyond description beautiful she moves
Like heav'nly *Venus*, 'midst her smiles and loves:
She views around the supplicating train,
60   And shakes her graceful head with stern disdain,
Proudly she turns around her lofty eyes,
And thus reviles celestial deities:
"What madness drives the *Theban* ladies fair
To give their incense to surrounding air?
65   Say why this new sprung deity preferr'd?
Why vainly fancy your petitions heard?
Or say why *Coeus'* offspring is obey'd,
While to my goddeship no tribute's paid?
For me no altars blaze with living fires,
70   No bullock bleeds, no frankincense transpires,
Tho' *Cadmus'* palace, not unknown to fame,
And *Phrygian* nations all revere my name.
Where'er I turn my eyes vast wealth I find.
Lo! here an empress with a goddess join'd.
75   What, shall a *Titaness* be deify'd,
To whom the spacious earth a couch deny'd?
Nor heav'n, nor earth, nor sea receiv'd your queen,
'Till pitying *Delos* took the wand'rer in.
Round me what a large progeny is spread!
80   No frowns of fortune has my soul to dread.
What if indignant she decrease my train
More than *Latona's* number will remain?
Then hence, ye *Theban* dames, hence haste away,
Nor longer off'rings to *Latona* pay?
85   Regard the orders of *Amphion's* spouse,
And take the leaves of laurel from your brows."
Niobe spoke. The *Theban* maids obey'd,
Their brows unbound, and left the rights unpaid.

        The angry goddess heard, then silence broke
90   On *Cynthus'* summit, and indignant spoke;
"*Phoebus!* behold, thy mother in disgrace,
Who to no goddess yields the prior place
Except to *Juno's* self, who reigns above,

The spouse and sister of the thund'ring *Jove*.
95   *Niobe* sprung from *Tantalus* inspires
Each *Theban* bosom with rebellious fires;
No reason her imperious temper quells,
But all her father in her tongue rebels;
Wrap her own sons for her blaspheming breath,
100 *Apollo!* wrap them in the shades of death."
Latona ceas'd and ardent thus replies,
The God, whose glory decks th' expanded skies.

       "Cease thy complaints, mine be the task assign'd
To punish pride, and scourge the rebel mind."
105 This *Phoebe* join'd.—They wing their instant flight;
Thebes trembled as th' immortal pow'rs alight.

       With clouds incompass'd glorious *Phoebus* stands;
The feather'd vengeance quiv'ring in his hands.

       Near *Cadmus'* walls a plain extended lay,
110 Where *Thebes'* young princes pass'd in sport the day:
There the bold coursers bounded o'er the plains,
While their great masters held the golden reins.
Ismenus first the racing pastime led,
And rul'd the fury of his flying steed.
115 "Ah me," he sudden cries, with shrieking breath,
While in his breast he feels the shaft of death;
He drops the bridle on his courser's mane,
Before his eyes in shadows swims the plain,
He, the first-born of great *Amphion's* bed,
120 Was struck the first, first mingled with the dead.

       Then didst thou, *Sipylus,* the language hear
Of fate portentous whistling in the air:
As when th' impending storm the sailor sees
He spreads his canvas to the fav'ring breeze,
125 So to thine horse thou gav'st the golden reins,
Gav'st him to rush impetuous o'er the plains:
But ah! a fatal shaft from *Phoebus'* hand
Smites through thy neck, and sinks thee on the sand.

Two other brothers were at *wrestling* found,
130 And in their pastime claspt each other round:
A shaft that instant from *Apollo's* hand
Transfixt them both, and stretcht them on the sand:
Together they their cruel fate bemoan'd,
Together languish'd, and together groan'd:
135 Together too th'unbodied spirits fled,
And sought the gloomy mansions of the dead.

Alphenor saw, and trembling at the view,
Beat his torn breast, that chang'd its snowy hue.
He flies to raise them in a kind embrace;
140 A brother's fondness triumphs in his face:
Alphenor fails in this fraternal deed,
A dart dispatch'd him (so the fates decreed:)
Soon as the arrow left the deadly wound,
His issuing entrails smoak'd upon the ground.

145 What woes on blooming *Damasichon* wait!
His sighs portend his near impending fate.
Just where the well-made leg begins to be,
And the soft sinews form the supple knee,
The youth sore wounded by the *Delian* god
150 Attempts t'extract the crime-avenging rod,
But, whilst he strives the will of fate t'avert,
Divine *Apollo* sends a second dart;
Swift thro' his throat the feather'd mischief flies,
Bereft of sense, he drops his head, and dies.

155 Young *Ilioneus*, the last, directs his pray'r,
And cries, "My life, ye gods celestial! spare."
Apollo heard, and pity touch'd his heart,
But ah! too late, for he had sent the dart:
Thou too, O *Ilioneus*, art doom'd to fall,
160 The fates refuse that arrow to recal.

On the swift wings of ever-flying *Fame*
To *Cadmus'* palace soon the tidings came:
Niobe heard, and with indignant eyes

She thus express'd her anger and surprize:
165 "Why is such privilege to them allow'd?
Why thus insulted by the *Delian* god?
Dwells there such mischief in the pow'rs above?
Why sleeps the vengeance of immortal *Jove*"
For now *Amphion* too, with grief oppress'd,
170 Had plung'd the deadly dagger in his breast.
Niobe now, less haughty than before,
With lofty head directs her steps no more.
She, who late told her pedigree divine,
And drove the *Thebans* from *Latona's* shrine,
175 How strangely chang'd!—yet beautiful in woe,
She weeps, nor weeps unpity'd by the foe.
On each pale corse the wretched mother spread
Lay overwhelm'd with grief, and kiss'd her dead,
Then rais'd her arms, and thus, in accents slow,
180 "Be sated cruel *Goddess*! with my woe;
If I've offended, let these streaming eyes,
And let this sev'nfold funeral suffice:
Ah! take this wretched life you deign'd to save,
With them I too am carried to the grave.
185 Rejoice triumphant, my victorious foe,
But show the cause from whence your triumphs flow?
Tho' I unhappy mourn these children slain,
Yet greater numbers to my lot remain."
She ceas'd, the bow string twang'd with awful sound,
190 Which struck with terror all th'assembly round,
Except the queen, who stood unmov'd alone,
By her distresses more presumptuous grown.
Near the pale corses stood their sisters fair
In sable vestures and dishevell'd hair;
195 One, while she draws the fatal shaft away,
Faints, falls, and sickens at the light of day.
To sooth her mother, lo! another flies,
And blames the fury of inclement skies,
And, while her words a filial pity show,
200 Struck dumb—indignant seeks the shades below.
Now from the fatal place another flies,

Falls in her flight, and languishes, and dies.
Another on her sister drops in death;
A fifth in trembling terrors yields her breath;
205 While the sixth seeks some gloomy cave in vain,
Struck with the rest, and mingled with the slain.

One only daughter lives, and she the least;
The queen close clasp'd the daughter to her breast:
"Ye heav'nly pow'rs, ah spare me one," she cry'd,
210 "Ah! spare me one," the vocal hills reply'd:
In vain she begs, the Fates her suit deny,
In her embrace she sees her daughter die.

*"The queen of all her family bereft,
Without or husband, son, or daughter left,
215 Grew stupid at the shock. The passing air
Made no impression on her stiff'ning hair.
The blood forsook her face: amidst the flood
Pour'd from her cheeks, quite fix'd her eye-balls stood.
Her tongue, her palate both obdurate grew,
220 Her curdled veins no longer motion knew;
The use of neck, and arms, and feet was gone,
And ev'n her bowels hard'ned into stone:
A marble statue now the queen appears,
But from the marble steal the silent tears."

*This Verse to the End is the Work of another Hand.

To S. M. a young *African* Painter, on seeing his Works.

TO show the lab'ring bosom's deep intent,
And thought in living characters to paint,
When first thy pencil did those beauties give,
And breathing figures learnt from thee to live,
5 How did those prospects give my soul delight,
A new creation rushing on my sight?

Still, wond'rous youth! each noble path pursue,
On deathless glories fix thine ardent view:
Still may the painter's and the poet's fire
10   To aid thy pencil, and thy verse conspire!
And may the charms of each seraphic theme
Conduct thy footsteps to immortal fame!
High to the blissful wonders of the skies
Elate thy soul, and raise thy wishful eyes.
15   Thrice happy, when exalted to survey
That splendid city, crown'd with endless day,
Whose twice six gates on radiant hinges ring:
Celestial *Salem* blooms in endless spring.

Calm and serene thy moments glide along,
20   And may the muse inspire each future song!
Still, with the sweets of contemplation bless'd,
May peace with balmy wings your soul invest!
But when these shades of time are chas'd away,
And darkness ends in everlasting day,
25   On what seraphic pinions shall we move,
And view the landscapes in the realms above?
There shall thy tongue in heav'nly murmurs flow,
And there my muse with heav'nly transport glow:
No more to tell of *Damon's* tender sighs,
30   Or rising radiance of *Aurora's* eyes,
For nobler themes demand a nobler strain,
And purer language on th' ethereal plain.
Cease, gentle muse! the solemn gloom of night
Now seals the fair creation from my sight.

To His Honour the Lieutenant-Governor,
on the Death of his Lady. *March* 24, 1773.

ALL-conquering Death! by thy resistless pow'r,
Hope's tow'ring plumage falls to rise no more!
Of scenes terrestrial how the glories fly,

Forget their splendors, and submit to die!
5   Who ere escap'd thee, but the saint* of old
Beyond the flood in sacred annals told,
And the great sage,* whom fiery courses drew
To heav'n's bright portals from *Elisha*'s view;
Wond'ring he gaz'd at the refulgent car,
10   Then snatch'd the mantle floating on the air.
From *Death* these only could exemption boast,
And without dying gain'd th' immortal coast.
Not falling millions sate the tyrant's mind,
Nor can the victor's progress be confin'd.
15   But cease thy strife with *Death,* fond *Nature,* cease:
He leads the *virtuous* to the realms of peace;
His to conduct to the immortal plains,
Where heav'n's Supreme in bliss and glory reigns.

There sits, illustrious Sir, thy beauteous spouse;
20   A gem-blaz'd circle beaming on her brows.
Hail'd with acclaim among the heav'nly choirs,
Her soul new-kindling with seraphic fires,
To notes divine she tunes the vocal strings,
While heav'n's high concave with the music rings.
25   *Virtue*'s rewards can mortal pencil paint?
No—all descriptive arts, and eloquence are faint;
Nor canst thou, *Oliver,* assent refuse
To heav'nly tidings from the *Afric* muse.

As soon may change thy laws, eternal *fate,*
30   As the saint miss the glories I relate;
Or her *Benevolence* forgotten lie,
Which wip'd the trick'ling tear from *Mis'ry*'s eye.
Whene'er the adverse winds were known to blow,
When loss to loss* ensu'd, and woe to woe,
35   Calm and serene beneath her father's hand
She sat resign'd to the divine command.

No longer then, great Sir, her death deplore,
And let us hear the mournful sigh no more,

Restrain the sorrow streaming from thine eye,
40 Be all thy future moments crown'd with joy!
Nor let thy wishes be to earth confin'd,
But soaring high pursue th'unbodied mind.
Forgive the muse, forgive th'advent'rous lays,
That fain thy soul to heav'nly scenes would raise.

*Enoch
*Elijah
*Three amiable Daughters who died when just arrived to Womens Estate.

A Farewel to AMERICA. To Mrs. S.W.

I.
ADIEU, *New-England's* smiling meads,
    Adieu, the flow'ry plain:
I leave thine op'ning charms, O spring,
    And tempt the roaring main.

II.
5 In vain for me the flow'rets rise,
    And boast their gaudy pride,
While here beneath the northern skies
    I mourn for *health* deny'd.

III.
Celestial maid of rosy hue,
10   O let me feel thy reign!
I languish till thy face I view,
    Thy vanish'd joys regain.

IV.
Susannah mourns, nor can I bear
    To see the crystal show'r,
15 Or mark the tender falling tear
    At sad departure's hour;

V.
Nor unregarding can I see
  Her soul with grief opprest:
But let no sighs, no groans for me,
20   Steal from her pensive breast.

VI.
In vain the feather'd warblers sing,
  In vain the garden blooms,
And on the bosom of the spring
  Breathes out her sweet perfumes,

VII.
25 While for *Britannia's* distant shore
  We sweep the liquid plain,
And with astonish'd eyes explore
  The wide-extended main.

VIII.
Lo! *Health* appears! celestial dame!
30 Complacent and serene,
With *Hebe's* mantle o'er her Frame,
  With soul-delighting mein.

IX.
To mark the vale where *London* lies
  With misty vapours crown'd,
35 Which cloud *Aurora's* thousand dyes,
  And veil her charms around,

X.
Why, *Phoebus*, moves thy car so slow?
  So slow thy rising ray?
Give us the famous town to view
40 Thou glorious king of day!

XI.

For thee, *Britannia*, I resign
   New-England's smiling fields;
To view again her charms divine,
   What joy the prospect yields!

XII.

45 But thou! Temptation hence away,
   With all thy fatal train
Nor once seduce my soul away,
   By thine enchanting strain.

XIII.

Thrice happy they, whose heav'nly shield
50   Secures their souls from harms,
And fell *Temptation* on the field
   Of all its pow'r disarms!

         Boston, May 7, 1773.

A REBUS, by *I. B.*

I.

A BIRD delicious to the taste,
On which an army once did feast,
   Sent by an hand unseen;
A creature of the horned race,
5 Which *Britain's* royal standards grace;
   A gem of vivid green;

II.

A town of gaiety and sport,
Where beaux and beauteous nymphs resort,
   And gallantry doth reign;
10 A *Dardan* hero fam'd of old
For youth and beauty, as we're told,
   And by a monarch slain;

III.
A peer of popular applause,
Who doth our violated laws,
15   And grievances proclaim.
Th'initials show a vanquish'd town,
That adds fresh glory and renown
        To old *Britannia's* fame.

An ANSWER to the *Rebus*, by the Author of these POEMS.

THE poet asks, and *Phillis* can't refuse
To shew th'obedience of the Infant muse.
She knows the *Quail* of most inviting taste
Fed *Israel's* army in the dreary waste;
5 And what's on *Britain's* royal standard borne,
But the tall, graceful, rampant *Unicorn*?
The *Emerald* with a vivid verdure glows
Among the gems which regal crowns compose;
Boston's a town, polite and debonair,
10 To which the beaux and beauteous nymphs repair,
Each *Helen* strikes the mind with sweet surprise,
While living lightning flashes from her eyes.
See young *Euphorbus* of the *Dardan* line
By *Menelaus'* hand to death resign:
15 The well known peer of popular applause
Is *C—m* zealous to support our laws.
        Quebec now vanquish'd must obey,
        She too must annual tribute pay
        To *Britain* of immortal fame,
20   And add new glory to her name.

                FINIS.

III.

A bent of popular applause,
Who doubly her violated laws,
And grievances proclaim
Th' annals show a vanquish'd town,
That adds fresh glory and renown
To old Britannia's fame.

An ANSWER to the Above, by the Author of these POEMS.

THE poet asks, and Phillis can't refuse
To show th' obedience of the Infant muse.
She knows the Quail of most inviting taste,
Fed Ibrael's army in the dreary waste;
And what is on Britain's royal standard borne,
But the tall, graceful, rampant Unicorn?
The Emerald with a wild verdure glows
Among the gems which regal crowns compose;
Boston's a town, polite and debonair,
To which the beaux and beauteous nymphs repair,
Each Helen strikes the mind with sweet surprise,
While living lightning flashes from her eyes,
See young Euphorbus of the Dardan line
By Menelaus' hand to death resign;
The well known peer of popular applause
Is C—zealous to support our laws.
(No're now vanquish'd must obey,
She too must annual tribute pay,
To Britain of immortal fame,
And add new glory to her name.

FINIS.

EXTANT POEMS NOT PUBLISHED IN

POEMS ON VARIOUS SUBJECTS

[manuscript at the Historical Society of Pennsylvania]

Atheism—

> Where now shall I begin this Spacious Feild
> To tell what curses unbeleif doth yield
> Thou that dost daily feel his hand and rod
> And dare deny the essence of a god
> 5   If there's no god from whence did all things spring
> He made the greatest and minutest thing
> If there's no heaven whither wilt thou go
> Make thy Elysium in the Shades below
> With great astonishment any soul is struck
> 10   O rashness great hast thou thy sense forsook
> Hast thou forgot the preterperfect days
> They are recorded in the Book of praise
> If twas not written by the hand of God
> Why was it sealed with Immanuel's blood
> 15   Tho 'tis a second point thou dost deny
> Unmeasur'd vengeance Scarlet sins do cry
> Turn now I pray thee from the dangerous road
> Rise from the dust and seek the mighty God
> By whose great mercy we do move and live
> 20   Whose Loving kindness doth our sins forgive
> Tis Beelzebub our adversary great
> Withholds from us the kingdom and the seat
> Bliss weeping waits us in her arms to fly
> To the vast regions of Felicity
> 25   Perhaps thy Ignorance will ask us where

Go to the corner stone it will declare
Thy heart in unbeleif will harder grow
Altho thou hidest it for pleasure now
Thou tak'st unusual means, the path forbear
30   Unkind to Others to thyself severe
Methinks I see the consequence thou art blind
Thy unbeleif disturbs the peaceful mind
The endless Scene too far for me to tread
Too great to Accomplish from so weak a head
35   If men Such wise inventions then should know
In the high Firmament who made the bow
That covenant was made for to ensure
Made to establish lasting to endure
Who made the heavens and earth a lasting Spring
40   Of Admiration. to whom dost thou bring
Thy thanks, and tribute, Adoration pay,
To heathen Gods, can wise Apollo say
Tis I that saves thee from the deepest hell
Minerva teach thee all thy days to tell
45   Doth Pluto tell thee thou shalt see the Shade
Of fell perdition for thy learning made
Doth Cupid in thy breast that warmth inspire
To Love thy brother which is Gods desire
Look thou above and see who made the sky
50   Nothing more Lucid to an Atheist's eye
Look thou beneath, behold each purling stream
It surely can not a Delusion Seem
Mark rising Pheobus when he spreads his ray
And his commission for to guide the day
55   At night keep watch, and see a Cynthia bright
And her commission for to guide the night
See how the stars when the[y] do sing his praise
Witness his essence in celestial Lays

[1767]

[manuscript at the Massachusetts Historical Society]

An Address to the Atheist, by P. Wheatley
at the Age of 14 Years—1767—.

      Muse! where shall I begin the spacious feild
      To tell what curses unbeleif doth yeild?
      Thou who dost daily feel his hand, and rod
      Darest thou deny the Essence of a God!—
5   If there's no heav'n, ah! whither wilt thou go
      Make thy Ilysium in the shades below?
      If there's no God from whom did all things Spring
      He made the *greatest* and *minutest* Thing
      Angelic ranks no less his Power display
10   Than the least mite scarce visible to Day
      With vast astonishment my soul is struck
      Have Reason'g powers thy darken'd breast forsook?
      The Laws deep Graven by the hand of God,
      Seal'd with Immanuel's all-redeeming blood:
15   This second point thy folly dares deny
      On thy devoted head for vengeance cry—
      Turn then I pray thee from the dangerous road
      Rise from the dust and seek the mighty God.
      His is bright truth without a dark disguise
20   And his are wisdom's all beholding Eyes:
      With labour'd snares our Adversary great
      Withholds from us the Kingdom and the seat.
      Bliss weeping waits thee, in her Arms to fly
      To her own regions of felicity—
25   Perhaps thy ignorance will ask us where?
      Go to the *Corner stone* he will declare.
      Thy heart in unbelief will harden'd grow
      Tho' much indulg'd in vicious pleasure now—
      Thou tak'st unusual means; the path forbear
30   Unkind to others to thy self Severe—
      Methinks I see the consequence thou'rt blind
      Thy unbelief disturbs the peaceful Mind.
      The endless scene too far for me to tread

Too great to utter from so weak a head.
35   That man his maker's love divine might know
In heavens high firmament he placed his Bow
To shew his covenant for ever sure
To endless Age unchanging to endure—
He made the Heavens and earth that lasting Spring
40   Of admiration! To whom dost thou bring
Thy grateful tribute? Adoration pay
To heathen Gods? Can wise *Apollo* say
Tis I that saves thee from the deepest hell;
Minerva teach thee all thy days to tell?
45   Doth *Pluto* tell thee thou Shalt see the shade
Of fell perdition for transgression made?
Doth *Cupid* in thy breast that warmth inspire
To love thy Brother, which is God's desire?
Atheist! behold the wide extended skies
50   And wisdom infinite shall strike thine eyes
Mark rising Sol when far he spreads his Ray
And his Commission read—To rule the Day
At night behold that silver Regent bright
And her command to lead the train of Night
55   Lo! how the Stars all vocal in his praise
Witness his Essence in celestial lays!

[1767]

[manuscript at the Historical Society of Pennsylvania]

Deism

Must Ethiopians be imploy'd for you
Greatly rejoice if any good I do
I ask O unbeleiver satan's child
Has not thy saviour been to meek & mild
5   The auspicious rays that round his head do shine
Do still declare him to be christ divine

Doth not the Omnipotent call him son?
And is well pleas'd with his beloved One
How canst thou thus divide the trinity
10   What can'st thou take up for to make the three
Tis satan snares a Fluttering in the wind
Whereby he hath ensnar'd thy Foolish mind
God the eternal Orders this to be
Sees thy vain arg'ments to divide the three
15   Canst thou not see the consequence in store
Begin the Omnipotent to adore
Arise the pinions of Persuasions here
Seek the Eternal while he is so near
At the last day where wilt thou hide thy face
20   The day approaching is no time for grace
Then wilt thou cry thyself undone and lost
Proclaiming Father, Son, and Holy Ghost
Who trod the wine press of Jehovahs wrath
Who taught us prayer and gave us grace and faith
25   Who but the great and the Supreme who bless'd
Ever and ever in Immortal rest
The meanest prodigal that comes to God
Is not cast off, but brought by Jesus Blood
When to the faithless Jews he oft did cry
30   One call'd him Teacher some made him a lye
He came to you in mean apparell clad
He came to save you from your sins and had
Far more Compassion than I can express
Pains his companions, and his Friends Distress
35   Immanuel God with us these pains did bear
Must the Eternal our Petitions hear?
Ah! cruel distiny his life he Laid
Father Forgive them thus the saviour said
They nail'd King Jesus to the cross for us
40   For our Transgressions he did bear the curse.

   May I O Eternal salute aurora to begin thy Praise, shall mortal dust do that which immortals scarcely can comprehend, then O omnipotent I will humbly ask, after imploring thy pardon for this presumption, when shall we approach thy majestys presence crown'd with celestial Dignities When shall we see the resting place of the great Supreme When shall we behold thee. O redeemer in all the respendent Graces of a Suffering God,

    yet wise men Sent from the Orient clime
    Now led by seraphs to the bless'd abode

[1767]

[manuscript at the Massachusetts Historical Society]

An Address to the Deist—1767—

      Must Ethiopians be employ'd for you?
      Much I rejoice if any good I do.
      I ask O unbeleiver, Satan's child
      Hath not thy Saviour been too much revil'd
5   Th' auspicious rays that round his temples shine
      Do still declare him to be Christ divine
      Doth not the great *Eternal* call him Son
      Is he not pleas'd with his beloved One—?
      How canst thou thus divide the Trinity—
10   The blest the Holy the eternal three
      Tis Satan's Snares are fluttering in the wind
      Whereby he doth insnare thy foolish mind
      God, the Eternal Orders this to be
      Sees thy vain arg'ments to divide the three
15   Cans't thou not see the Consequence in store?
      Begin th' Almighty monarch to adore
      Attend to Reason whispering in thine ear
      Seek the Eternal while he is so near.
      Full in thy view I point each path I know
20   Lest to the vale of black dispair I go.
      At the last day where wilt thou hide thy face
      That *Day* approaching is no time for Grace.
      Too late percieve thyself undone and lost

To late own Father, Son, and Holy Ghost.
25 Who trod the wine-press of Jehovah's wrath?
Who taught us prayer, and promis'd grace and faith—?
Who but the Son, who reigns supremely blest
Ever, and ever, in immortal rest.? [sic]
The vilest prodigal who comes to God
30 Is not cast out but bro't by Jesus' blood.
When to the faithless Jews he oft did cry
Some own'd this teacher Some made him a lye
He came to you in mean apparel clad
He came to Save us from our Sins, and had
35 Compassion more than language can express.
Pains his companions, and his friends distress
Immanuel on the cross those pains did bear—
Will the eternal our petitions hear?
Ah! wondrous Distiny his life he laid.
40 "Father forgive them," thus the Saviour pray'd
Nail'd was King Jesus on the cross for us.
For our transgressions he sustain'd the Curse.

[1767]

On Messrs Hussey and Coffin.
TO THE PRINTER
[*Newport Mercury*, December 21, 1767].

Please to insert the following Lines, composed by a Negro Girl
(belonging to one Mr. Wheatley of Boston) on the following
Occasion, viz. Messrs Hussey and Coffin, as undermentioned,
belonging to Nantucket, being bound from thence to Boston,
narrowly escaped being cast away on Cape-Cod, in one of the
late Storms; upon their Arrival, being at Mr. Wheatley's, and,
while at Dinner, told of their narrow Escape, this Negro Girl at
the same Time 'tending Table, heard the Relation, from which
she composed the following Verses.

Did Fear and Danger so perplex your Mind,
As made you fearful of the Whistling Wind?
Was it not Boreas knit his angry Brow
Against you? or did Consideration bow?
5   To lend you Aid, did not his Winds combine?
To stop your passage with a churlish Line,
Did haughty Eolus with Contempt look down
With Aspect windy, and a study'd Frown?
Regard them not;—the Great Supreme, the Wise,
10   Intends for something hidden from our Eyes.
Suppose the groundless Gulph had snatch'd away
Hussey and Coffin to the raging Sea;
Where wou'd they go? where wou'd be their Abode?
With the supreme and independent God,
15   Or made their Beds down in the Shades below,
Where neither Pleasure nor Content can flow.
To Heaven their Souls with eager Raptures soar,
Enjoy the Bliss of him they wou'd adore.
Had the soft gliding Streams of Grace been near,
20   Some favourite Hope their fainting hearts to cheer,
Doubtless the Fear of Danger far had fled:
No more repeated Victory crown their Heads.

*Had I the Tongue of a Seraphim, how would I exalt thy
Praise; thy Name as Incense to the Heavens should fly, and the
Remembrance of thy Goodness to the shoreless Ocean of Beati-
tude!—Then should the Earth glow with seraphick Ardour.*

Blest Soul, which sees the Day while Light doth shine,
To guide his Steps to trace the Mark divine.

Phillis Wheatley

[manuscript at the Historical Society of Pennsylvania]

America

    New England first a wilderness was found
    Till for a continent 'twas destin'd round
    From feild to feild the savage monsters run
    E'r yet Brittania had her work begun
5   Thy Power, O Liberty, makes strong the weak
    And (wond'rous instinct) Ethiopians speak
    Sometimes by Simile, a victory's won
    A certain lady had an only son
    He grew up daily virtuous as he grew
10   Fearing his Strength which she undoubted knew
    She laid some taxes on her darling son
    And would have laid another act there on
    Amend your manners I'll the task remove
    Was said with seeming Sympathy and Love
15   By many Scourges she his goodness try'd
    Untill at length the Best of Infants cry'd
    He wept, Brittania turn'd a senseless ear
    At last awaken'd by maternal fear
    Why weeps americus why weeps my Child
20   Thus spake Brittania, thus benign and mild
    My dear mama said he, shall I repeat—
    Then Prostrate fell, at her maternal feet
    What ails the rebel, great Brittania Cry'd
    Indeed said he, you have no cause to Chide
25   You see each day my fluent tears my food.
    Without regard, what no more English blood?
    Has length of time drove from our English veins
    The kindred he to Great Brittania deigns?
    Tis thus with thee O Brittain keeping down
30   New English force, thou fear'st his Tyranny and thou
       didst frown
    He weeps afresh to feel this Iron chain
    Turn, O Brittania claim thy child again
    Riecho Love drive by thy powerful charms

Indolence Slumbering in forgetful arms
35   See Agenoria diligent imploy's
Her sons, and thus with rapture she replys
Arise my sons with one consent arise
Lest distant continents with vult'ring eyes
Should charge America with Negligence
40   They praise Industry but no pride commence
To raise their own Profusion, O Brittain See
By this, New England will increase like thee

[1768]

[manuscript at the Historical Society of Pennsylvania]

To the Hon.ble Commodore Hood on his Pardoning a Deserter

It was thy noble soul and high desert
That caus'd these breathings of my grateful heart
You sav'd a soul from Pluto's dreary shore
You sav'd his body and he asks no more
5   This generous act Immortal wreaths shall bring
To thee for meritorious was the Spring
From whence from whence, [sic] this candid ardor
    flow'd
To grace thy name, and Glorify thy God
The Eatherial spirits in the realms above
10   Rejoice to see thee exercise thy Love
Hail: Commodore may heaven delighted pour
Its blessings plentious in a silent shower
The voice of pardon did resound on high
While heaven consented, and he must not die
15   On thee, fair victor be the Blessing shed
And rest for ever on thy matchless Head

Phillis
[1769]

[manuscript at the Moorland-Spingarn Research Center at Howard University]

On Friendship

> Let amicitia in her ample reign
> Extend her notes to a Celestial strain
> Benevolent far more divinely Bright
> Amor like me doth triumph at the sight
> 5 When my thoughts in gratitude imploy
> Mental Imaginations give me Joy
> Now let my thoughts in Contemplation steer
> The Footsteps of the Superlative fair

Written by   Phillis Wheatley
Boston July 15 1769

[manuscript at the Historical Society of Pennsylvania]

On the Death of Mr. Snider Murder'd by Richardson

> In heavens eternal court it was decreed
> How the first martyr for the cause should bleed
> To clear the country of the hated brood
> He whet his courage for the common good
> 5 Long hid before, a vile infernal here
> Prevents Achilles in his mid career
> Where'er this fury darts his Pois'nous breath
> All are endanger'd to the shafts of death
> The generous Sires beheld the fatal wound
> 10 Saw their young champion gasping on the ground
> They rais'd him up. but to each present ear
> What martial glories did his tongue declare
> The wretch appal'd no longer can despise
> But from the Striking victim turns his eyes—
> 15 When this young martial genius did appear
> The Tory cheifs no longer could forbear.

Ripe for destruction, see the wretches doom
He waits the curses of the age to come
In vain he flies, by Justice Swiftly chaced
20   With unexpected infamy disgraced
Be Richardson for ever banish'd here
The grand Usurpers bravely vaunted Heir.
We bring the body from the watry bower
To lodge it where it shall remove no more.
25   Snider behold with what Majestic Love
The Illustrious retinue begins to move
With Secret rage fair freedoms foes beneath
See in thy corse ev'n Majesty in Death

                              Phillis
                              [Late February or early March 1770]

[manuscript owned by Mark E. Mitchell]

Ocean

Now muse divine, thy heav'nly aid impart,
The feast of Genius, and the play of Art.
From high Parnassus' radiant top repair,
Celestial Nine! propitious to my pray'r.
5   In vain my Eyes explore the wat'ry reign,
By you unaided with the flowing strain.
            When first old Chaos of tyrannic soul
Wav'd his dread Sceptre o'er the boundless whole,
Confusion reign'd till the divine Command
10   On floating azure fix'd the Solid Land,
Till first he call'd the latent seeds of light,
And gave dominion o'er eternal Night.
From deepest glooms he rais'd this ample Ball,
And round its walls he bade its surges roll;
15   With instant haste the new made seas complyd,
And the globe rolls impervious to the Tide;
Yet when the mighty Sire of Ocean frownd

"His awful trident shook the solid Ground."
The King of Tempests thunders o'er the plain,
20 And scorns the azure monarch of the main,
He sweeps the surface, makes the billows rore,
And furious, lash the loud resounding shore.
His pinion'd race his dread commands obey,
Syb's, Eurus, Boreas, drive the foaming sea!
25 See the whole stormy progeny descend!
And waves on waves devolving without End,
But cease Eolus, all thy winds restrain,
And let us view the wonders of the main
Where the proud Courser paws the blue abode,
30 Impetuous bounds, and mocks the driver's rod.
There, too, the Heifer fair as that which bore
Divine Europa to the Cretan shore.
With guileless mein the gentle Creature strays[,]
Quaffs the pure stream, and crops ambrosial Grass[.]
35   Again with recent wonder I survey
The finny sov'reign bask in hideous play[.]
(So fancy sees) he makes a tempest rise
And intercept the azure vaulted skies[.]
Such is his sport:—but if his anger glow
40 What kindling vengeance boils the deep below!
          Twas but e'er now an Eagle young and gay
Pursu'd his passage thro' the aierial way[.]
He aim'd his piece, would C[ale]f's hand do more [?]
Yes, him he brought to pluto's dreary shore[.]
45 Slow breathed his last, the painful minutes move
With lingring pace his rashness to reprove;
Perhaps his father's Just commands he bore
To fix dominion on some distant shore[.]
Ah! me unblest he cries[.] Oh! had I staid
50 Or swift my Father's mandate had obey['d.]
But ah! too late.—Old Ocean heard his cries[.]
He stroakes his hoary tresses and replies[:]
What mean these plaints so near our wat'ry throne,
And what the Cause of this distressful moan?
55 Confess[,] Iscarius, let thy words be true
Not let me find a faithless Bird in you[.]

His voice struck terror thro' the whole domain[.]
Aw'd by his frowns the royal youth began,
Saw you not[,] Sire, a tall and Gallant ship
60   Which proudly skims the surface of the deep[?]
With pompous form from Boston's port she came[,]
She flies, and London her resounding name[.]
O'er the rough surge the dauntless Chief prevails
For partial Aura fills his swelling sails[.]
65   His fatal musket shortens thus my day
And thus the victor takes my life away[.]
          Faint with his wound Iscarius said no more[,]
His Spirit sought Oblivion's sable shore.
This Neptune saw, and with a hollow groan
70   Resum'd the azure honours of his Throne.

[Written in another hand on page four of the manuscript:]

                              OCEAN
                              A poem by Phillis
                              in her handwriting
                              made on her return from
                              England in Capt Calef
                              Sept. 1773—

An ELEGY, To Miss. Mary Moorhead, on the DEATH of her
Father, *The Rev. Mr.* JOHN MOORHEAD.

          INVOLV'D in Clouds of Wo, *Maria* mourns,
And various Anguish wracks her Soul by turns;
See thy lov'd Parent languishing in Death,
His Exit watch, and catch his flying Breath;
5   "Stay happy Shade," distress'd *Maria* cries;
"Stay happy Shade," the hapless Church replies;
"Suspend a while, suspend thy rapid flight,
Still with thy Friendship, chear our sullen Night;
The sullen Night of Error, Sin, and Pain;
10   See Earth astonish'd at the Loss, complain;"

Thine, and the Church's Sorrows I deplore;
Moorhead is dead, and Friendship is no more;
From Earth she flies, nor mingles with our Wo,
Since cold the Breast, where once she deign'd to glow;
15   Here shone the heavenly Virtue, there confess'd,
Celestial Love, reign'd joyous in his Breast;
Till Death grown jealous for his drear Domain,
Sent his dread Offspring, unrelenting Pain.
With hasty Wing, the Son of Terror flies,
20   Lest *Moorhead* find the Portal of the Skies;
Without a Passage through the Shades below,
Like great *Elijah*, Death's triumphant Foe;
Death follows soon, nor leaves the Prophet long,
His Eyes are seal'd, and every Nerve unstrung;
25   Forever silent is the stiff'ning Clay,
While the rapt Soul, explores the Realms of Day.
Oft has he strove to raise the Soul from Earth,
Oft has he travail'd in the heavenly Birth;
Till JESUS took possession of the Soul,
30   Till the new Creature liv'd throughout the whole.

When the fierce conviction seiz'd the Sinner's Mind,
The Law-loud thundering he to Death consign'd;
JEHOVAH'S Wrath revolving, he surveys,
The Fancy's terror, and the Soul's amaze.
35   Say, what is Death? The Gloom of endless Night,
Which from the Sinner, bars the Gates of Light:
Say, what is Hell? In Horrors passing strange;
His Vengeance views, who seals his final Change;
The winged Hours, the final Judgment brings,
40   Decides his Fate, and that of Gods and Kings;
Tremendous Doom! And dreadful to be told,
To dwell in Tophet 'stead of shrines of Gold.
"Gods! Ye shall die like Men," the Herald cries,
"And stil'd no more the Children of the Skies."

45   Trembling he sees the horrid Gulf appear,
Creation quakes, and no Deliverer near;
With Heart relenting to his Feelings kind,

See *Moorhead* hasten to relieve his Mind.
See him the Gospel's healing Balm impart,
50 To sooth the Anguish of his tortur'd Heart.
He points the trembling Mountain, and the Tree,
Which bent beneath th' incarnate Deity,
How God descended, wonderous to relate,
To bear our Crimes, a dread enormous Weight;
55 Seraphic Strains too feeble to repeat,
Half the dread Punishment the GOD-HEAD meet.
Suspended there, (till Heaven was reconcil'd,)
Like MOSES' Serpent in the Desert wild.
The Mind appeas'd what new Devotion glows,
60 With Joy unknown, the raptur'd Soul o'erflows;
While on his GOD-like Savior's Glory bent,
His Life proves witness of his Heart's intent.
Lament ye indigent the Friendly Mind,
Which oft relented, to your Mis'ry kind.

65   With humble Gratitude he render'd Praise,
To Him whose Spirit had inspir'd his Lays;
To Him whose Guidance gave his Words to flow,
Divine instruction, and the Balm of Wo:
To you his Offspring, and his Church, be given,
70 A triple Portion of his Thirst for Heaven;
Such was the Prophet; we the Stroke deplore,
Which let's us hear his warning Voice no more.
But cease complaining, hush each murm'ring Tongue,
Pursue the Example which inspires my Song.
75 Let his Example in your Conduct shine;
Own the afflicting Providence, divine;
So shall bright Periods grace your joyful Days,
And heavenly Anthems swell your Songs of Praise.

Boston, Decem. 15 1773. Phillis Wheatley.

Printed from the Original Manuscript, and Sold by WILLIAM M'ALPINE, at his Shop in *Marlborough-Street*, 1773.

[To a Gentleman of the Navy.]
For the ROYAL AMERICAN MAGAZINE [December 1774].

*By particular request we insert the following Poem addressed,
by Philis [sic], (a young African, of surprising genius) to a gentle-
man of the navy, with his reply.*

*By this single instance may be seen, the importance of educa-
tion.—Uncultivated nature is much the same in every part of the
globe. It is probable* Europe *and* Affrica *would be alike savage or
polite in the same circumstances; though, it may be questioned,
whether men who have no artificial wants, are capable of becom-
ing so ferocious as those, who by faring sumptuously every day,
are reduced to a habit of thinking it necessary to their happiness,
to plunder the whole human race.*

> Celestial muse! for sweetness fam'd inspire
> My wondrous theme with true poetic fire,
> Rochfort, for thee! And Greaves deserve my lays
> The sacred tribute of ingenuous praise.
5> For here, true merit shuns the glare of light,
> She loves oblivion, and evades the sight.
> At sight of her, see dawning genius rise
> And stretch her pinions to her native skies.
>
> Paris, for Helen's bright resistless charms,
10> Made Illion bleed and set the world in arms.
> Had you appear'd on the Achaian shore
> Troy now had stood, and Helen charm'd no more.
> The Phrygian hero had resign'd the dame
> For purer joys in friendship's sacred flame,
15> The noblest gift, and of immortal kind,
> That brightens, dignifies the manly mind.
>
> Calliope, half gracious to my prayer,
> Grants but the half and scatters half in air.
>
> Far in the space where ancient Albion keeps
20> Amidst the roarings of the sacred deeps,

Where willing forests leave their native plain,
Descend, and instant, plough the wat'ry main.
Strange to relate! with canvas wings they speed
To distant worlds; of distant worlds the dread.
25   The trembling natives of the peaceful plain,
Astonish'd view the heroes of the main,
Wond'ring to see two chiefs of matchless grace,
Of generous bosom, and ingenuous face,
From ocean sprung, like ocean foes to rest,
30   The thirst of glory burns each youthful breast.

In virtue's cause, the muse implores for grace,
These blooming sons of Neptune's royal race;
Cerulean youths! your joint assent declare,
Virtue to rev'rence, more than mortal fair,
35   A crown of glory, which the muse will twine,
Immortal trophy! Rochfort shall be thine!
Thine too O Greaves! for virtue's offspring share,
Celestial friendship and the muse's care.
Yours is the song, and your's the honest praise,
40   Lo! Rochfort smiles, and Greaves approves my lays.

BOSTON; October 30th. 1774.

[from the *Royal American Magazine*, December 1774]

The Answer [By the Gentleman of the Navy].

Celestial muse! sublimest of the nine,
Assist my song, and dictate every line:
Inspire me once, nor with imperfect lays,
To sing this great, this lovely virgins praise:
5   But yet, alas! what tribute can I bring,
WH—TL—Y but smiles, whilst I thus faintly sing,

Behold with reverence, and with joy adore;
The lovely daughter of the Affric shore,

Where every grace, and every virtue join,
10   That kindles friendship and makes love divine;
In hue as diff'rent as in souls above;
The rest of mortals who in vain have strove,
Th' immortal wreathe, the muse's gift to share,
Which heav'n reserv'd for this angelic fair.

15   Blest be the guilded shore, the happy land,
Where spring and autumn gently hand in hand;
O'er shady forests that scarce know a bound,
In vivid blaze alternately dance round:
Where cancers torrid heat the soul inspires;
20   With strains divine and true poetic fires;
(Far from the reach of Hudson's chilly bay)
Where cheerful phoebus makes all nature gay;
Where sweet refreshing breezes gently fan;
The flow'ry path, the ever verdent lawn,
25   The artless grottos, and the soft retreats;
"At once the lover and the muse's seats."
Where nature taught, (tho' strange it is to tell,)
Her flowing pencil Europe to excell.
Britania's glory long hath fill'd the skies;
30   Whilst other nations, tho' with envious eyes,
Have view'd her growing greatness, and the rules,
That's long been taught in her untainted schools:
Where great Sir Isaac! whose immortal name;
Still shines the brightest on the seat of fame;
35   By ways and methods never known before;
The sacred depth of nature did explore:
And like a God, on philosophic wings;
Rode with the planets thro' their circling rings:
Surveying nature with a curious eye,
40   And viewing other systems in the sky.

     Where nature's bard with true poetic lays,
The pristine state of paradise displays,
And with a genius that's but very rare
Describes the first the only happy pair
45   That in terrestial mansions ever reign'd,

     View'd hapiness now lost, and now regain'd,
     Unravel'd all the battles of the Gods,
     And view'd old night below the antipodes.
     On his imperious throne, with awful sway,
50   Commanding regions yet unknown today,

        Or where those lofty bards have dwelt so long,
     That ravish'd Europe with their heavenly song,

        But now this blissful clime, this happy land,
     That all the neighbouring nations did command;
55   Whose royal navy neptunes waves did sweep,
     Reign'd Prince alone, and sov'reign of the deep:
     No more can boast, but of the power to kill,
     By force of arms, or diabolic skill.
     For softer strains we quickly must repair
60   To Wheatly's song, for Wheatly is the fair;
     That has the art, which art could ne'er acquire;
     To dress each sentence with seraphic fire.

        Her wondrous virtues I could ne'er express!
     To paint her charms, would only make them less.

                              December 2nd. 1774.

[from the *Royal American Magazine*, January 1775]

PHILIS'S [*sic*] Reply to the Answer in our last by the
Gentleman in the Navy.

        For one bright moment, heavenly goddess! shine,
     Inspire my song and form the lays divine.
     Rochford, attend. Beloved of Phoebus! hear,
     A truer sentence never reach'd thine ear;
5   Struck with thy song, each vain conceit resign'd
     A soft affection seiz'd my grateful mind,

While I each golden sentiment admire
In thee, the muse's bright celestial fire.
The generous plaudit 'tis not mine to claim,
10   A muse untutor'd, and unknown to fame.

       The heavenly sisters pour thy notes along
And crown their bard with every grace of song.
My pen, least favour'd by the tuneful nine,
Can never rival, never equal thine;
15   Then fix the humble Afric muse's seat
At British Homer's and Sir Isaac's feet.
Those bards whose fame in deathless strains arise
Creation's boast, and fav'rites of the skies.

       In fair description are thy powers display'd
20   In artless grottos, and the sylvan shade;
Charm'd with thy painting, how my bosom burns!
And pleasing Gambia on my soul returns,
With native grace in spring's luxuriant reign,
Smiles the gay mead, and Eden blooms again,
25   The various bower, the tuneful flowing stream,
The soft retreats, the lovers golden dream,
Her soil spontaneous, yields exhaustless stores;
For phoebus revels on her verdant shores.
Whose flowery births, a fragrant train appear,
30   And crown the youth throughout the smiling year,

       There, as in Britain's favour'd isle, behold
The bending harvest ripen into gold!
Just are thy views of Afric's blissful plain,
On the warm limits of the land and main.

35   Pleas'd with the theme, see sportive fancy play,
In realms devoted to the God of day!

       Europa's bard, who the great depth explor'd,
Of nature, and thro' boundless systems soar'd,
Thro' earth, thro' heaven, and hell's profound domain,

40   Where night eternal holds her awful reign.
        But, lo! in him Britania's prophet dies,
        And whence, ah! whence, shall other *Newton's* rise?
        Muse, bid thy Rochford's matchless pen display
        The charms of friendship in the sprightly lay.
45   Queen of his song, thro' all his numbers shine,
        And plausive glories, goddess! shall be thine.
        With partial grace thou mak'st his verse excel,
        And *his* the glory to describe so well.
        Cerulean bard! to thee these strains belong,
50   The Muse's darling and the prince of song.

                                    DECEMBER 5th, 1774.

[from the *Pennsylvania Magazine* 2 (April 1776)]

To His Excellency General Washington.

The following LETTER *and* VERSES, *were written by the famous* Phillis Wheatley, *the African Poetess, and presented to his Excellency Gen.* Washington.

SIR,

I Have taken the freedom to address your Excellency in the enclosed poem, and entreat your acceptance, though I am not insensible of its inaccuracies. Your being appointed by the Grand Continental Congress to be Generalissimo of the armies of North America, together with the fame of your virtues, excite sensations not easy to suppress. Your generosity, therefore, I presume, will pardon the attempt. Wishing your Excellency all possible success in the great cause you are so generously engaged in. I am,

    Your Excellency's most obedient humble servant, PHILLIS WHEATLEY. *Providence, Oct. 26, 1775. His Excellency Gen. Washington.*

Celestial choir! enthron'd in realms of light
Columbia's scenes of glorious toils I write.
While freedom's cause her anxious breast alarms,
She flashes dreadful in refulgent arms.
5   See mother earth her offspring's fate bemoan,
And nations gaze at scenes before unknown!
See the bright beams of heaven's revolving light
Involved in sorrows and the veil of night!

The goddess comes, she moves divinely fair,
10   Olive and laurel binds her golden hair:
Wherever shines this native of the skies,
Unnumber'd charms and recent graces rise.

Muse! bow propitious while my pen relates
How pour her armies through a thousand gates:
15   As when Eolus heaven's fair face deforms,
Enwrapp'd in tempest and a night of storms;
Astonish'd ocean feels the wild uproar,
The refluent surges beat the sounding shore;
Or thick as leaves in Autumn's golden reign,
20   Such, and so many, moves the warrior's train.
In bright array they seek the work of war,
Where high unfurl'd the ensign waves in air.
Shall I to Washington their praise recite?
Enough thou know'st them in the fields of fight.
25   Thee, first in place and honours,—we demand
The grace and glory of thy martial band.
Fam'd for thy valour, for thy virtues more,
Hear every tongue thy guardian aid implore!

One century scarce perform'd its destin'd round,
30   When Gallic powers Columbia's fury found;
And so may you, whoever dares disgrace
The land of freedom's heaven-defended race!
Fix'd are the eyes of nations on the scales,
For in their hopes Columbia's arm prevails.
35   Anon Britannia droops the pensive head,
While round increase the rising hills of dead.

Ah! cruel blindness to Columbia's state!
Lament thy thirst of boundless power too late.

Proceed, great chief, with virtue on thy side,
40   Thy ev'ry action let the goddess guide.
A crown, a mansion, and a throne that shine,
With gold unfading, WASHINGTON! be thine.

[manuscript at Bowdoin College library]

On the Capture of General Lee

The following thoughts on his Excellency Major General Lee being betray'd into the hands of the Enemy by the treachery of a pretended Friend; To the Honourable James Bowdoin Esq.r are most respectfully Inscrib'd, By his most obedient and devoted humble Servant.

The deed perfidious, and the Hero's fate,
In tender strains, celestial Muse! relate.
The latent foe to friendship makes pretence
The name assumes without the sacred sense!
5   He, with a rapture well dissembl'd, press'd
The hero's hand, and fraudful, thus address'd.

"O friend belov'd! may heaven its aid afford,
And spread yon troops beneath thy conquering sword!
Grant to America's united prayer
10   A glorious conquest on the field of war.
But thou indulgent to my warm request
Vouchsafe thy presence as my honour'd guest:
From martial cares a space unbend thy soul
In social banquet, and the sprightly bowl."
15   Thus spoke the foe; and warlike *Lee* reply'd,
"Ill fits it me, who such an army guide;
To whom his conduct each brave soldier owes

To waste an hour in banquets or repose:
This day important, with loud voice demands
20   Our wisest Counsels, and our bravest hands."
Thus having said he heav'd a boding sigh.
The hour approach'd that damps Columbia's Joy.
Inform'd, conducted, by the treach'rous friend
With winged speed the adverse train attend
25   Ascend the Dome, and seize with frantic air
The self surrender'd glorious prize of war!
On sixty coursers, swifter than the wind
They fly, and reach the British camp assign'd.
Arriv'd, what transport touch'd their leader's breast!
30   Who thus deriding, the brave Chief address'd.
"Say, art thou he, beneath whose vengeful hands
Our best of heroes grasp'd in death the sands?
One fierce regard of thine indignant eye
Turn'd Brittain pale, and made her armies fly;
35   But Oh! how chang'd! a prisoner in our arms
Till martial honour, dreadful in her charms,
Shall grace Britannia at her sons' return,
And widow'd thousands in our triumphs mourn."
While thus he spoke, the hero of renown
40   Survey'd the boaster with a gloomy frown
And stern reply'd. "Oh arrogance of tongue!
And wild ambition, ever prone to wrong!
Believ'st thou Chief, that armies such as thine
Can stretch in dust that heaven-defended line?
45   In vain allies may swarm from distant lands
And demons aid in formidable bands.
Great as thou art, thou shun'st the field of fame
Disgrace to Brittain, and the British name!
When offer'd combat by the noble foe,
50   (Foe to mis-rule,) why did thy sword forgo
The easy conquest of the rebel-land?
Perhaps *too* easy for thy martial hand.
What various causes to the field invite!
For plunder *you*, and we for freedom fight:
55   Her cause divine with generous ardor fires,

And every bosom glows as she inspires!
Already, thousands of your troops are fled
To the drear mansions of the silent dead:
Columbia too, beholds with streaming eyes
60   Her heroes fall—'tis freedom's sacrifice!
So wills the Power who with convulsive storms
Shakes impious realms, and nature's face deforms.
Yet those brave troops innum'rous as the sands
One soul inspires, one General Chief commands
65   Find in your train of boasted heroes, one
To match the praise of Godlike Washington.
Thrice happy Chief! in whom the virtues join,
And heaven-taught prudence speaks the man divine!"

          He ceas'd. Amazement struck the warrior-train,
70   And doubt of conquest, on the hostile plain.

                                        BOSTON. Dec.r 30, 1776

[manuscript at the Massachusetts Historical Society]

On the Death of General Wooster

Madam [Mary Wooster],

I recd your favour by Mr Dennison inclosing a paper containing
the Character of the truely worthy General Wooster. It was with
the most sensible regret that I heard of his fall in battle, but the
pain of so afflicting a dispensation of Providence must be greatly
alleviated to you and all his friends in the consideration that he
fell a martyr in the Cause of Freedom—

          From this the muse rich consolation draws
          He nobly perish'd in his Country's cause
          His Country's Cause that ever fir'd his mind
          Where martial flames, and Christian virtues join'd.
5   How shall my pen his warlike deeds proclaim

Or paint them fairer on the list of Fame—
Enough great Cheif—now wrapt in shades around
Thy grateful Country shall thy praise resound
Tho' not with mortals' empty praise elate
10 That vainest vapour to th' immortal State
Inly serene the expiring hero lies
And thus (while heav'nward roll his swimming eyes)[:]
["]Permit, great power while yet my fleeting breath
And Spirits wander to the verge of Death—
15 Permit me yet to paint fair freedom's charms
For her the Continent shines bright in arms
By thy high will, celestial prize she came—
For her we combat on the feild of fame
Without her presence vice maintains full sway
20 And social love and virtue wing their way
O still propitious be thy guardian care
And lead *Columbia* thro' the toils of war.
With thine own hand conduct them and defend
And bring the dreadful contest to an end—
25 For ever grateful let them live to thee
And keep them ever virtuous, brave, and free—
But how, presumptuous shall we hope to find
Divine acceptance with th' Almighty mind—
While yet (O deed ungenerous!) they disgrace
30 And hold in bondage Afric's blameless race?
Let virtue reign—And thou accord our prayers
Be victory our's, and generous freedom theirs."
The hero pray'd—the wond'ring Spirit fled
And Sought the unknown regions of the dead—
35 Tis thine fair partner of his life, to find
His virtuous path and follow close behind—
A little moment steals him from thy Sight
He waits thy coming to the realms of light
Freed from his labours in the ethereal Skies
40 Where in Succession endless pleasures rise!

You will do me a great favour by returning to me by the first
oppy those books that remain unsold and remitting the money
for those that are sold—I can easily dispose of them here for

12/Lm.o each—I am greatly obliged to you for the care you show me, and your condescention in taking so much pains for my Interest—I am extremely Sorry not to have been honour'd with a personal acquaintance with you—if the foregoing lines meet with your acceptance and approbation I shall think them highly honour'd. I hope you will pardon the length of my letter, when the reason is apparent—fondness of the Subject &—the highest respect for the deceas'd—I sincerely sympathize with you in the great loss you and your family Sustain and am Sincerely

> Your friend & very humble Servt Phillis
> Wheatley Queenstreet Boston July—15*th* 1778

[written before Wheatley's marriage in April 1778; published in the *Boston Magazine*, September 1784]

To Mr. and Mrs.—, on the Death of their Infant Son,
By Phillis Wheatly [*sic*].

     O DEATH! whose sceptre, trembling realms obey,
     And weeping millions mourn thy savage sway;
     Say, shall we call thee by the name of friend,
     Who blasts our joys, and bids our glories end?
5   Behold, a child who rivals op'ning morn,
     When its first beams the eastern hills adorn;
     So sweetly blooming once that lovely boy,
     His father's hope, his mother's only joy,
     Nor charms nor innocence prevail to save,
10   From the grim monarch of the gloomy grave!
     Two moons revolve when lo! among the dead
     The beauteous infant lays his weary head:
     For long he strove the tyrant to withstand,
     And the dread terrors of his iron hand;
15   Vain was his strife, with the relentless power,
     His efforts weak; and this his mortal hour;
     He sinks—he dies—celestial muse, relate,

His spirit's entrance at the sacred gate.
Methinks I hear the heav'nly courts resound,
20 The recent theme inspires the choirs around.
His guardian angel with delight unknown,
Hails his bless'd charge on his immortal throne;
His heart expands at scenes unknown before,
Dominions praise, and prostate thrones adore;
25 Before the Eternal's feet their crowns are laid,
The glowing seraph vails his sacred head.
Spirits redeem'd, that more than angels shine,
For nobler praises tune their harps divine:
These saw his entrance; his soft hand they press'd,
30 Sat on his throne, and smiling thus address'd,
"Hail: thou! thrice welcome to this happy shore,
Born to new life where changes are no more;
Glad heaven receives thee, and thy God bestows,
Immortal youth exempt from pain and woes.
35 Sorrow and sin, those foes to human rest,
Forever banish'd from thy happy breast."
Gazing they spoke, and raptur'd thus replies,
The beauteous stranger in the etherial skies.
"Thus safe conducted to your bless'd abodes,
40 With sweet surprize I mix among the Gods;
The vast profound of this amazing grace,
Beyond your search, immortal powers, I praise;
Great Sire, I sing thy boundless love divine,
Mine is the bliss, but all the glory thine."

45   All heav'n rejoices as your . . . sings,
To heavenly airs he tunes the sounding strings;
Mean time on earth the hapless parents mourn,
"Too quickly fled, ah! never to return."
Thee, the vain visions of the night restore,
50 Illusive fancy paints the phantom o'er;
Fain would we clasp him, but he wings his flight;
Deceives our arms, and mixes with the night;
But oh! suppress the clouds of grief that roll,
Invading peace, and dark'ning all the soul.
55 Should heaven restore him to your arms again,

Oppress'd with woes, a painful endless train,
How would your prayers, your ardent wishes, rise,
Safe to repose him in his native skies.

[manuscript at the Schomburg Center for Research in Black Culture,
The New York Public Library]

Prayer
Sabbath—June 13, 1779

Oh my Gracious Preserver!
hitehero thou hast brot [me,]
be pleased when thou bringest
to the birth to give [me] strength
5   to bring forth living & perfect a
being who shall be greatly in-
strumental in promoting thy [glory]
Tho conceived in Sin & brot forth
in iniquity yet thy infinite wisdom
10 can bring a clean thing out of an
unclean, a vess[el] of Honor filled
for thy glory—grant me
to live a life of gratitude to thee
for the innumerable benefits—
15 O Lord my God! instruct my ignorance
& enlighten my Darkness
Thou art my King, take [thou]
the entire possession of [all] my
powers & faculties & let me be
20 no longer under the dominion
of sin—Give me a sincere &
hearty repentance for all my
[grievous?] offences & strengthen
by thy grace my resolutions
25 on amendment & circumspection
for the time to come—Grant me

[also] the spirit of Prayer & Suppli[cation]
according to thy own
most gracious Promises.

[manuscript at the Massachusetts Historical Society]

An Elegy Sacred to the Memory of the
Rev'd Samuel Cooper, D.D.

O Thou whose exit wraps in boundless woe,
For Thee the tears of various Nations flow
For Thee the floods of virtuous sorrows rise
From the full heart and burst from streaming eyes,
5   Far from our view to heaven's eternal height
The seat of bliss divine, and glory bright;
Far from the restless turbulence of life,
The war of factions, and impassion'd strife.
From every ill mortality indur'd,
10   Safe in Celestial Salem's walls secur'd.

E'er yet from this terrestrial state retir'd,
The Virtuous lov'd Thee, and the wise admir'd.
The gay approv'd Thee, and the grave rever'd.
And all thy words with rapt attention heard!
15   The Sons of learning on thy lessons hung,
While soft persuasion mov'd th' illit'rate throng.
Who, drawn by rhetoric's commanding laws,
Comply'd obedient, nor conceived the cause.
Thy every sentence was with grace inspir'd,
20   And every period with devotion fir'd,
Bright Truth thy guide without disguise,
And penetration's all discerning eyes.

Thy Country mourns th' afflicting hand divine
That now forbids thy radient lamp to shine,

25 Which, like the sun, resplendent source of light
    Diffus'd its beams, and chear'd our gloom of night.

    What deep felt sorrow in each *kindred* breast
    With keen sensation rends the heart distress'd!
    Fraternal love sustains a tenderer part
30 And mourns a Brother with a Brother's heart.

    Thy Church laments her faithful Pastor fled
    To the cold mansions of the silent dead
    There hush'd forever, cease the heavenly strain
    That wak'd the soul but here resounds in vain.
35 Still live thy merits, where thy name is known,
    As the sweet Rose, its blooming beauty gone
    Retains its fragrance with a long perfume:
    Thus Cooper! thus thy deathless name shall bloom
    Unfading, in thy *Church* and *Country's* love,
40 While Winter frowns or Spring renews the grove.
    The hapless Muse, her loss in Cooper mourns,
    And as she sits, she writes, and weeps, by turns;
    A Friend sincere, whose mild indulgent rays
    Encouraged oft, and oft approv'd her lays.

45   With all their charms terrestrial objects strove,
    But vain their pleasures to attract his love.
    Such Cooper was—at Heaven's high call he flies,
    His task well finished, to his native skies.
    Yet to his fate reluctant we resign,
50 Tho' our's to copy conduct such as thine:
    Such was thy wish, th' observant Muse survey'd
    Thy latest breath, and this advice convey'd.

                                    [December 30 or 31, 1783]

AN ELEGY, SACRED TO THE MEMORY OF THAT
GREAT DIVINE, THE REVEREND AND LEARNED
DR. SAMUEL COOPER, *Who departed this Life December
29, 1783, AETATIS 59. BY PHILLIS PETERS. BOSTON:
Printed and Sold by E. Russell, in Essex-Street,
near Liberty-Pole,* M,DCC,LXXXIV.

To the CHURCH *and* CONGREGATION *assembling in
Brattle-Street, the following,* ELEGY, *Sacred to the* MEMORY
of their late Reverend and Worthy PASTOR, *Dr.* SAMUEL
COOPER, *is, with the greatest Sympathy, most respectfully in-
scribed by their Obedient,*

> *Humble Servant,*
> PHILLIS PETERS.

> BOSTON, Jan. 1784.

O THOU whose exit wraps in boundless woe,
   For Thee the tears of various Nations flow:
For Thee the floods of virtuous sorrows rise
From the full heart and burst from streaming eyes,
5   Far from our view to Heaven's eternal height,
The Seat of bliss divine, and glory bright;
Far from the restless turbulence of life,
The war of factions, and impassion'd strife.
From every ill mortality endur'd,
10   Safe in celestial *Salem's* walls secur'd.

   E'ER yet from this terrestrial state retir'd,
The Virtuous lov'd Thee, and the Wise admir'd.
The gay approv'd Thee, and the grave rever'd;
And all thy words with rapt attention heard!
15   The Sons of Learning on thy lessons hung,
While soft persuasion mov'd th' illit'rate throng.
Who, drawn by rhetoric's commanding laws,
Comply'd obedient, nor conceiv'd the cause.

Thy every sentence was with grace inspir'd,
20 And every period with devotion fir'd;
Bright Truth thy guide without a dark disguise,
And penetration's all-discerning eyes.

THY COUNTRY mourn's th' afflicting Hand
        divine
That now forbids thy radiant lamp to shine,
25 Which, like the sun, resplendent source of light
Diffus'd its beams, and chear'd our gloom of night.

WHAT deep-felt sorrow in each *Kindred* breast
With keen sensation rends the heart distress'd!
Fraternal love sustains a tenderer part,
30 And mourns a BROTHER with a BROTHER'S heart.

THY CHURCH laments her faithful PASTOR fled
To the cold mansions of the silent dead.
There hush'd forever, cease the heavenly strain,
That wak'd the soul, but here resounds in vain.
35 Still live thy merits, where thy name is known,
As the sweet Rose, its blooming beauty gone
Retains its fragrance with a long perfume:
Thus COOPER! thus thy death-less name shall bloom
Unfading, in thy *Church* and *Country's* love,
40 While Winter frowns, or spring renews the grove.
The hapless Muse, her loss in COOPER mourns,
And as she sits, she writes, and weeps, by turns;
A Friend sincere, whose mild indulgent grace
Encourag'd oft, and oft approv'd her lays.

45 WITH all their charms, terrestrial objects strove,
But vain their pleasures to attract his love.
Such COOPER was—at Heaven's high call he flies;
His task well finish'd, to his native skies.
Yet to his fate reluctant we resign,
50 Tho' our's to copy conduct such as thine:
Such was thy wish, th' observant Muse survey'd
Thy latest breath, and this advice convey'd.

LIBERTY AND PEACE, A POEM. *By* PHILLIS PETERS, BOSTON: *Printed by* WARDEN and RUSSELL, *At Their Office in Marlborough-Street.* M,DCC,LXXXIV.

LO! Freedom comes. Th' prescient Muse foretold,
All Eyes th' accomplish'd Prophecy behold:
Her Port describ'd, *"She moves divinely fair,*
Olive and Laurel bind her golden Hair."

5   She, the bright Progeny of Heaven, descends,
And every Grace her sovereign Step attends;
For now kind Heaven, indulgent to our Prayer,
In smiling *Peace* resolves the Din of *War*.
Fix'd in *Columbia* her illustrious Line,

10   And bids in thee her future Councils shine.
To every Realm her Portals open'd wide,
Receives from each the full commercial Tide.
Each Art and Science now with rising Charms
Th' expanding Heart with Emulation warms.

15   E'en great *Britannia* sees with dread Surprize,
And from the dazzl'ing Splendors turns her Eyes!
Britain, whose Navies swept th' *Atlantic* o'er,
And Thunder sent to every distant Shore:
E'en thou, in Manners cruel as thou art,

20   The Sword resign'd, resume the friendly Part!
For *Galia's* Power espous'd *Columbia's* Cause,
And new-born *Rome* shall give *Britannia* Law,
Nor unremember'd in the grateful Strain,
Shall princely *Louis'* friendly Deeds remain;

25   The generous Prince th' impending Vengeance eye's,
Sees the fierce Wrong, and to the rescue flies.
Perish that Thirst of boundless Power, that drew
On *Albion's* Head the Curse to Tyrants due.
But thou appeas'd submit to Heaven's decree,

30   That bids this Realm of Freedom rival thee!
Now sheathe the Sword that bade the Brave attone
With guiltless Blood for Madness not their own.
Sent from th' Enjoyment of their native Shore
Ill-fated—never to behold her more!

35   From every Kingdom on *Europa's* Coast
      Throng'd various Troops, their Glory, Strength and
         Boast.
      With heart-felt pity fair *Hibernia* saw
      Columbia menac'd by the Tyrant's Law:
      On hostile Fields fraternal Arms engage,
40   And mutual Deaths, all dealt with mutual Rage;
      The Muse's Ear hears mother Earth deplore
      Her ample Surface smoak with kindred Gore:
      The hostile Field destroys the social Ties,
      And ever-lasting Slumber seals their Eyes.
45   *Columbia* mourns, the haughty Foes deride,
      Her Treasures plunder'd, and her Towns destroy'd:
      Witness how *Charlestown's* curling Smoaks arise,
      In sable Columns to the clouded Skies!
      The ample Dome, high-wrought with curious Toil,
50   In one sad Hour the savage Troops despoil.
      Descending *Peace* the Power of War confounds;
      From every Tongue celestial *Peace* resounds:
      As from the East th' illustrious King of Day,
      With rising Radiance drives the Shades away,
55   So Freedom comes array'd with Charms divine,
      And in her Train Commerce and Plenty shine.
      Britannia owns her Independent Reign,
      Hibernia, Scotia, and the Realms of *Spain;*
      And great *Germania's* ample Coast admires
60   The generous Spirit that *Columbia* fires.
      Auspicious Heaven shall fill with fav'ring Gales,
      Where e'er *Columbia* spreads her swelling Sails:
      To every Realm shall *Peace* her Charms display,
      And Heavenly *Freedom* spread her golden Ray.

[The London *Arminian Magazine* 7 (July 1784)]

An ELEGY *on Leaving—.*

      FAREWEL! ye friendly bow'rs, ye streams adieu,
         I leave with sorrow each sequester'd seat:

The lawns, where oft I swept the morning dew,
  The groves, from noon-tide rays a kind retreat.

5 Yon wood-crown'd hill, whose far projecting shade,
  Inverted trembles in the limpid lake:
Where wrapt in thought I pensively have stray'd,
  For crowds and noise, reluctant, I forsake.

The solemn pines, that, winding through the vale.
10 In graceful rows attract the wand'ring eye,
Where the soft ring-dove pours her soothing tale,
  No more must veil me from the fervid sky.

Beneath yon aged oak's protecting arms,
  Oft-times beside the pebbl'd brook I lay;
15 Where, pleas'd with simple Nature's various charms,
  I pass'd in grateful solitude the day.

Rapt with the melody of Cynthio's strain,
  There first my bosom felt poetic flame;
Mute was the bleating language of the plain,
20 And with his lays the wanton fawns grew tame.

But, ah! those pleasing hours are ever flown;
  Ye scenes of transport from my thoughts retire;
Those rural joys no more the day shall crown,
  No more my hand shall wake the warbling lyre.

25 But come, sweet Hope, from thy divine retreat,
  Come to my breast, and chase my cares away,
Bring calm Content to gild my gloomy seat,
  And cheer my bosom with her heav'nly ray.

VARIANTS OF POEMS PUBLISHED IN

POEMS ON VARIOUS SUBJECTS

[manuscript at the American Antiquarian Society]

To the University of Cambridge, wrote in 1767—

> While an intrinsic ardor bids me write
> The muse doth promise to assist my pen.
> 'Twas but e'en now I left my native Shore
> The sable Land of error's darkest night
> 5   There, sacred Nine! for you no place was found,
> Parent of mercy, 'twas thy Powerfull hand
> Brought me in Safety from the dark adobe.
>
>   To you, Bright youths! he points the heights of
>   Heav'n
> To you, the knowledge of the depths profound.
> 10   Above, contemplate the ethereal Space
> And glorious Systems of revolving worlds.
>
>   Still more, ye Sons of Science! you've reciev'd
> The pleasing Sound by messengers from heav'n,
> The Saviour's blood, for your Redemption flows.
> 15   S[ee] Him, with hands stretch'd out upon the Cross!
> Divine compassion in his bosom glows.
> He hears revilers with oblique regard.
> What Condescention in the Son of God!
> When the whole human race, by Sin had fal'n;
> 20   He deign'd to Die, that they might rise again,
> To live with him beyond the Starry Sky
> Life without death, and Glory without End.—

Improve your privileges while they Stay:
Caress, redeem each moment, which with haste
25 Bears on its rapid wing Eternal bliss.
Let hateful vice so baneful to the Soul,
Be still avoided with becoming care;
Suppress the sable monster in its growth,
Ye blooming plants of human race, divine
30 An Ethiop tells you, tis your greatest foe
Its present sweetness turns to endless pain
And brings eternal ruin on the Soul.

[manuscript at the Historical Society of Pennsylvania]

To the King's Most Excellent Majesty on his
Repealing the American Stamp Act

Your Subjects hope
The crown upon your head may flourish long
And in great wars your royal arms be strong
May your Sceptre many nations sway
5   Resent it on them that dislike Obey
But how shall we exalt the British king
Who ruleth france Possessing every thing
The sweet remembrance of whose favours past
The meanest peasants bless the great the last
10 May George belov'd of all the nations round
Live and by earths and heavens blessings crownd
May heaven protect and Guard him from on high
And at his presence every evil fly
Thus every clime with equal gladness See
15 When kings do Smile it sets their Subjects free
When wars came on the proudest rebel fled
God thunder'd fury on their guilty head

                                    Phillis
                                    [1768]

[holograph manuscript at the Dartmouth College Library sent "To the
Revd. Mr. Jeremy Belknap In Dover New Hampshire"; given the general
lack of punctuation and the subsequent substantive revisions, the Dartmouth
holograph is probably the earliest known version of this poem.
Belknap (1744–1798), pastor of a Congregational church in Dover,
New Hampshire (1767–1786), was the author of a three-volume *History of New
Hampshire* (1784, 1791, 1792), a two-volume *American Biography* (1794, 1798),
The Foresters (1792), and *Sacred Poetry* (1795).]

On the Decease of the Rev'd Doctr. Sewall [variant 1]

E're yet the morning heav'd its Orient head
Behold him praising with the happy dead—
Hail happy Saint, on the Immortal Shore
We hear thy warnings and advice no more
5   Then let each one behold with wishful eyes
The saint ascending to his native skies
From hence the prophet wing'd his rapturous way
To mansions pure to fair Celestial day—
Then begging for the Spirit of the Gods
10   And panting eager for the bless'd Abodes
Let every one with the same vigour Soar
To bliss and happiness Unseen before
Then be Christs Image on our minds impressd
And plant a Saviour in each glowing breast
15   Thrice happy thou Arriv'd to Joy at last
What compensation for the evil past
Thou Lord incomprehensible, unknown—
By sense; we bow at thy exalted throne—
While thus we beg thy excellence to feel
20   Thy sacred spirit, in our hearts reveal
To make each One of us that grace partake
Which thus we ask for the redeemers Sake—
["]Sewall is dead[,"] Swift-piniond fame thus cryd
["]Is Sewall dead[?"] my trembling heart replyd
25   Behold to us a benefit denyd
But when Our Jesus had ascended high

With captive bands he led captivity
And gifts receiv'd for such as knew not God
Lord send a Pastor for thy Churches Good
30   ["]O ruin'd world[,"] my mournful tho'ts replyd
["]And ruin'd continent[,"] the mountains cryd
How Oft for us the Holy prophet prayd
But now behold him in his clay cold bed
Ye Powers above my weeping verse to close
35   I'll on his tomb an epitaph compose—

Here lies a man bought with Christs precious blood
Once a Poor sinner now a saint with God
Behold ye rich and poor and fools and wise
Nor let this monitor your hearts surprize
40   I'll tell you all what this great saint has done
That makes him Brighter than the Glorious Sun
Listen ye Happy from the seats above
I speak Sincerely and with truth and Love
He sought the Paths of virtue and of truth
45   Twas this, that made him happy in his youth
In Blooming years he found that grace divine
That gives admittance to the sacred Shrine—
Mourn him ye Indigent whom he has fed
Seek yet more earnest for the Living bread
50   E'n Christ your bread descend from above
Implore his pity and his grace and Love.
Mourn him ye youth whom he has Often told
Gods bounteous mercy from the times of Old
I too, have cause this heavy loss to mourn:
55   Because my monitor will not return
Now this faint semblance of his complete:
He is thro' Jesus made divinely great
And set a Glorious Pattern to repeat
But when shall we to this blessd State arrive?
60   When the Same graces in Our hearts do thrive

Phillis Wheatley
[1769]

[manuscript in Huntingdon Papers at the Chestunt Foundation, Cambridge
University; a second manuscript version in the Huntingdon Papers, with slight
differences in punctuation, lacks lines 36–37 of the version below]

On the Decease of the rev'd Dr. Sewell—[variant 2].

E'r yet the morning heav'd its Orient head
Behold him praising with the happy dead,
Hail happy Saint, on the Immortal Shore.
We heard thy warnings and advice no more
5 Then let each one behold with wishful eyes
The saint ascending to his native Skies
From hence the Prophet wing'd his rapturous way
To mansions pure, to fair celestial day—
Then begging for the Spirit of his God
10 And panting eager for the blest abode
Let every one with the same vigour soar
To bliss and happiness unseen before
Then be christs image on our minds impress'd
And plant a Saviour in each glowing Breast
15 Thrice happy thou, arriv'd to Joy at last
What compensation for the evil past—
Thou Lord incomprehensible unknown
By sense;—we bow at thy exalted throne
While thus we beg thy excellence to feel
20 Thy Sacred Spirit in our hearts reveal
To make each one of us thy grace partake
Which thus we ask for the Redeemers Sake
["]Sewell is dead[,"] swift-pinion'd fame thus cry'd
["]Is Sewell dead,["] my trembling heart reply'd
25 Behold, to us, a benefit deny'd
But when our Jesus had ascended high
With captive bands he led captivity
And gifts receiv'd for such as knew not God
Lord, send a Pastor for thy Churches good;
30 ["]O ruin'd world,["] my mournful tho'ts reply'd
["]And ruin'd continent[,"] the ecco cry'd
How oft for us the holy Prophet pray'd

But now behold him in his clay cold bed
By duty urg'd my weeping verse to close
35   I'll on his Tomb, an Epitaph compose.

Here lies a man brought with Christ's precious blood
Once a poor Sinner, now a saint with God
Behold ye rich and poor and fools and wise
Nor let this monitor your hearts Surprize
40   I'll tell you all, what this great saint has done
That makes him brighter than the glorious Sun
Listen ye happy, from the Seats above
I speak Sincerely and with truth and Love
He sought the paths of virtue and of truth
45   Twas this that made him happy in his Youth
In blooming years he found that grace divine
That gives admittance to the Sacred Shrine
Mourn him ye indigent, whom he has fed
Seek yet more earnest for the living bread
50   Even Christ, your bread that cometh from above
Implore his pity and his grace and Love
Mourn him ye youth whom he hath often told
Gods bounteous mercy from the times of old
I too, have cause this heavy loss to mourn
55   For this my monitor will not return
Now this faint semblance of his complete
He is thro' Jesus made divinely great
And Set a Glorious pattern to repeat
But when shall we to this bless'd State Arrive
60   When the same graces in our hearts do thrive

                              Phillis Wheatley
                              [1769]

[manuscript at the American Antiquarian Society]

On the Death of the Rev'd Dr. Sewall. 1769. [variant 3].—

E'er yet the morning heav'd its Orient head
Behold him praising with the happy dead.
Hail! happy Saint, on the immortal Shore.
We hear thy warnings and advice no more:
5   Then let each one behold with wishful eyes
The saint ascending to his native Skies,
From hence the Prophet wing'd his rapturous way
To mansions pure, to fair celestial day.—

Then begging for the Spirit of his God
10   And panting eager for the bless'd abode,
Let every one, with the Same vigour Soar
To bliss, and happiness, unseen before
Then be Christ's image on our minds impress'd
And plant a Saviour in each glowing Breast.
15   Thrice happy thou, arriv'd to Joy at last;
What compensation for the evil past!

Thou Lord, incomprehensible, unknown,
To Sense, we bow, at thy exalted Throne!
While thus we beg thy excellence to feel,
20   Thy Sacred Spirit, in our hearts reveal
And make each one of us, that grace partake
Which thus we ask for the Redeemer's Sake

"Sewall is dead," Swift pinion'd fame thus cry'd.
"Is Sewall dead?" my trembling heart reply'd
25   O what a blessing in thy flight deny'd!
But when our Jesus had ascended high,
With Captive bands he led Captivity;
And gifts reciev'd for such as knew not God
Lord! Send a Pastor, for thy Churche's [good]
30   O ruin'd world! bereft of thee, we cryd,
(The rocks responsive to the voice, reply'd.)

How oft for us this holy Prophet pray'd;
But ah! behold him in his Clay-cold bed
By duty urg'd, my weeping verse to close,
35   I'll on his Tomb, an Epitaph compose.

Lo! here, a man bought with Christ's precious blood
Once a poor Sinner, now a Saint with God.—
Behold ye rich and poor, and fools and wise;
Nor Let this monitor your hearts Surprize!
40   I'll tell you all, what this great Saint has done
Which makes him Brighter than the Glorious Sun.—
Listen ye happy from your Seats above
I Speak Sincerely and with truth and Love.
He Sought the Paths of virtue and of Truth
45   Twas this which made him happy in his Youth.
In Blooming years he found that grace divine
Which gives admittance to the sacred Shrine.
Mourn him, ye Indigent, Whom he has fed,
Seek yet more earnest for the living Bread:
50   E'en Christ your Bread, who cometh from above
Implore his pity and his grace and Love.
Mourn him ye Youth, whom he hath often told
God's bounteous Mercy from the times of Old.
I too, have cause this mighty loss to mourn
55   For this my monitor will not return.

Now this faint Semblance of his life complete
He is, thro' Jesus, made divinely great
And left a glorious pattern to repeat
But when Shall we, to this bless'd State arrive?
60   When the same graces in our hearts do thrive.

AN ELEGIAC POEM, On the DEATH of that celebrated
Divine, and eminent Servant of JESUS CHRIST, the late
Reverend, and pious GEORGE WHITEFIELD, Chaplain to
the Right Honourable the Countess of Huntingdon, &c &c.
Who made his Exit from this transitory State, to dwell in the
celestial Realms of Bliss, on LORD'S-DAY, 30th of September,
1770, when he was seiz'd with a Fit of the Asthma, at
NEWBURY-PORT, near BOSTON, in NEW-ENGLAND. In
which is a Condolatory Address to His truly noble Benefactress
the worthy and pious Lady HUNTINGDON,—and the
Orphan-Children in GEORGIA; who, with many Thousands,
are left, by the Death of this great Man, to lament the Loss of a
Father, Friend, and Benefactor.

*By PHILLIS, a Servant Girl of 17 Years of Age, belonging to
Mr. J. WHEATLEY, of Boston:—And has been but 9 Years in
this Country from Africa.*

Hail happy Saint on thy immortal throne!
To thee complaints of grievance are unknown;
We hear no more the music of thy tongue,
Thy wonted auditories cease to throng.
5   Thy lessons in unequal'd accents flow'd!
While emulation in each bosom glow'd;
Thou didst, in strains of eloquence refin'd,
Inflame the soul, and captivate the mind.
Unhappy we, the setting Sun deplore!
10   Which once was splendid, but it shines no more;
He leaves this earth for Heaven's unmeasur'd height:
And worlds unknown, receive him from our sight;
There WHITEFIELD wings, with rapid course his way,
And sails to Zion, through vast seas of day.

15   When his AMERICANS were burden'd sore,
When streets were crimson'd with their guiltless gore!
Unrival'd friendship in his breast now strove:
The fruit thereof was charity and love

Towards *America*—couldst thou do more
20   Than leave thy native home, the *British* shore,
To cross the great Atlantic's wat'ry road,
To see *America's* distress'd abode?
Thy prayers, great Saint, and thy incessant cries,
Have pierc'd the bosom of thy native skies!
25   Thou moon hast seen, and ye bright stars of light
Have witness been of his requests by night!
He pray'd that grace in every heart might dwell:
He long'd to see *America* excell;
He charg'd its youth to let the grace divine
30   Arise, and in their future actions shine;
He offer'd THAT he did himself receive,
A greater gift not GOD himself can give:
He urg'd the need of HIM to every one;
It was no less than GOD's co-equal SON!
35   Take HIM ye wretched for your only good;
Take HIM ye starving souls to be your food.
Ye thirsty, come to his life giving stream:
Ye Preachers, take him for your joyful theme:
Take HIM, "my dear AMERICANS," he said,
40   Be your complaints in his kind bosom laid:
Take HIM ye *Africans*, he longs for you;
Impartial SAVIOUR, is his title due;
If you will chuse to walk in grace's road,
You shall be sons, and kings, and priests to GOD.

45   Great COUNTESS! we *Americans* revere
Thy name, and thus condole thy grief sincere:
We mourn with thee, that TOMB obscurely plac'd,
In which thy Chaplain undisturb'd doth rest.
New-England sure, doth feel the ORPHAN's smart:
50   Reveals the true sensations of his heart:
Since this fair Sun, withdraws his golden rays,
No more to brighten these distressful days!
His lonely *Tabernacle*, sees no more
A WHITEFIELD landing on the *British* shore:
55   Then let us view him in yon azure skies:

Let every mind with this lov'd object rise.
No more can he exert his lab'ring breath,
Seiz'd by the cruel messenger of death.
What can his dear AMERICA return?
60 But drop a tear upon his happy urn,
Thou tomb, shalt safe retain thy sacred trust,
Till life divine re-animate his dust.

> Sold by EZEKIEL
> RUSSELL, in Queen-
> Street, and JOHN BOYLES,
> in Marlboro-Street
> [October 1770].

[October 1770 broadside at the Henry E. Huntington Library and Art Gallery]

An Ode of VERSES On the much-lamented Death of the REV.
MR. GEORGE WHITEFIELD, Late Chaplain to the Countess
of *Huntingdon;* Who departed this Life, at *Newberry* near
Boston in *New England,* on the Thirtieth of *September,* 1770, in
the Fifty-seventh Year of his Age.

Compos'd in America *by a Negro Girl Seventeen Years of Age,
and sent over to a Gentleman of Character in* London.

HAIL Happy Saint, on thy Immortal Throne!
To thee Complaints of Grievance are unknown.
We hear no more the Music of thy Tongue,
Thy wonted Auditories cease to throng.
5 Thy Lessons in unequal'd Accents flow'd,
While Emulation in each Bosom glow'd.
Thou didst, in Strains of Eloquence refin'd,
Inflame the Soul, and captivate the Mind.
Unhappy we thy setting Sun deplore,
10 Which once was splendid, but it shines no more.
He leaves the Earth for Heaven's unmeasur'd Height,

And Worlds unknown receive him out of Sight.
There *Whitefield* wings with rapid Course his Way,
And sails to *Zion* thro' vast Seas of Day.

15 When his *Americans* were burthen'd sore,
When Streets were crimson'd with their guiltless Gore,
Wond'rous Compassion in his Breast now strove,
The Fruit thereof was Charity and Love.
Towards *America* what could he more!

20 Than leave his native Home, the *British* Shore,
To cross the Great *Atlantick* wat'ry Road,
To see *New England's* much-distress'd Abode.
Thy Prayers, great Saint, and thy incessant Cries,
Have often pierc'd the Bosom of the Skies.

25 Thou, Moon, hast seen, and thou, bright Star of Light,
Hast Witness been of his Requests by Night.
He pray'd for Grace in ev'ry Heart to dwell,
He long'd to see *America* excel.
He charg'd its Youth to let the Grace Divine

30 Arise, and in their future Actions shine.
He offer'd that he did himself receive:
A greater Gift not God himself could give.
He urg'd the Need of Him to ev'ry one,
It was no less than God's co-equal Son.

35 Take him, ye Wretched, for your only Good;
Take him, ye hungry Souls, to be your Food;
Take him, ye Thirsty, for your cooling Stream;
Ye Preachers, take him for your joyful Theme;
Take him, my dear *Americans*, he said,

40 Be your Complaints in his kind Bosom laid;
Take him, ye *Africans*, he longs for you,
Impartial Saviour is his Title due.
If you will walk in Grace's heavenly Road,
He'll make you free, and Kings, and Priests to God.

45 No more can he exert his lab'ring Breath,
Seiz'd by the cruel Messenger of Death.
What can his dear *America* return,
But drop a Tear upon his happy Urn.
Thou, Tomb, shalt safe retain thy sacred Trust,

50 Till Life Divine reanimate his Dust.

Our *Whitefield* the Haven has gain'd,
    Outflying the Tempest and Wind;
His Rest he has sooner obtain'd,
    And left his Companions behind.

55   With Songs let us follow his Flight,
    And mount with his Spirit above;
Escap'd to the Mansions of Light,
    And lodg'd in the *Eden* of Love.

THE CONCLUSION.
May *Whitefield's* Virtues flourish with his Fame,
60   And Ages yet unborn record his Name.
All Praise and Glory be to God on High,
Whose dread Command is, That we all must die.
To live to Life eternal, may we emulate
The worthy Man that's gone, e'er tis too late.

Printed and sold for the Benefit of a poor Family burnt out a few
Weeks since near *Shoreditch Church,* that lost all they possessed,
having nothing insur'd. Price a Penny apiece, or 5 s. a Hundred
to those that sell them again.

[1770 Boston broadside at the Historical Society of Pennsylvania]

To Mrs. Leonard, on the Death of her Husband.

    GRIM Monarch! see depriv'd of vital breath,
A young Physician in the dust of death!
Dost thou go on incessant to destroy:
The grief to double, and impair the joy?
5   Enough thou never yet wast known to say,
Tho' millions die thy mandate to obey.
Nor youth, nor science nor the charms of love,
Nor aught on earth thy rocky heart can move.
The friend, the spouse, from his dark realm to save,
10   In vain we ask the tyrant of the grave.

Fair mourner, there see thy own LEONARD
     spread,
Lies undistinguish'd from the vulgar dead;
Clos'd are his eyes, eternal slumbers keep,
His senses bound in never-waking sleep,
15   Till time shall cease; till many a shining world,
Shall fall from Heav'n, in dire confusion hurl'd:
Till dying Nature in wild torture lies;
Till her last groans shall rend the brazen skies!
And not till then, his active Soul shall claim,
20   Its body, now, of more than mortal frame.
But ah! methinks the rolling tears apace,
Pursue each other down the alter'd face.
Ah! cease ye sighs, nor rend the mourner's heart:
Cease thy complaints, no more thy griefs impart.
25   From the cold shell of his great soul arise!
And look above, thou native of the skies!
There fix thy view, where fleeter than the wind
Thy LEONARD flies, and leaves the earth behind.

Thyself prepare to pass the gloomy night,
30   To join forever in the fields of light;
To thy embrace, his joyful spirit moves,
To thee the partner of his earthly loves;
He welcomes thee to pleasures more refin'd
And better suited to the deathless mind.

                              Phillis Wheatley.
                              [June 1771]

[manuscript at the Connecticut Historical Society]

On the Death of Dr. Samuel Marshall [variant 1]

     Thro' thickest glooms, Look back, immortal Shade;
     On that confusion which thy flight hath made.
     Or from Olympus height, look down, and see,

A Town involv'd in grief, bereft of thee.
5   His Lucy sees him mix among the Dead,
And rends the gracefull tresses from her head.
Frantic with woe, with griefs unknown, oppress'd,
Sigh follows Sigh, and heaves the downy breast;
Too quickly fled, ah! whither art thou gone?
10 Ah! lost forever to thy wife and son!
The hapless child, thy only hope, and heir,
Clings round the neck, and weeps his Sorrows there
The loss of thee, on Tyler's Soul returns.
And Boston too, for her Physician mourns.
15 When Sickness call'd for Marshall's kindly hand,
Lo! how with pitty would his heart expand!
The Sire, the friend in him we oft have found;
With gen'rous friendship, did his Soul abound.
Could Esculapius then no Longer stay,
20 To bring his lingring Infant in to Day?
The Babe unborn, in dark confiens is toss'd
And Seems in anguish for its Father Lost.
Gone is Apollo! from his house of earth!
And leaves the memorial of his worth.
25 From yonder worlds unseen he Comes no more,
The common parent, whom we thus deplore:
Yet in our hopes, immortal Joys attend,
The Sire, the Spouse, the universal freind.

[from the *Boston Evening-Post*, October 14, 1771]

On the Death of Doctor SAMUEL MARSHALL. [variant 2]

Thro' thickest glooms, look back, immortal Shade!
On that confusion which thy flight has made.
Or from Olympus' height look down, and see
A Town involv'd in grief for thee:
5   His *Lucy* sees him mix among the dead.
And rends the graceful tresses from her head:
Frantic with woe, with griefs unknown, oppres'd,
Sigh follows sigh, and heaves the downy breast.

Tóo quickly fled, ah! whither art thou gone!
10   Ah! lost for ever to thy Wife and Son!
The hapless child, thy only hope and heir,
Clings round her neck, and weeps his sorrows there.
The loss of thee on *Tyler's* soul returns,
And *Boston* too, for her Physician mourns.
15   When sickness call'd for *Marshall's* kindly hand,
Lo! how with pity would his heart expand!
The sire, the friend, in him we oft have found,
With gen'rous friendship did his soul abound.
Could Esculapius then no longer stay?
20   To bring his ling'ring infant into day!
The babe unborn, in dark confines is toss'd
And seems in anguish for it's father lost.

Gone, is Apollo! from his house of earth,
And leaves the sweet memorials of his worth.
25   From yonder world unseen, he comes no more,
The common parent, whom we thus deplore:
Yet, in our hopes, immortal joys attend
The Sire, the Spouse, the universal Friend.

Recollection.

To the AUTHOR *of the* LONDON MAGAZINE [March 1772].

Boston, in New-England, Jan. 1, 1772.

SIR,
    As your Magazine is a proper repository for any thing valu-
able or curious, I hope you will excuse the communicating the
following by one of your subscribers.

    There is in this town a young *Negro woman*, who left *her*
country at ten years of age, and has been in *this* eight years. She
is a compleat sempstress, an accomplished mistress of her pen,

and discovers a most surprising genius. Some of her productions
have seen the light, among which is a poem on the death of the
Rev. Mr. George Whitefield.—The following was occasioned by
her being in company with some young ladies of family, when
one of them said she did not remember, among all the poetical
pieces she had seen, ever to have met with a poem upon REC-
OLLECTION. The *African* (so let me call her, for so in fact she
is) took the hint, went home to her master's, and soon sent what
follows.

"MADAM,

Agreeable to your proposing *Recollection* as a subject proper
for me to write upon, I enclose these few thoughts upon it; and,
as you was the first person who mentioned it, I thought none
more proper to dedicate it to; and, if it meets with your approba-
tion, the poem is honoured, and the authoress satisfied. I am,
Madam,

Your very humble servant, PHILLIS."

RECOLLECTION.
To Miss A—M—, humbly inscribed by the Authoress.

    MNEME, begin; inspire, ye sacred Nine!
    Your vent'rous *Afric* in the deep design.
    Do ye rekindle the coelestial fire,
    Ye god-like powers! the glowing thoughts inspire,
5   *Immortal Pow'r!* I trace thy sacred spring,
    Assist my strains, while I *thy* glories sing.
    By *thee*, past acts of many thousand years,
    Rang'd in due order, to the mind appears;
    The *long-forgot* thy gentle hand conveys,
10   *Returns*, and soft upon the fancy plays.
    Calm, in the visions of the night he pours
    Th' exhaustless treasures of his secret stores.

Swift from above he wings his downy flight
Thro' *Phoebe's* realm, fair regent of the night.
15　Thence to the raptur'd poet gives his aid,
Dwells in his heart, or hovers round his head;
To give instruction to the lab'ring mind,
Diffusing light coelestial and refin'd.
Still he pursues, unweary'd in the race,
20　And wraps his senses in the pleasing maze.
The Heav'nly Phantom *points* the actions done
In the past worlds, and tribes beneath the sun.
He, from his throne in ev'ry human breast,
Has *vice* condemn'd, and ev'ry *virtue* bless'd.
25　Sweet are the sounds in which thy words we hear,
Coelestial musick to the ravish'd ear.
We hear thy voice, resounding o'er the plains,
Excelling Maro's sweet Menellian strains.
But awful *Thou!* to that perfidious race,
30　Who scorn thy warnings, nor the good embrace;
By *Thee* unveil'd, the horrid crime appears,
Thy mighty hand redoubled fury bears;
The time mis-spent augments their hell of woes,
While through each breast the dire contagion flows.
35　Now turn and leave the rude ungraceful scene,
And paint fair Virtue in immortal green.
For ever flourish in the glowing veins,
For ever flourish in poetick strains.
Be *Thy* employ to guide my early days,
40　And *Thine* the tribute of my youthful lays.

Now **eighteen years* their destin'd course have run,
In due succession, round the central sun;
How did each folly unregarded pass!
But sure 'tis graven on eternal brass!
45　To *recollect,* inglorious I return;
'Tis mine past follies and past crimes to mourn.
The *virtue,* ah! unequal to the *vice,*
Will scarce afford small reason to rejoice.

Such, RECOLLECTION! is thy pow'r, high-
thron'd

50   In ev'ry breast of mortals, ever own'd.
        The wretch, who dar'd the vengeance of the skies,
        At last awakes with horror and surprise.
        By *Thee* alarm'd, he sees impending fate,
        He howls in anguish, and repents too late.
55   But oft *thy* kindness moves with timely fear
        The furious rebel in his mad career.
        Thrice bless'd the man, who in *thy* sacred shrine
        Improves the REFUGE from the wrath divine.

*Her age.

[broadside at the Library of Congress]

To the Rev. Mr. *Pitkin*, on the DEATH of his LADY.

      WHERE Contemplation finds her sacred Spring;
      Where heav'nly Music makes the Centre ring;
      Where Virtue reigns unsull[i]ed, and divine;
      Where Wisdom thron'd, and all the Graces shine;
5   There sits thy Spouse, amid the glitt'ring Throng;
      There central Beauty feasts the ravish'd Tongue;
      With recent Powers, with recent glories crown'd,
      The Choirs angelic shout her Welcome round.

      The virtuous Dead, demand a grateful Tear—
10   But cease thy Grief a-while, thy Tears forbear,
      Not thine alone, the Sorrow I relate,
      Thy blooming Off-spring feel the mighty Weight;
      Thus, from the Bosom of the tender Vine,
      The Branches torn, fall, wither, sink supine.

15   Now flies the Soul, thro' Aether unconfin'd.
      Thrice happy State of the immortal Mind!
      Still in thy Breast tumultuous Passions rise,
      And urge the lucent Torrent from thine Eyes.
      Amidst the Seats of Heaven, a Place is free

20   Among those bright angelic Ranks for thee.
      For thee, they wait—and with expectant Eye,
      Thy Spouse leans forward from th' ethereal Sky,
      Thus in my Hearing, "Come away," she cries,
      "Partake the sacred Raptures of the Skies!
25   Our Bliss divine, to Mortals is unknown,
      And endless Scenes of Happiness our own;
      May the dear Off-spring of our earthly Love,
      Receive Admittance to the Joys above!
      Attune the Harp to more than mortal Lays,
30   And pay with us, the Tribute of their Praise
      To Him, who died, dread Justice to appease,
      Which reconcil'd, holds Mercy in Embrace;
      Creation too, her MAKER'S Death bemoan'd,
      Retir'd the Sun, and deep the Centre groan'd.
35   He in his Death slew ours, and as he rose,
      He crush'd the Empire of our hated Foes.
      How vain their Hopes to put the GOD to flight,
      And render Vengeance to the Sons of Light!"

          Thus having spoke she turn'd away her Eyes,
40   Which beam'd celestial Radiance o'er the Skies.
      Let Grief no longer damp the sacred Fire,
      But rise sublime, to equal Bliss aspire;
      Thy Sighs no more be wafted by the Wind,
      Complain no more, but be to Heav'n resign'd.
45   'Twas thine to shew those Treasures all divine,
      To sooth our Woes, the Task was also thine.
      Now Sorrow is recumbent on thy Heart,
      Permit the Muse that healing to impart,
      Nor can the World, a pitying tear refuse,
50   They weep, and with them, ev'ry heavenly Muse.

                              Phillis Wheatley.
                              Boston, June 16th, 1772.

The above *Phillis Wheatley*, is a Negro Girl, about 18 Years
old, who has been in this Country 11 Years.

[manuscript at the Massachusetts Historical Society]

A POEM ON THE DEATH OF *CHARLES ELIOT,*
AGED 12 MONTHS [variant 1]

Thro' airy realms, he wings his instant flight,
To purer regions of celestial light;
Unmov'd he sees unnumber'd systems roll.
Beneath his feet, the universal whole
5   In just succession run their destin'd round,
And circling wonders spread the dread profound;
Th' etherial now, and now the starry skies,
With glowing splendors, strike his wond'ring eyes.

The heav'nly legions, view, with joy unknown,
10   Press his soft hand, and seat him on the throne,
And smiling, thus: "To this divine abode,
The seat of Saints, of Angels, and of GOD:
Thrice welcome thou,"—The raptur'd babe replies,
"Thanks to my God, who snatch'd me to the skies,
15   Ere vice triumphant had possess'd my heart;
Ere yet the tempter claim'd my better part;
Ere yet on sin's most deadly actions bent;
Ere yet I knew temptation's dread intent;
Ere yet the rod for horrid crimes I knew,
20   Not rais'd with vanity, or press'd with wo;
But soon arriv'd to heav'n's bright port assign'd.
New glories rush on my expanding mind;
A noble ardor now, my bosom fires,
To utter what the heav'nly muse inspires!"

25   Joyful he spoke—exulting cherubs round
Clap loud their pinions, and the plains resound.
Say, parents! why this unavailing moan?
Why heave your bosoms with the rising groan?
To CHARLES, the happy subject of my song,
30   A happier world, and nobler strains belong.
Say, would you tear him from the realms above?

Or make less happy, frantic in your love?
Doth his beatitude increase your pain,
Or could you welcome to this earth again
35   The son of bliss?—No, with superior air,
Methinks he answers with a smile severe,
"Thrones and dominions cannot tempt me there!"

But still you cry, "O Charles! thy manly mind,
Enwrap our souls, and all thy actions bind;
40   Our only hope, more dear than vital breath,
Twelve moons revolv'd, and sunk in shades of death!
Engaging infant! Nightly visions give
Thee to our arms, and we with joy recieve:
We fain would clasp the phantom to our breast,
45   The phantom flies, and leaves the soul unblest!"

Prepare to meet your dearest infant friend
Where joys are pure, and glory's without end.

Boston, Sept.r 1.st 1772.   Phillis Wheatley.

[holograph manuscript at the Dartmouth College Library]

A Poem on the death of Charles Eliot aged 12 months.
[variant 2]

Thro' Airy realms, he wings his instant flight
To purer regions of celestial Light,
Unmov'd he Sees unnumber'd Systems roll,
Beneath his feet, the Universal whole
5   In Just Succession run their destin'd round
And circling wonders Spread the dread Profound,
Th'etherial now, and now the Starry Skies;
With glowing Splendors, Strike his wondring eyes.
The heav'nly legions, view with Joy unknown,
10   Press his soft hand, & Seat him on the throne,

And Smiling, thus. ["]To this divine abode,
The Seat of Saints, of Angels and of God:
Thrice welcome thou.["]—The raptur'd babe replies,
"Thanks to my God, who Snatch'd me to the Skies!
15 "E'er Vice triumphant had Posses'd my heart;
"E'er yet the tempter claim'd my better part:
"E'er yet on sins most deadly Actions bent;
"E'er yet I knew temptation's dread intent:
"E'er yet the rod for horrid crimes I knew,
20 "Not raisd with vanity or press'd with woe;
"But soon Arriv'd to heav'ns bright Port assign'd
"New glories rush on my expanding Mind.
A noble ardor now, my bosom fires
To utter what the heavnly muse inspires!"
25   Joyful he Spoke.—exulting cherubs round.
Clap loud their pinions, and the plains resound.
Say, parents why this unavailing moan?
Why heave your bosoms with the rising groan?
To Charles the happy Subject of my Song
30 A happier world, and nobler Strains belong
Say, would you tear him from the realms above?
Or make less happy, frantic in your Love.
Doth his beatitude increase your Pain,
Or could you welcome to this earth again
35 The Son of bliss—No with Superior Air
Methink he answers with a Smile Severe,
"Thrones and Dominions cannot tempt me there!["]
     But Still you cry. "O Charles! thy manly mind
"Enwrap our Souls, and all thy actions bind,
40 "Our only hope, more dear than vital breath,
"Twelve moons revolv'd, and Sunk in shades of death
"Engaging Infant! Nightly visions give
"Thee to our Arms, and we with Joy receive,
"We fain would clasp, the Phantom to our breast
45 "The Phantom flies, and leaves the Soul unblest."
Prepare to meet your dearest Infant friend,
Where Joys are pure, and Glory without end.

Boston, Sept.r 1.st 1772.   Phillis Wheatley

[manuscript at the Staffordshire Records Office in Stafford, United Kingdom]

TO THE RIGHT HONL. WILLIAM LEGGE, EARL OF DARTMOUTH, HIS MAJESTY'S SECRETARY OF STATE FOR NORTH AMERICA &.c &.c &.c [variant 1]

Hail! happy day! when Smiling like the Morn,
Fair Freedom rose, New England to adorn.
The northern clime, beneath her genial ray,
Beholds, exulting, thy Paternal Sway,
5   For big with hope, her race no longer mourns,
Each Soul expands, each ardent bosom burns,
While in thy hand, with pleasure, we behold
The Silken reins, and Freedom's charms unfold!
Long lost to Realms beneath the northern Skies,
10   She Shines supreme, while hated Faction dies,
Soon as he Saw the triumph long desir'd
Sick at the view, he languish'd and expir'd.
Thus from the Splendors of the rising Sun.
The Sickning Owl explores the dark unknown.

15   No more of grievance unredress'd complain;
Or injur'd Rights, or groan beneath the chain,
Which Wanton Tyranny with lawless hand,
Made to enslave, O Liberty! thy Land.
My Soul rekindles at thy glorious name
20   Thy beams essential to the vital Flame.

The Patrio'ts' breast, what Heav'nly virtue warms!
[sic]
And adds new lustre to his mental charms;
While in thy Speech, the Graces all combine;

Apollos too, with Sons of Thunder Join,
25   Then Shall the Race of injur'd Freedom bless
The Sire, the Friend, and messenger of Peace.

While you, my Lord, read o'er th' advent'rous Song
And wonder whence Such daring boldness Sprung:
Hence, flow my wishes for the common good
30   By feeling hearts alone, best understood.

From Native clime, when Seeming cruel fate
Me snatch'd from Afric's fancy'd happy Seat
Impetuous.—Ah! what bitter pangs molest
What Sorrows labour'd in the Parent breast!
35   That more than Stone, ne'er Soft compassion mov'd
Who from its Father Seiz'd his much belov'd.
Such once my case.—Thus I deplore the day
When Britons weep beneath Tyrannic sway.
To thee, our thanks for favours past are due,
40   To thee, we still Solicite for the new;
Since in thy pow'r as in thy Will before,
To Sooth the griefs which thou didst then deplore.

May heav'nly grace, the Sacred Sanction give
To all thy works, and thou for ever live,
45   Not only on the wing of fleeting Fame,
(Immortal Honours grace the Patriots' name!)
Thee to conduct to Heav'ns refulgent fane;
May feiry coursers sweep th' ethereal plain!
Thou, like the Prophet, find the bright abode
50   Where dwells thy Sire, the Everlasting God.

[dated Boston, October 10, 1772; printed in the
New-York Journal, June 3, 1773]

TO THE RIGHT HONL. WILLIAM LEGGE, EARL OF DARTMOUTH, HIS MAJESTY'S SECRETARY OF STATE FOR NORTH AMERICA &.c &.c &.c [variant 2]

    HAIL! happy Day! when Smiling like the Morn,
    Fair *Freedom* rose, New England to adorn:
    The Northern Clime beneath her genial Ray
    Beholds, exulting, thy paternal Sway;
5   For, big with Hopes, her Race no longer mourns;
    Each Soul expands, every Bosom burns:
    While in thy Hand, with Pleasure, we behold,
    The silken Reins, and *Freedom's* charms unfold!
    Long lost to Realms beneath the Northern skies,
10   She shines supreme; while hated *Faction* dies:
    Soon as appear'd the Triumph long desir'd,
    Sick at the View, he languish'd and expir'd.

    No more, of Grievance unredress'd complain,
    Or injur'd Rights, or groan beneath the Chain,
15   Which wanton Tyranny, with lawless Hand,
    Made to enslave, O *Liberty!* thy Land.—
    My Soul rekindles, at thy glorious Name,
    Thy Beams, essential to the vital Flame.—
    The Patriots' Breast, what Heavenly Virtue warms,
20   And adds new Lustre to his mental Charms!
    While in thy Speech, the Graces all combine,
    Apollo's too, with Sons of Thunder join.
    Then shall the Race of injur'd Freedom bless,
    The Sire, the Friend, and Messenger of Peace.

25   While you, my Lord, read o'er the advent'rous Song
    And wonder, whence such daring Boldness sprung;
    Whence flow my Wishes for the common Good,
    By feeling Hearts alone best understood?
    From native Clime, when seeming cruel Fate
30   Me snatch'd from Afric's fancy'd happy Seat,

Impetuous.—Ah! what bitter pangs molest,
What Sorrows labour'd in the Parent breast?
That more than Stone, ne'er Soft compassion mov'd,
Who from its Father seiz'd his much belov'd.
35 Such once my Case.—Thus I deplore the Day,
When Britons weep beneath Tyrannic Sway.
To thee our Thanks for Favours past are due;
To thee we still solicit for the new:
Since in thy Pow'r as in thy will before,
40 To sooth the Griefs which thou di[d]st then deplore;
May Heav'nly Grace, the sacred Sanction give,
To all thy Works, and thou for ever live;
Not only on the Wing of fleeting Fame,
(Immortal Honours Grace the Patriot's Name,)
45 Thee to conduct to Heaven's refulgent Fane;
May feiry Courses sweep the ethereal Plain,
There, like the Prophet, find the bright Abode,
Where dwells thy Sire, the Everlasting GOD.

[broadside at the Historical Society of Pennsylvania]

To the Hon'ble Thomas Hubbard, *Esq;*
On the Death of Mrs. Thankfull Leonard.

WHILE thus you mourn beneath the Cypress shade
That hand of Death, a kind conductor made
To her whose flight commands your tears to flow
And wracks your bosom with a scene of wo:
5 Let Recollection bear a tender part
To sooth and calm the tortures of your heart:
To still the tempest of tumultous grief;
To give the heav'nly Nectar of relief;
Ah! cease, no more her unknown bliss bemoan!
10 Suspend the sigh, and check the rising groan.
Her virtues shone with rays divinely bright,
But ah! soon clouded with the shades of night.
How free from tow'ring pride, that gentle mind!

Which ne'er the hapless indigent declin'd,
15 Expanding free, it sought the means to prove
Unfailing Charity, unbounded Love!

She unreluctant flies, to see no more
Her much lov'd Parents on Earth's dusky shore,
'Till dark mortality shall be withdrawn,
20 And your bless'd eyes salute the op'ning morn.*
Impatient heav'n's resplendent goal to gain
She with swift progress scours the azure plain,
Where grief subsides, where passion is no more
And life's tumultous billows cease to roar,
25 She leaves her earthly mansions for the skies
Where new creations feast her won'dring eyes.
To heav'n's high mandate chearfully resign'd
She mounts, she flies, and leaves the rolling Globe
     behind.
She who late sigh'd for LEONARD to return
30 Has ceas'd to languish, and forgot to mourn.
Since to the same divine dominions come
She joins her Spouse, and smiles upon the Tomb:
And thus addresses;—(let Idea rove)—
["]Lo! this the Kingdom of celestial Love!
35 Could our fond Parents view our endless Joy,
Soon would the fountain of their sorrows dry;
Then would delightful retrospect inspire,
Their kindling bosoms with the sacred fire!
Amidst unutter'd pleasures, whilst I play,
40 In the fair sunshine of celestial day:
As far as grief affects a deathless Soul,
So far doth grief my better mind controul:
To see on Earth, my aged Parents mourn,
And secret, wish for THANKFULL to return!
45 Let not such thought their latest hours employ
But as advancing fast, prepare for equal Joy."

*Meaning the Resurrection.

                    Boston, January 2. 1773.   *Phillis Wheatley.*

[dated May 7, 1773; published in *The Massachusetts Gazette and Boston Post-Boy*, May 10]

To the Empire of America, Beneath the Western Hemisphere.
Farewell to America. To Mrs. S. W. [variant 1]

ADIEU NEW ENGLAND'S smiling Meads,
    Adieu the flow'ry Plain:
I leave thy op'ning Charms, O Spring!
    To try the Azure Reign.—

5   In vain for me the Flowrets rise,
        And show their guady [*sic*] Pride,
While here beneath the Northern Skies
    I mourn for Health deny'd.

Thee, charming Maid, while I pursue,
10   In thy luxuriant Reign,
And sigh, and languish thee to view,
    Thy Pleasures to regain:—

SUSANNA mourns, nor can I bear
    To see the Christal Show'r
15   Fast falling,—the indulgent Tear,
    In sad Departure's Hour!

Not unregarding lo! I see
    Thy Soul with Grief oppress'd:
Ah! curb the rising Groan for me,
20   Nor Sighs disturb thy Breast.

In vain the feather'd Songsters sing,
    In vain the Garden blooms,
And on the Bosom of the Spring
    Breathes out her sweet Perfumes;—

25   While for Britannia's distant Shore
    We sweep the liquid Plain,

'Till Aura to the Arms restore,
   Of this belov'd Domain.

Lo, Health appears, Celestial Dame!
30   Complacent and serene,
With Hebe's Mantle o'er her Frame,
   With Soul-delighting Mein.

Deep in a Vale, where London lies,
   With misty Vapours crown'd;
35 Which cloud Aurora's thousand Dyes,
   And veil her Charms around.

Why, P[h]oebus, moves thy Car so slow,
   So slow thy rising Ray;—
Nor give the mantl'd Town to View
40   Thee, glorious King of Day!

But late from Orient Skies behold,
   He shines benignly bright,
He decks his native Plains with Gold,
   With chearing Rays of Light.

45 For thee, Britannia, I resign
   New England's smiling Face,
To view again her Charms divine,
   One short reluctant Space.

But thou, Temptation, hence away,
50   With all thy hated Train
Of Ills,—nor tempt my Mind astray
   From Virtue's sacred Strain.

Most happy! who with Sword and Shield
   Is screen'd from dire Alarms,
55 And fell Temptation on the Field
   Of fatal Pow'r disarms.

But cease thy Lays: my Lute forbear;
      Nor frown, my gentle Muse,
To see the secret, falling Tear,
60   Nor pitying look refuse.

[From the *Massachusetts Gazette: and the Boston
Weekly News-Letter*, May 13, 1773]

BOSTON, *MAY* 10, 1773 Saturday last Capt. Calef sailed for
London, in [with] whom went Passengers Mr. Nathaniel Wheat-
ley, Merchant; also, Phillis, the extraordinary Negro Poet, Ser-
vant to Mr. John Wheatley.

FAREWELL TO AMERICA.
To Mrs. S— W—. By Phillis Wheatley. [variant 2]

    ADIEU New England's smiling Meads;
        Adieu the flow'ry Plain,
    I leave thy opening Charms, O Spring!
        To try the Azure Reign.

5   In vain for me the Flow'rets rise
        And show their gawdy Pride,
    While here beneath the Northern Skies
        I mourn for Health deny'd.

    Thee, charming Maid! while I pursue
10   In thy luxuriant Reign;
    And sigh and languish, thee to view,
        Thy Pleasures to regain.

    Susanna mourns, nor can I bear
        To see the Christal Show'r
15   Fast falling—the indulgent Tear
        In sad Departure's Hour.

Not unregarding lo! I see
          Thy Soul with Grief oppress'd;
Ah! curb the rising Groan for me,
20   Nor Sighs disturb thy Breast.

In vain the feather'd Songsters sing,
          In vain the Garden Blooms,
And on the Bosom of the Spring,
          Breaths out her sweet Perfumes.

25 While for Britannia's distant Shore,
          We sweep the liquid Plain,
Till Aura to the Arms restore
          Of this belov'd Domain.

Lo! Health appears! Celestial Dame,
30   Complacent and serene,
With Hebe's Mantle o'er her Frame,
          With Soul-delighting Mein.

Deep in a Vale where London lies,
          With misty Vapours crown'd,
35 Which cloud Aurora's thousand Dyes,
          And Veil her Charms around.

Why Phoebus! moves thy Car so slow,
          So slow thy rising Ray;
Nor gives the mantled Town to View
40   Thee glorious King of Day!

But late from Orient Skies, behold!
          He Shines benignly bright,
He decks his native Plains with Gold,
          With chearing Rays of Light.

45 For thee Britannia! I resign
          New-England's smiling Face,
To view again her Charms divine,
          One short reluctant Space.

But thou Temptation! hence, away,
50   With all thy hated Train
Of Ills—nor tempt my Mind astray
          From Virtue's sacred Strain.

Most happy! who with Sword and Shield
          Is screen'd from dire Alarms,
55 And fell Temptation, on the Field,
          Of fatal Power disarms.

But cease thy Lays, my Lute forbear
          Nor frown my gentle Muse,
To see the secret falling Tear,
60   Nor pitying look refuse.

It was mentioned in our last that Phillis[,] the Negro Poet, had taken her Passage for England, in consequence of an Invitation from the Countess of Huntingdon, which was a mistake.

LETTERS

[manuscript in Huntingdon Papers at the
Cheshunt Foundation, Cambridge University]

To the Rt. Hon'ble the Countess of Huntingdon

Most noble Lady,

The Occasion of my addressing your Ladiship will, I hope, Apologize for this my boldness in doing it: it is to enclose a few lines on the decease of your worthy Chaplain, the Rev'd Mr. Whitefield, in the loss of whom I Sincerely sympathize with your Ladiship; but your great loss which is his Greater gain, will, I hope, meet with infinite reparation, in the presence of God, the Divine Benefactor whose image you bear by filial imitation.

The Tongues of the Learned are insufficient, much less the pen of an untutor'd African, to paint in lively characters, the excellencies of this Citizen of Zion! I beg an Interest in your Ladiship's Prayers and Am,

With great humility
your Ladiship's most
Obedient Humble Servant
Phillis Wheatley
[Boston Oct. 25, 1770]

[The London Magazine: Or, Gentleman's Monthly Intelligencer 41 (March 1772)]

Madam [to Abigail May?],

Agreeable to your proposing Recollection as a subject proper
for me to write upon, I enclose these few thoughts upon it; and,
as you was the first person who mentioned it, I thought none
more proper to dedicate it to; and, if it meets with your approba-
tion, the poem is honoured, and the authoress satisfied. I am,
Madam,

> Your very humble servant,
> Phillis
> [November or December 1771]

[The variant version of Wheatley's poem "Recollection" follows.]

[manuscript in the Scottish Record Office, Edinburgh]

To John Thornton in London

> Boston April 21st, 1772

Hon'd Sir,

I rec'd your instructive favr. of Feb. 29, for which, return you
ten thousand thanks, I did not flatter myself with the tho'ts of
your honouring me with an Answer to my letter, I thank you for
recommending the Bible to be my cheif Study, I find and Ac-
knowledge it the best of Books, it contains an endless treasure of
wisdom and knowledge. O that my eyes were more open'd to
see the real worth, and true excellence of the word of truth, my
flinty heart Soften'd with the grateful dews of divine grace and
the Stubborn will, and affections, bent on God alone their proper
object, and the vitiated palate may be corrected to relish heav'nly
things. It has pleasd God to lay me on a bed of Sickness, and I
knew not but my deathbed, but he has been graciously pleas'd to
restore me in a great measure. I beg your prayers, that I may be

made thankful for his paternal corrections, and that I may make proper use of them to the glory of his grace. I am Still very weak & the Physicians, seem to think there is danger of a consumpsion. And O that when my flesh and my heart fail me God would be my strength and portion for ever, that I might put my whole trust and Confidence in him, who has promis'd never to forsake those who Seek him with the whole heart. You could not, I am sure have express [sic] greater tenderness and affection for me, than by being a welwisher to my Soul, the friends of Souls bear Some resemblance to the father of Spirits and are made partakers of his divine Nature.

I am affraid I have entruded on your patient [patience], but if I had not tho't it ungrateful to omit writing in answer to your favour Should not have troubl'd you, but I can't expect you to answer this,

> I am Sir with greatest respect,
> your very hum. sert.
> Phillis Wheatley

[manuscript in the Roberts Autograph Collection in the Quaker Collection, Haverford College Library]

To Arbour Tanner in New Port [Rhode Island]
                                    Boston, May 19th 1772

Dear Sister

I rec'd your favour of February 6th for which I give you my sincere thanks. I greatly rejoice with you in that realizing view, and I hope experience, of the Saving change which you So emphatically describe. Happy were it for us if we could arrive to that evangelical Repentance, and the true holiness of heart which you mention. Inexpressibly happy Should we be could we have a due Sense of Beauties and excellence of the Crucified Saviour. In his Crucifixion may be seen marvellous displays of Grace and Love, Sufficient to draw and invite us to the rich and endless treasures of his mercy; let us rejoice in and adore the wonders of God's infinite Love in bringing us from a land Semblant of darkness itself, and where the divine light of revelation (being obscur'd) is as darkness. Here, the knowledge of the true God and eternal life are made manifest; But there, profound ignorance overshadows the Land. Your observation is true, namely, that there was nothing in us to recommend us to God. Many of our fellow creatures are pass'd by, when the bowels of divine love expanded towards us. May this goodness & long Suffering of God lead us to unfeign'd repentance.

It gives me very great pleasure to hear of so many of my Nation, Seeking with eagerness the way to true felicity. O may we all meet at length in that happy mansion. I hope the correspondence between us will continue, (my being much indispos'd this winter past was the reason of my not answering yours before now) which correspondence I hope may have the happy effect of improving our mutual friendship. Till we meet in the regions of consummate blessedness, let us endeavor by the assistance of divine grace, to live the life, and we Shall die the death of the Righteous. May this be our happy case and of those who are travelling to the region of Felicity, is the earnest request of your affectionate

Friend & hum. Sert. Phillis Wheatley

[manuscript at the Massachusetts Historical Society]

To Arbour Tanner in New Port Rhode Island
To the care of Mr. Pease's Servant

Boston, July 19th 1772
My dear friend
I rec'd your kind Epistle a few days ago; much disappointed to hear that you had not rec'd my answer to your first letter.* I have been in a very poor state of health all the past winter and spring, and now reside in the country for the benefit of its more wholesome air. I came to town this morning to spend the Sabbath with my master and mistress: Let me be interested in yr. Prayers that God would please to bless to me the means us'd for my recovery, if agreeable to his holy Will. While my outward man languishes under weakness and pa[in], may the inward be refresh'd and Strengthend more abundantly by him who declar'd

from heaven that his strength was made perfect in weakness!
May he correct our vitiated taste, that the meditation of him may
be delightful to us. No longer to be so excessively charm'd with
fleeting vanities: But pressing forward to the fix'd mark f[or] the
prize. How happy that man who is prepar'd for that Nig[ht]
Wherein no man can work! Let us be mindful of our high calling,
continually on our guard, lest our treacherous hearts Should give
the adversary an advantage over us. O! who can think without
horror of the Snares of the Devil. Let us, by freque[nt] medita-
tion on the eternal Judgment, prepare for it. May the Lord bless
to us these thoughts, and teach us by his Spirit to live to him
alone, and when we leave this world may We be his: That this
may be our happy case, is the sincere desire

                              Of, your affectionate friend, & humble Servt.
                                                          Phillis Wheatley

*I sent the letter to Mr. Whitwell's who said he would forward it.

[manuscript in the Staffordshire Records Office in Stafford, United Kingdom]

To the Right Hon'ble The Earl of Dartmouth &c. &c. &c. p[e]r
favour of Mr. Wooldridge.

My Lord,
     The Joyful occasion which has given me this Confidence in
addressing your Lordship in the enclos'd Peice will, I hope, Suf-
ficiently apologize for this freedom from an African, who with
the (now) happy America, exults with equal transport, in the
view of one of its greatest advocates Presiding, with the Special
tenderness of a Fatherly heart, over the American department.
     Nor can they, my Lord, be insensible of the Friendship so
much exemplified in your endeavours in their behalf, during the
late unhappy disturbances. I sincerely wish your Lordship all
Possible Success, in your undertakings for the Interest of North
America.
     That the united Blessings of Heaven and Earth, may attend
you here, and the endless Felicity of the invisible State, in the

presence of the Divine Benefactor, may be your portion here after, is the hearty desire

> Of, My Lord
> Your Lordship's
> Most Obt. & devoted Huml.
> Servt.

Boston N[ew]. E[ngland]. Oct. 10th 1772   Phillis Wheatley

[manuscript in Huntingdon Papers at the Cheshunt Foundation, Cambridge University]

The Right Honourable The Countess of Huntington [*sic*] At Talgarth South Wales.—

Madam   London June 27, 1773

It is with pleasure I acquaint your Ladyship of my safe arrival in London after a fine passage of 5 weeks, in the Ship London with my young Master (advis'd by my Physicians for my Health) have Brought a letter from Richd. Carey Esqr. but was disappointed by your absence of the honour of waiting upon your Ladyship with it. I would have inclos'd it, but was doubtful of the safety of the conveyance.

I should think my self very happy in Seeing your Ladyship, and if you was So desirous of the Image of the Author as to propose it for a Frontispiece I flatter myself that you would accept the Reality.

I conclude with thanking your Ladyship for permitting the Dedication of my Poems to you; and am not insensible, that, under the patronage of your Ladyship, not more eminent in the Station of Life than in your exemplary Piety and Virtue, my feeble efforts will be Shielded from the Severe trials of unpitying Criticism and, being encourag'd by your Ladyship's Indulgence, I the more freely resign to the world these Juvenile productions, And Am Madam, with greatest humility, your Dutiful Huml Sert,

> Phillis Wheatley

[manuscript in Huntingdon Papers at the Cheshunt Foundation, Cambridge University]

The Right Hon'ble The Countess of Huntingdon

Madam,

I rec'd with mixed sensations of pleasure & disappointment your Ladiship's message favored by Mr. Rien Acquainting us with your pleasure that my Master & I Should wait upon you in So[uth]. Wales, delighted with your Ladiship Condescention to me so unworthy of it. Am sorry [to a]cquaint your Ladiship that the Ship is certainly to Sail next Thurs[day on] which I must return to America. I long to see my Friends there. [I am ex]tremely reluctant to go without having first Seen your Ladiship.

It gives me very great satisfaction to hear of an African so worthy to be honour'd with your Ladiship's approbation & Friendship as him whom you call your Brother. I rejoice with your Ladiship in that Fund of Mental Felicity which you cannot but be possessed of, in the consideration of your exceeding great reward. My great opinion of your Ladiship's goodness, leads to believe, I have an interest in your most happy hours of communion, with your most indulgent Father and our great and common Benefactor. With greatest humility I am,

most dutifully
your Ladiship's Obedt. Sert.
Phillis Wheatley.

London July 17
1773

My master is yet undetermined about
going home, and Sends his dutiful
respects to your Ladiship.

[copy at the Massachusetts Historical Society]

To Col. David Worcester in New Haven, Connecticut. favour'd by Mr. Badcock's Servant.

Sir,

Having an opportunity by a Servant of Mr. Badcock's who lives near you, I am glad to hear you and your Family are well. I take the Freedom to transmit to you, a short Sketch of my voyage and return from London where I went for the recovery of my health as advisd by my Physician. I was receiv'd in England with such kindness[,] Complaisance, and so many marks of esteem and real Friendship as astonishes me on the reflection, for I was no more than 6 weeks there.—Was introduced to Lord Dartmouth and had near half an hour's conversation with his Lordship, with whom was Alderman Kirkman.—Then to Lord Lincoln, who visited me at my own Lodgings with the Famous Dr. Solander, who accompany'd Mr. Banks in his late expedition round the World.

Then to Lady Cavendish, and Lady Carteret Webb,—Mrs. Palmer a Poetess, an accomplished Lady.—[To] Dr. Thos. Gibbons, Rhetoric Proffesor, To Israel Mauduit Esqr.[,] Benjamin Franklin Esqr. F[ellow]. R[oyal]. S[ociety]., Grenville [sic] Sharp Esqr. who attended me to the Tower & Show'd the Lions, Panthers, Tigers, &c. The Horse Armoury, Sma[ll] Armoury, the Crowns, Sceptres, Diadems, the Font for christin[in]g the Royal Family. Saw Westminster Abbey, British Museum[,] Coxe's Museum, Saddler's wells, Greenwich Hospital, Park and Chapel, the royal Observatory at Greenwich, &c. &c. too many things and Places to trouble you with in a Letter.—The Earl of Dartmouth made me a Compliment of 5 guineas, and desird me to get the whole of Mr. Pope's Works, as the best he could recommend to my perusal, this I did, also got Hudibrass, Don Quixot, & Gay's Fables—was presented with a Folio Edition of Milton's Paradise Lost, printed on a Silver Type, so call'd from its elegance, (I suppose) By Mr. Brook Watson Mercht.[,] whose Coat of

Arms is prefix'd.—Since my return to America my Master, has at the desire of my friends in England given me my freedom. The Instrument is drawn, so as to secure me and my property from the hands of Exectutrs.[,] administrators, &c. of my master, and secure whatsoever Should be given me as my Own. A Copy is Sent to Isra. Mauduit Esqr. F[ellow], [of the] R[oyal], S[ociety].

I expect my Books which are publishd in London in [the vessel commanded by] Capt. Hall, who will be here I believe in 8 or 10 days. I beg the favour that you would honour the enclos'd Proposals, & use your interest with Gentlemen & Ladies of your acquaintance to subscribe also, for the more subscribers there are, the more it will be for my advantage as I am to have half the Sale of the Books. This I am the more Solicitous for, as I am now upon my own footing and whatever I get by this is entirely mine, & it is the Chief I have to depend upon. I must also request you would desire the Printers in New Haven, not to reprint that Book, as it will be a great hurt to me, preventing any further Benefit that I might receive from the Sale of my Copies from England. The price is 2/6d [two shillings, six pence] Bound or 2 [shillings]/Sterling Sewed.—If any should be so ungenerous as to reprint them the Genuine Copy may be known, for it is sign'd in my own handwriting. My dutiful respects attend your Lady and Children and I am

ever respectfully your oblig'd Huml. Sert.
Phillis Wheatley

Boston October
18th 1773

I found my mistress very sick on my return But she is somewhat better. We wish we could depend on it. She gives her Compliments to you & your Lady.

[manuscript at the Massachusetts Historical Society]

To Obour Tanner in New Port

Boston Oct. 30, 1773

Dear Obour,

I rec'd your most kind Epistles of Augt. 27th, & Oct. 13th by a young man of your Acquaintance, for which I am obligd to you. I hear of your welfare with pleasure; but this acquaints you that I am at present indisposd by a cold, & Since my arrival have been visited by the asthma.—

Your observations on our dependence on the Deity, & your hopes that my wants will be supply'd from his fulness which is in Christ Jesus, is truely worthy of your self.—I can't say but my voyage to England has conduced to the recovery (in a great measure) of my Health. The Friends I found there among the Nobility and Gentry, Their Benevolent conduct towards me, the unexpected, and unmerited civility and Complaisance with which I was treated by all, fills me with astonishment. I can scarcely Realize it.—This I humbly hope has the happy Effect of lessning me in my own Esteem. Your Reflections on the sufferings of the Son of God, & the inestimable price of our immortal Souls, Plainly dem[on]-strate the sensations of a Soul united to Jesus. What you observe of Esau is true of all mankind, who, (left to themselves) would sell their heavenly Birth Rights for a few moments of sensual pleasure whose wages at last (dreadful wages!) is eternal condemnation. Dear Obour let us not sell our Birth right for a thousand worlds, which indeed would be as dust upon the Ballance.—The God of the Seas and dry Land, has graciously Brought me home in safety. Join with me in thanks to him for so great a mercy, & that it may excite me to praise him with cheerfulness, to Persevere in Grace & Faith, & in the Knowledge of our Creator and Redeemer,—that my heart may be filld with gratitude. I should have been pleasd greatly to see Miss West, as I imagine she knew you. I have been very Busy ever since my arrival or should have, now wrote a more particular account of my voyage, but must submit that satisfaction to some other Opportunity. I am Dear friend,

most affectionately ever yours,
Phillis Wheatley

my mistress has been very sick above 14 weeks & confined to her Bed the whole time, but is I hope s[om]e what Better, now.

The young man by whom this is handed you seems to me to be a very clever man, knows you very well, & is very Complaisant and agreable.—

P.W.

I enclose Proposals for my Book, and beg youd use your interest to get Subscriptions as it is for my Benefit.

[manuscript in the Scottish Record Office, Edinburgh]

To John Thornton Esqre. Merchant London

Hon'd Sir,

It is with great satisfaction, I acquaint you with my experience of the goodness of God in safely conducting my passage over the mighty waters, and returning me in safety to my American Friends. I presume you will Join with them and m[e] in praise to God for so distinguishing a favour, it was amazing Mercy, altogether unmerited by me: and if possible it is augmented by the consideration of the bitter r[e]verse, which is the deserved wages of my evil doings. The Apostle Paul, tells us that the wages of Sin is death. I don't imagine he excepted any sin whatsoever, being equally hateful in its nature in the sight of God, who is essential Purity.

Should we not sink hon'd Sir, under this Sentence of Death, pronounced on every Sin, from the comparatively least to the greatest, were not this blessed Co[n]trast annexed to it, "But the Gift of God is eternal Life, through Jesus Christ our Lord?" It is his Gift. O let us be thankful for it! What a load is taken from the Sinner's Shoulder when he thinks that Jesus has done that work for him which he could never have done, and Suffer'd, that punishment of his imputed Rebellions, for which a long Eternity of Torments could not have made sufficient expiation. O that I could meditate continually on this work of wonde[r] in Deity itself. This, which Kings & Prophets have desir'd to see, & have not See[n.] This, which Angels are continually exploring, yet are not equal to the search.—Millions of Ages shall roll away, and they may try in vain to find out to perfection, the sublime mysteries of Christ's Incarnation. Nor will this desir[e] to look into the deep things of God, cease, in the Breasts of glorified Saints & Angels. It's duration will be coeval with Eternity. This Eternity how dreadf[ul,] how delightful! Delightful to those who have an interest in the Crucifi[ed] Saviour, who has dignified our Nature, by seating it at the Right Hand of the divine Majesty.—They alone who are thus interested have Cause to rejoi[ce] even on the brink of that Bottomless Profound: and I doubt not (without the [lea]st Adulation) that you are one of that happy number. O pray that I may be one also, who Shall Join with you in Songs of praise at the Throne of him, who is no respecter of Persons: being equally the great Maker of all:—Therefor disdain not to be called the Father of Humble Africans and Indians; though despis'd on earth on account of our colour, we have this Consolation, if he enables us to deserve it. "That God dwells in the humble & contrite heart." O that I were more & more possess'd of this inestimable blessing; to be directed by the immediate influence of the divine Spirit in my daily walk & Conversation.

Do you, my hon'd Sir, who have abundant Reason to be thankful for the great Share you possess of it, be always mindful in your Closet, of those who want it—of me in particular.—

When I first arrived at home my mistress was so bad as not to be expected to live above two or three days, but through the goodness of God She is still alive but remains in a very weak & languishing Condition. She begs a continued interest in your most earnest prayers, that she may be surly prepar'd for that great Change which [she] is likely Soon to undergo; She intreats you, as her Son is Still in England, that you would take all opportun[i]ties to advise & counsel him; She says she is going to leave him & desires you'd be a Spiritual Fath[er] to h[im]. *She will take it very kind. She thanks you heartily for the kind notice you took of me while in England.* Pleas[e] to give my best Respects to Mrs. & miss Thorton, and masters Henry and Robert who held with me a long conversation on many subjects which

Mrs. Drinkwater knows very well. I hope she is in better Health than when I left her. Please to remember me to your whole family & I than[k] them for their kindness to me, begging Still an interest in your best hours
I am Hon'd Sir

most respectfully your Humble Servt.
Phillis Wheatley
Boston Dec. 1, 1773

I have written to Mrs. Wilberforce, Sometime since Please to give my duty to her; Since writing the above the Rev'd Mr. Moorhead has made his Exit from this world, in whom we lament the loss of the Zealous Pious & true christian.

[manuscript at the Historical Society of Pennsylvania]

To the Rev. Samuel Hopkins Newport Rhode Island
p[e]r Post

Boston, Feb. 9, 1774
Rev'd Sir,

I take with pleasure the opportunity by the Post, to acquaint you of the arr[iva]l of my books from London. I have Seal'd up a package, containing 17 for you 2 for Mr. Tanner and one for Mrs. Mason, and only wait for you to appoint some proper person by whom I may convey them to you. I rec[eive]d some time ago 20/sterling upon them by the hands of your Son, in a Letter from Obour Tanner. I received at the same time a paper by which I understand there are two Negro men who are desirous of returning to their native Country, to preach the Gospel; But being much indispos'd by the return of my Asthmatic complaint, besides, the sickness of my mistress who has been long confin'd to her bed, & is not expected to live a great while; all these things render it impracticable for me to do anything at present with regard to that paper, but what I can do in influencing my Christian friends and acquaintance, to promote this laudable design shall not be wanting. Methinks Rev'd Sir, this is the beginning of that happy period foretold by the Prophets, when all shall know the Lord from the least to the greatest, and that without the assistance of human Art & Eloquence. My heart expands with sympathetic Joy to see at distant time the thick cloud of ignorance dispersing from the face of my benighted Country; Europe and America have long been fed with the heavenly provision, and I fear they loathe it, while Africa is perishing with a Spiritual Famine. O that they could partake of the crumbs, the precious crumbs, Which fall from the table, of these distinguished children of the Kingdome.

Their minds are unprejudiced against the truth therefore tis to be hoped they woud recieve it with their Whole heart. I hope that which the divine royal Psalmist Says by inspiration is now on the point of being Accomplish'd, namely, Ethiopia Shall Soon Stretch forth her hands Unto God. Of this, Obour Tanner and I trust many others within your knowledge are living witnesses. Please to give my love to her & I intend to write her soon. My best respects attend every kind inquirer after your obligd Humble Servant,

Phillis Wheatley

[from the *Connecticut Gazette; and the Universal Intelligencer*, March 11, 1774]

The following is an extract of a Letter from Phillis, a Negro Girl of Mr. Wheatley's, in Boston, to the Rev. Samson Occom, which we are desired to insert as a Specimen of her Ingenuity.—It is dated 11th Feb., 1774.

"Rev'd and honor'd Sir,
I have this Day received your obliging kind Epistle, and am greatly satisfied with your Reasons respecting the Negroes, and think highly reasonable what you offer in Vindication of their natural Rights: Those that invade them cannot be insensible that the divine Light is chasing away the thick Darkness which

broods over the Land of Africa; and the Chaos which has reign'd
so long, is converting into beautiful Order, and [r]eveals more
and more clearly, the glorious Dispensation of civil and religious
Liberty, which are so inseparably united, that there is little or no
Enjoyment of one without the other: Otherwise, perhaps, the Is-
raelites had been less solicitous for their Freedom from Egyptian
Slavery; I do not say they would have been contented without it,
by no means, for in every human Breast, God has implanted a
Principle, which we call Love of Freedom; it is impatient of Op-
pression, and pants for Deliverance; and by the Leave of our
Modern Egyptians I will assert, that the same Principle lives in
us. God grant Deliverance in his own Way and Time, and get
him honor upon all those whose Avarice impels them to counte-
nance and help forward the Calamities of their Fellow Creatures.
This I desire not for their Hurt, but to convince them of the
strange Absurdity of their Conduct whose Words and Actions
are so diametrically opposite. How well the Cry for Liberty, and
the reverse Disposition for the Exercise of oppressive Power
over others agree,—I humbly think it does not require the Pene-
tration of a Philosopher to determine."—

[manuscript at the Massachusetts Historical Society]

To Miss Obour Tanner Newport

Boston, March 21, 1774

Dear Obour,

I rec'd your obliging Letter, enclosd, in your revd. Pastor's &
handed me by his Son. I have lately met with a great trial in the
death of my mistress; let us imagine the loss of a Parent, Sister or
Brother the tenderness of all these were united in her.—I was a
poor little outcast & a stranger when she took me in: not only
into her house but I presently became a sharer in her most tender
affections. I was treated by her more like her child than her Ser-
vant; no opportunity was left unimprov'd, of giving me the best
of advice, but in terms how tender! how engaging! This I hope
ever to keep in remembrance. Her exemplary life was a greater

monitor than all her precepts and Instruction, thus we may ob-
serve of how much greater force example is than instruction. To
alleviate our sorrows we had the satisfaction to se[e] her depart
in inexpresible raptures, earnest longings & impatient thirstings
for the *upper* Courts of the Lord. Do, my dear friend, remember
me & this family in your Closet, that this afflicting dispensation
may be sanctify'd to us. I am very sorry to hear that you are in-
dispo[sd] but hope this will find you in better health. I have been
unwell the great Part of the winter, but am much better as the
Spring approache[s]. Pray excuse my not writing to you so long
before, for I have been so busy lately, that I could not find
leizure. I shall send the 5 Books you wrote for, the first conve-
nient Opportunity; if you want more, they Shall be ready for
you. I am very affectionately your Friend,

                                            Phillis Wheatley

[manuscript in the Scottish Record Office, Edinburgh]

John Thornton Esqr Merchant at Clapham Near London P[e]r
Capt hood

Much honoured Sir,

I should not so soon have troubled you with the 2d. Letter,
but the mournful *Occasion* will sufficiently Apologize. It is the
death of Mrs. Wheatley. She has been labouring under a lan-
guishing illness for many months past and has at length took her
flight from hence to those blissful regions, which need not the
light of any, but the Sun of Righteousness. O could you have
been present, to See how She long'd to drop the tabernacle of
Clay, and to be freed from the cumbrous Shackles of a mortal
Body, which had so many Times retarded her desires when Soar-
ing upward. She has often told me how your Letters hav[e]
quicken'd her in her Spiritual Course: when She has been in
darkness of mind they have rais'd and enliven'd her insomuch,
that She went on, with chearfuln[ess] and alacrity in the path of

her duty. She did truely, *run with patience the race that was Set before her,* and hath, at length obtained the celestial Goal. She is now Sure, that the afflictions of this present time, were not worthy to be compared to the Glory, which is now, revealed in her, Seeing they have wrought out for her, *a far more exceeding and eternal weight of Glory.* This, Sure, is sufficient encouragement under the bitterest Sufferings, which we can endure.—About half an hour before her Death, She Spoke with a more audible voice, than She had for 3 months before. She calld her friends & relations around her, and charg'd them not to leave their great work undone till *that* hour, but to fear God, and keep his Commandments, being ask'd if her faith faild her She answer'd, No. Then Spr[ead] out her arms crying come! come quickly! come, come! O pray for an eas[y] and quick Passage! She eagerly longed to depart to be with Christ. She retaind her Senses till the very last moment when "fare well, fare well" with a very low voice, were the last words She utter'd. I sat the whole time by her bed Side, and Saw with Grief and Wonder, the Effects of Sin on the human race. Had not Christ taken away the envenom'd Sting, where had been our hopes? what might we not have fear'd, what might we not have expectd from the dreadful King of Terrors? But *this* is matter of endless praise, to the King eternal immortal, invisible, that, *it is finished.* I hope her Son will be interested in Your Closet duties, & that the prayers which she was continually putting up, & wch are recorded before God, in the Book of his remembrance for her Son & for me may be answer'd. I can Scarcely think that an Object of so many prayers, will fail of the Blessings implor'd for him ever Since he was born. I intreat the same Interest in your best thoughts for my Self, that her prayers, in my behalf, may be favour'd with an Answer of *Peace.* We received and forwarded your Letter to the rev'd Mr. Occom, but first, took the freedom to peruse it, and are exceeding glad, that you have order'd him to draw immediately for £25, for I really think he is in absolute necessity for that and as much more, he is so loth to run in debt for fear he Shall not be able to repay, that he has not the least Shelter for his Creatures to defend them from the inclemencies of the weather, and he has lost some already for want of it. His hay is quite as defenceless, thus the

former are in a fair way of being lost, and the latter to be wasted;
It were to be wished that his *dwelling house* was like the Ark,
with appartments, to contain the beasts and their provision; He
Said Mrs. Wheatley and the rev'd Mr. Moorhead were his best
friends in Boston. But alass! they are gone. I trust gone to recieve
the rewards promis'd to those, who Offer a Cup of cold water in
the name & for the sake of Jesus—They have both been very in-
strum[ental in meetin]g the wants of that child of God, Mr. Oc-
com—but I fear your [patience has been] exhausted, it remains
only that we thank you for your kind Letter to my mistress it
came above a fortnight after her Death.—Hoping for an interest
in your prayers for these Sanctificiation [*sic*] of this bereaving
Providence, I am hon'd Sir with dutiful respect ever your obliged

               and devoted Humble Servant Phillis Wheatley
Boston
N[ew] England March 29th
1774
John Thornton Esqr.

[manuscript at the Massachusetts Historical Society]

To Miss Obour Tanner New Port Rhode Island
favd by Mr. Pemberton

Dear Obour,

I recd last evening your kind & friendly Letter, and am *not* a
little animated thereby. I hope ever to follow your good advices
and be resigned to the afflicting hand of a Seemingly frowning
Providence. I have recd the money you sent for the 5 books &
2/6 [2 shillings, six pence] more for another, which I now Send &
wish safe to hand. Your tenderness for my welfare demands my
gratitu[de]. Assist me, dear Obour! to praise our great benefac-
tor, for the innumerable Benefits continually pour'd upon me,
that while he strikes one Comfort *dead* he raises up another. But
O, that I could dwell on, & delight in him alone above every

other Object! While the world hangs loose about us we Shall not
be in painful *anxiety* in giving up to God, that which he first gave
to us. Your letter came by Mr. Pemberton who brings you the
book you wrote for. I shall wait upon Mr. Whitwell with your
Letter, and am

> Dear Sister, ever Affectionately, your
> Phillis Wheatley

I have recd by some of the last ships 300 more of my Poems.
Boston May 6, 1774

[manuscript in the Chamberlin Collection, Boston Public Library]

To the Rev'd Mr. Saml. Hopkins New Port Rhode Island fav'd.
by Mr. Pemberton

Rev'd Sir,

I recieved your kind letter last Evening by Mr. Pemberton, by
whom also this is to be handed you. I have also recd the money
for the 5 Books I sent Obour, & 2/6 more for another. She had
wrote me, but the date is 29 April. I am very sorry to hear, that
Philip Quaque has very little or no *apparent* Success in his mis-
sion.—Yet, I wish that what you hear respecting him, may be
only a misrepresentation.—Let us not be discouraged, but still
hope that God will bring about his great work, tho' Philip may
not be the Instrument in the Divine Hand to perform this work
of wonder, turning the Africans *"from darkness to light."* Possi-
bly, if Philip would introduce himself properly to them, (I don't
know the reverse) he might be more Successful; and in setting a
good example which is more powerfully winning than Instruc-
tion. I Observe your Reference to the Maps of Guinea &
Salmon's Gazetteer, and shall consult them. I have recd in some
of the last Ships from London 300 more copies of my Poems,
and wish to dispose of them as Soon as Possible. If you know of
any being wanted I flatter myself you will be pleas'd to let me

know it, which will be adding one more to the many Obligations already confer'd on her, who is, with a due Sense of your kindness,

Your most humble,
And Obedient Servant
Phillis Wheatley

Boston
May 6, 1774
The revd S. Hopkins

[manuscript in the Scottish Record Office, Edinburgh]

To John Thornton Esqr. Merchant London

Much hond. Sir,

I have the honour of your obliging favour of August 1st by Mr. Wheatley who arriv'd not before the 27th. Ultimo after a tedious passage of near two months; the obligations I am under to the family I desire to retain a grateful Sense of, And consequently rejoice in the bountiful dealings of providence towards him—

By the great loss I have Sustain'd of my best friend, I feel like One [fo]rsaken by her parent in a desolate wilderness, for Such the world appears to [me], wandring thus without my friendly guide. I fear lest every step Should lead me [in]to error and confusion. She gave me many precepts and instructions; which I hope I shall never forget. Hon'd sir, pardon me if after the retrospect of such uncommon tenderness for thirteen years from my earliest youth—such unwearied diligence to instruct me in the principles of the true Religion, this in some degree Justifies me while I deplore my misery—If I readily Join with you in wishing that you could in these respects Supply her place, but this does not seem probable from the great distance of your residence. However I will endeavour to compensate it by a Strict Observance of hers and your good advice from time to time, which you have given me encouragement to hope for—What a Blessed Source of consolation that our greatest friend is an immortal God whose friendship is invariable! from whom I have all that is *in me* praise worthy in mental possession. This Consideration humbles me much under ecomiums on the gifts of God, the fear that I should not improve them to his glory and the good of mankind, it almost hinders a commendable self estimation (at times) but quite beats down the boldness of presumption. The world is a severe Schoolmaster, for its frowns are less dang'rous than its Smiles and flatteries, and it is a difficult task to keep in the path of Wisdom. I attended, and find exactly true your thoughts on the behavior of those who seem'd to respect me while under my mistresses patronage: you said right, for Some of those have already put on a reserve; but I submit while God rules; who never forsakes any till they have ungratefully forsaken him—. My old master's generous behaviour in granting me my freedom, and still so kind to me I delight to acknowledge my great obligations to him, this he did about 3 months before the death of my dear mistress & at her desire, as well as his own humanity, of wch I hope ever to retain a grateful Sense, and treat him with that respect which is ever due to a paternal friendship—If this had not been the Case, yet I hope I should willingly Submit to Servitude to be free in Christ.—But since it is thus —Let me be a *Servant of Christ* and that is the most perfect freedom.—

You propose my returning to Africa with Bristol yamma and John Quamine if either of them upon Strict enquiry is Such, as I dare give my heart and hand to, I believe they are either of them good enough if not too good for me, or they would not be fit for missionaries; but why do you hon'd Sir, wish those poor men so much trouble as to carry me So long a voyage? Upon my arrival, how like a Barbarian Should I look to the Natives; I can promise that my tongue shall be quiet for a strong reason indeed being an utter stranger to the Language of Anamaboe. Now to be Serious, This undertaking appears too hazardous, and not sufficiently Eligible, to go—and leave my British & American Friends—I am also unacquainted with those Missionaries in Person. The reverend gentleman who unde[r] [ta]kes their Education has repeatedly informd me by Letters of their pro[gress] in Learning also an Account of John Quamine's family and Kingdo[m.] But be that as it will I resign it all to God's all wise governance; I thank you heartily for your generous Offer—With sincerity—

I am hond. Sir
most gratefully your devoted Servt.
Phillis Wheatley

Boston October 30th 1770 [1774]

[From the *Pennsylvania Magazine* (April 1776)]

The following LETTER *and* VERSES, *were written by the famous* Phillis Wheatley, *the African Poetess, and presented to his Excellency Gen.* Washington.

SIR,

I Have taken the freedom to address your Excellency in the enclosed poem, and entreat your acceptance, though I am not insensible of its inaccuracies. Your being appointed by the Grand Continental Congress to be Generalissimo of the armies of North America, together with the fame of your virtues, excite sensations not easy to suppress. Your generosity, therefore, I presume, will pardon the attempt. Wishing your Excellency all possible success in the great cause you are so generously engaged in. I am,

Your Excellency's most obedient humble servant, PHILLIS WHEATLEY. *Providence, Oct. 26, 1775. His Excellency Gen. Washington.*

[Wheatley's poem to Washington follows.]

[manuscript at the Massachusetts Historical Society]

Miss Obour Tanner Worcester

Boston May 29th '78

Dear Obour,

I am exceedingly glad to hear from you by Mrs. Tanner, and wish you had timely notice of her departure, so as to have wrote me; next to that is the pleasure of hearing that you are well. The vast variety of Scenes that have pass'd before us these 3 years past will to a reasonable mind serve to convince us of the uncertain duration of all things Temporal, and the proper result of such a consideration is an ardent desire of, & preparation for, a State and enjoyments which are more Suitable to the immortal mind.—You will do me a great favour if you'll write me by every Opp'y [opportunity].—Direct your letters under cover to Mr. John Peters in Queen Street. I have but half an hour's notice; and must apologize for this hasty scrawl. I am most affectionately, my dear Obour, your sincere friend

Phillis Wheatley

[manuscript at the Massachusetts Historical Society]

[15 July 1778]

Madam [Mary Wooster],

I recd your favour by Mr Dennison inclosing a paper containing the Character of the truely worthy General Wooster. It was with the most sensible regret that I heard of his fall in battle, but the pain of so afflicting a dispensation of Providence must be greatly alleviated to you and all his friends in the consideration that he fell a martyr in the Cause of Freedom—

[Wheatley's poem "On the Death of General Wooster"]

You will do me a great favour by returning to me by the first oppy those books that remain unsold and remitting the money for those that are sold—I can easily dispose of them here for 12/Lm.o each—I am greatly obliged to you for the care you show me, and your condescention in taking so much pains for my Interest—I am extremely Sorry not to have been honour'd with a personal acquaintance with you—if the foregoing lines meet with your acceptance and approbation I shall think them highly honour'd. I hope you will pardon the length of my letter, when the reason is apparent—fondness of the Subject &—the highest respect for the deceas'd—I sincerely sympathize with you in the great loss you and your family Sustain and am Sincerely

Your friend & very humble Servt Phillis Wheatley Queenstreet Boston July—15th 1778

Phillis Wheatley

[manuscript at the Massachusetts Historical Society]

Miss Obour Tanner Worcester
favd by Cumberland

Dr. Obour,
    By this opportunity I have the pleasure to inform you that I am well and hope you are so; tho' I have been Silent, I have not been unmindful of you but a variety of hindrances was the cause of my not writing to you.—But in time to Come I hope our correspondence will revive—and revive in better times—pray write me soon, for I long to hear from you—you may depend on constant replies—I wish you much happiness, and am

Dr. Obour, your friend & Sister
Phillis Peters

Boston May 10, 1779

VARIANT LETTERS

[manuscript in Huntingdon Papers at the Cheshunt Foundation, Cambridge University]

Most Noble Lady [the Countess of Huntingdon],

The occasion of my addressing your Ladiship will, I hope, apoligize for this my boldness in doing it; it is to inclose a few lines on the decease of your worthy Chaplain, The Reverend Mr. Whitefield, in the loss of whom, I sincerely sympathize with your Ladiship; but your great loss, which is his greater gain, will I hope, meet with infinite reparation in the presence of God the divine benefactor, whose image you are by filial imitation. The tongues of the learned are insufficient much less the pen of an untutor'd African, to paint in lively Characters, the excellencies of this Citizen of Zion—

> I am with great humility your Ladiship's
> Most obedient Humble Servant,
> Phillis Wheatley

I beg an interest in your Ladiship's Prayers
Boston Octr. 25th 1770

[from the *New-York Journal*, June 3, 1773]

We have had several Specimens of the poetical Genius of an African Negro Girl, belonging to Mr. Wheatley of Boston, in New England, who was Authoress of the following Epistle and Verses, addressed to Lord Dartmouth—They were written, we are told on the following Occasion, viz[:] A Gentleman had seen several of the Pieces ascribed to her, thought them so much superior to her Situation, and Opportunities of Knowledge, that he doubted their being genuine—And in order to be satisfied, went to her Master's House, told his Doubts, and to remove them, desired that she would write something before him. She told him she was then busy and engaged for the Day, but if he would propose a Subject, and call in the Morning, she would endeavour to satisfy him. Accordingly, he gave for a Subject, The Earl of Dartmouth, and calling the next Morning, she wrote in his presence, as follows.

My Lord,

The joyful Occasion which has given me this Confidence in addressing your Lordship in the inclos'd Piece, will I hope sufficiently apologize for this Freedom in an African, who, with the now happy America, exults with equal Transport, in the View of one of its greatest Advocates presiding with equal Tenderness of a fatherly Heart over that Department.

Nor can they, my Lord, be insensible of the Friendship so much exemplified in your Endeavours in their Behalf, during the late unhappy Disturbances,—I sincerely wish your Lordship all possible Success in your Undertakings, for the Interest of North America.—That the united Blessings of Heaven and Earth may attend you here; and that the endless Felicity of the invisible State in the Presence of the divine Benefactor, may be your Portion hereafter, is the hearty Desire of,

My LORD,
Your Lordship's
Most obedient humble Servant,
Phillis Wheatley

[A version of Wheatley's poem to Dartmouth follows.]

PROPOSALS FOR VOLUMES OF POETRY

[from the *Boston Censor*, February 29, March 14. April 18, 1772]

Proposals for Printing by Subscription

A Collection of POEMS, wrote at several times, and upon various occasions, by PHILLIS, a Negro Girl, from the strength of her own Genius, it being but a few Years since she came to this Town an uncultivated Barbarian from *Africa*. The Poems having been seen and read by the best Judges, who think them well worthy of the Publick View; and upon critical examination, they find that the declared Author was capable of writing them. The Order in which they were penned, together with the Occasion, are as follows;

[1] On the Death of the Rev. Dr. *Sewell*, when sick, 1765—;
[2] On Virtue, [17]66—;
[3] On two Friends, who were cast away, d[itt]o.—;
[4] To the University of Cambridge, 1767—;
[5] An Address to the Atheist, do.—;
[6] An Address to the Deist, do.—,
[7] On America, 1768—;
[8] On the King, do.—;
[9] On Friendship, do.—;
[10] Thoughts on being brought from Africa to America, do.—;
[11] On the Nuptials of Mr. *Spence* to Miss *Hooper*, do.—;
[12] On the Hon. Commodore Hood, on his pardoning a Deserter, 1769—;
[13] On the Death of Reverend Dr. *Sewell*, do.—;
[14] On the Death of Master *Seider*, who was killed by *Ebenezer Richardson*, 1770.—;

[15] On the Death of the Rev. *George Whitefield*, do.—;

[16] On the Death of a young Miss, aged 5 years, do—;

[17] On the Arrival of the Ships of War, and landing of the Troops. [undated]—;

[18] On the Affray in King-Street, on the Evening of the 5th of March. [undated]—;

[19] On the death of a young Gentleman. [undated]—;

[20] To *Samuel Quincy*, Esq; a Panegyrick. [undated]—,

[21] To a Lady on her coming to America for her Health. [undated]—,

[22] To Mrs. *Leonard*, on the Death of her Husband. [undated]—;

[23] To Mrs. Boylston and Children on the Death of her Son and their Brother. [undated]—;

[24] To a Gentleman and Lady on the Death of their Son, aged 9 Months. [undated]—;

[25] To a Lady on her remarkable Deliverance in a Hurricane. [undated]—,

[26] To *James Sullivan*, Esq; and Lady on the Death of her Brother and Sister, and a child *Avis*, aged 12 Months. [undated]—,

[27] *Goliah* [*sic* for Goliath] of Gath. [undated]—;

[28] On the Death of Dr. *Samuel* Marshall. [undated]—;

It is supposed they will make one small Octavo Volume, and will contain about 200 Pages.

They will be printed on Demy Paper, and beautiful Types.

The Price to Subscribers, handsomely bound and lettered, will be Four Shillings.—Stitched in blue, Three Shillings.

It is hoped Encouragement will be given to this Publication, as a reward to a very uncommon Genius, at present a Slave.

This Work will be put to the Press as soon as three Hundred Copies are subscribed for, and shall be published with all Speed.

Subscriptions are taken in by E. Russell, in Marlborough Street.

[from the *Massachusetts Gazette and the Boston News-Letter*, April 16, 1773]

PROPOSALS

For Printing in *London* by SUBSCRIPTION, A Volume of PO-EMS, Dedicated by Permission to the Right Hon. the Countess of Huntingdon. Written by PHILLIS, A Negro Servant to Mr. Wheatley of *Boston* in New-England. Terms of Subscription.

    I. The Book to be neatly printed in 12 mo. on a new Type and a fine Paper, adorned with an elegant Frontispiece, representing the Author.

    II. That the Price to Subscribers shall be Two Shillings Sewed or Two Shillings and Sixpence neatly bound.

II[I]. That every Subscriber deposit One Shilling at the Time of subscribing; and the Remainder to be paid on the Delivery of the Book.

Subscriptions are received by Cox & Berry, in *Boston*.

[from the *Boston Evening Post and General Advertiser*, October 30, November 6, 27, 1779]

Proposals

For Printing By Subscription a Volume of Poems And Letters on Various Subjects, Dedicated to the Right Honourable Benjamin Franklin Esq: One of the Ambassadors of the United States at the Court of France, By Phillis Peters

    POEMS
Thoughts on the Times.
On the Capture of General Lee, to I.B. Esq.
To his Excellency General Washington.
On the death of General Wooster.

An Address to Dr—.
To Lieut R— of the Royal Navy.
To the same.
To T.M. Esq. of Granada.
To Sophia of South Carolina.
To Mr. A. M'B— of the Navy.
To Lieut R— D— of the Navy.
Ocean.
The choice and advantages of a Friend; to Mr. T— M—
Farewell to England 1773.
To Mrs. W—ms on Anna Eliza.
To Mr. A McB—d.
Epithalamium to Mrs. H—
To P.N.S. & Lady on the death of their infant son.
To Mr. El—y on the death of his Lady.
On the death of Lieut. L—ds.
To Penelope.
To Mr. & Mrs. L— on the death of their daughter.
A Complaint.
To Mr. A.I.M. on Virtue.
To Dr. L—d and Lady on the death of their son aged 5 years
To Mr. L—g on the death of his son.
To Capt. F—r on the death of his granddaughter.
To Philandra an Elegy.
Niagara.
Chloe to Calliope.
To Musidora on Florello.
To Sir E.L— Esq.
To the Hon. John Montague Esq. Rear Admiral of the Blue.

LETTERS
1. To the Right Hon. Wm E. of Dartmouth, Sec. of State for
   N. America.
2. To the Rev. Mr. T.P. Farmington.
3. To Mr. T.W.—Dartmouth College.
4. To the Hon. T. H. Esq.
5. To Dr. B. Rush, Phila.

6. To the Rev. Dr. Thomas, London.
7. To the Right Hon. Countess of H—.
8. To I.M— Esq. London.
9. To Mrs. W—e in the County of Surrey.
10. To Mr. T.M. Homerton, near London.
11. To Mrs. S. W—
12. To the Rt. Hon. the Countess of H—.
13. To the same.

Messieurs Printers,—The above collection of Poems and Letters was put into my hands by the desire of the ingenious author, in order to be introduced to public View.

The subjects are various and curious, and the author a *Female African*, whose lot it was to fall into the hands of a *generous* master and *great* benefactor. The learned and ingenuous as well as those who are pleased with novelty, are invited to incourage the publication by a generous subscription—the former, that they may fan the sacred fire which, is self-enkindled in the breast of this *young* African—The ingenuous that they may by reading this collection, have a large play for their imaginations, and be ex[c]ited to please and benefit mankind, by some brilliant production of their own pens.—Those who are *always* in search of some *new* thing, that they may obtain a sight of this *rara avis in terra* [Latin for "rare bird in the land"]—And every one, that the ingenious author may be encouraged to improve her own mind, benefit and please mankind.

CONDITIONS

They will be printed on good paper and a neat Type, and will contain about 300 Pages in Octavo.

The price to Subscribers will be *Twelve Pounds*, neatly Bound & Lettered, and *Nine Pounds* sew'd in blue paper, one Half to be paid on Subscribing, the other Half on delivery of the Books.

The Work will be put to the Press as soon as a sufficient Number of Encouragers offer.

Those who subscribe for Six [books] will have a Seventh Gratis.

Subscriptions are taken by White and Adams, the Publishers, in School-Street, *Boston.*

[from *The Boston Magazine* (September 1784)]

Wheatley's Final Proposal

The Poem ["To Mr. and Mrs.—, On the Death of Their Infant Son"], in page 488, of this Number, was selected from a manuscript Volume of Poems, written by PHILLIS PETERS, formerly PHILLIS WHEATLEY—and is inserted as a Specimen of her Work; should this gain the approbation of the Publick and sufficient encouragement be given, a Volume will be shortly Published, by the Printers hereof, who received subscriptions for said Work.

NOTES

POEMS ON VARIOUS SUBJECTS, RELIGIOUS AND MORAL

Dedication.

Selina Hastings (1707–1791), Countess of Huntingdon, was the most socially prominent Methodist leader and patron of many writers besides Wheatley, including the African Britons James Albert Ukawsaw Gronniosaw (c. 1710–c. 1772), John Marrant (1755–1791), and Olaudah Equiano (1745?–1797). In 1748 the Countess chose the Calvinist George Whitefield (1714–1770) to be one of her personal chaplains and promoted his brand of Methodism (see the note below on "On the Death of the Rev. Mr. George Whitefield. 1770"), especially through the missionary associations she called her Connexion, conceived as mediating between the Church of England and the Dissenting sects. Forced by the Church in 1779 to register her chapels as Dissenting meeting houses, the Countess and her Connexion left the Church of England in 1782. Huntingdon and Susanna Wheatley were correspondents.

Preface.

New authors traditionally denied writing for publication and often claimed that they agreed to allow their work to be published only at the urging of friends.

Copy of a Letter Sent by the Author's Master to the Publisher.

The term *master* was used during the eighteenth century to mean either *owner* or *employer*. Note that the title page of Wheatley's *Poems* somewhat misleadingly calls her John Wheatley's "Negro Servant," rather than slave. The Mohegan minister Samson Occom (1732–1792) is discussed in the Introduction.

To the Publick.

Wheatley's publisher, Archibald Bell, also used this address to the public in his London newspaper advertisements for her *Poems* during September 1773. The signers represent an unlikely combination of religious denominations, political positions, and views on slavery, though many of them were related by blood or marriage. The Honourable ("The Hon.") names on the list were members of the governing council of the colony of Massachusetts, followed by the gentlemen ("Esq;"), ministers who were Doctors of Divinity ("D.D."), and other clergymen. Thomas Hutchinson (1711–1780) was governor of Massachusetts from 1771 to 1774, when he fled to England in the face of rising colonial opposition; Lieutenant-Governor Andrew Oliver (1706–1774) was Hutchinson's brother-in-law. Wheatley wrote a poem on the death of Oliver's wife in March 1773. Thomas Hubbard (1702–1773), a prominent merchant, was treasurer of Harvard College, deacon in the Old South Church, and a neighbor of the Wheatleys. In 1771 Phillis Wheatley published a poem on the death of the husband of Hubbard's daughter, Thankfull Hubbard Leonard (1745–1772), and in 1772 on the death of the daughter. John Erving (1728–1816) was a prominent Boston merchant, whose daughter married James Bowdoin (1726–1790), a politician and statesman (he became governor of Massachusetts in 1785, and Bowdoin College would be named after him). Bowdoin's sister married James Pitts (1710–1776). Harrison Gray (1711?–1794), another important merchant, was actively anti-slavery. Also an important merchant, John Hancock (1737–1793) is most famous for his signature on the Declaration of Independence. Joseph Green (1705?–1780) was a poet as well as a merchant, with one of the largest personal libraries in Boston. Richard Cary (1717–1790) wrote letters to the Countess of Huntingdon on May 25, 1772, April 3, and May 3, 1773, praising Phillis Wheatley. Charles Chauncy (1705–1787), minister of the First Unitarian Church and writer on religious subjects, opposed the emotional style of Whitefield's preaching. Mather Byles (1707–1788), a Congregational minister, was also well known as a wit and poet. Ebenezer Pemberton (1704–1777) was minister of the Congregational New Brick Church in the North End. When he published his sermon in London in 1771 on the death of Whitefield, Pemberton appended Wheatley's previously published elegy on his death. Andrew Eliot (1718–1778), minister of the Congregational New North Church, was an outspoken opponent of slavery. In 1784 Wheatley published an elegy on the death of Samuel Cooper (1725–1783), minister of the Brattle Street Congregational Church. Cooper baptized her. Samuel Mather (1706–1785), son of Cotton Mather (1663–1728), cousin of Mather Byles, and minister of the Tenth Congregational Church, married Governor Hutchinson's sister. John Moorhead (1703–1773), minister of the Federal Street Presbyterian Church, was the owner or employer of Scipio Moorhead, to whom Wheatley addressed a poem in 1773. In 1773 Wheatley published an elegy addressed to Reverend Moorhead's daughter on the death of her father. John Wheatley is discussed in the Introduction.

To Maecenas.

Not included in the 1772 Proposals. Probably composed between April 1772 and September 1773. Wheatley follows Classical tradition in opening her collected works with a poem addressed to her patron. For example, the Roman poet Horace (65–8 B.C.) begins his *Odes, Epodes, Satires,* and *Epistles* with poems adressed to Maecenas (d.8 B.C.), an extremely wealthy and politically powerful friend and supporter of Virgil (70–19 B.C.) as well as Horace. He is the dedicatee of Virgil's *Georgics.* The Countess of Huntingdon is probably Wheatley's Maecenas (see Introduction). Like most eighteenth-century writers lacking formal education, Wheatley most probably knew the second-century B.C. Greek epic poems the *Iliad* and *Odyssey,* attributed to Homer, through the translations of Alexander Pope (1688–1744), and the *Aeneid,* an epic poem by Virgil (also known as Maro and the Mantuan), through the translation by John Dryden (1631–1700). In lines 17–20, Wheatley alludes to the opening of *Iliad* xvi, in which Patroclus asks Achilles for permission to wear Achilles' armor and aid the Greeks against the Trojans. Because Achilles was the son of Peleus, king of Phthia, one of his epithets was Pelides. In line 19 "prone" is used to mean leaning forward. The nine Muses were the daughters of Zeus, king of the Greek gods, and Mnemosyne (Memory), who as mother of the muses inspired the arts and literature: Calliope (epic poetry), Clio (history), Euterpe (flute-playing), Terpsichore (lyric poetry and dancing, especially choral), Erato (lyric poetry), Melpomene (tragedy), Thalia (comedy), Polyhymnia (hymns and pantomime), and Urania (astronomy). One of the Muses' sacred residences was Helicon, a mountain in southwestern Boeotia. Parnassus was another Greek mountain, site of the Castalian fountain sacred to the Muses, as well as to Phoebus Apollo, god of the sun, and leader of the Muses, especially in music and poetry. Terence was the second-century B.C. Roman playwright whose cognomen, Afer, means *the African*. For much of his life he was a slave. Naiads, or nymphs, were mythological young female figures who inhabited and animated various places of nature. Aurora was the goddess of the dawn.

On Virtue.

Included in her 1772 Proposals, dated 1766. Published 1773.

To the University of Cambridge, in New-England.

Included in her 1772 Proposals, dated 1767. Published 1773. Harvard College was frequently referred to simply as Cambridge because of its location in the Boston suburb. During the eighteenth and nineteenth centuries the enslaved condition of Africans in America was often likened to the Egyptian bondage of the ancient Hebrews. *Ethiop* or *Ethiopian* was a name frequently applied to anyone from Africa. See the variant version of this poem.

To the King's Most Excellent Majesty. 1768.

Included in her 1772 Proposals, dated 1768. Published 1773. Like many colonists, Wheatley wanted to believe that by approving the repeal of the 1765 Stamp Act in 1766, George III (1738–1820) was expressing sympathy with colonial resistance to the principle of external taxation.

On Being Brought from Africa to America.

Included in her 1772 Proposals, dated 1768. Published 1773.

On the Death of the Rev. Dr. Sewell.

Included in her 1772 Proposals, dated 1769. Published 1773. Joseph Sewall (1688–1769), minister of the Congregational Old South Church, into which Phillis Wheatley was baptised, was the son of Chief Justice Samuel Sewall, author of one of the earliest American writings against slavery, *The Selling of Joseph* (Boston, 1700). See the variant version of this poem.

On the Death of the Rev. Mr. George Whitefield. 1770.

Included in her 1772 Proposals, dated 1770. Published 1770. George Whitefield (1714–1770), along with John (1703–1791) and Charles (1707–1788) Wesley, and others, began the Methodist movement within the Church of England during the 1730s. Except for the Huntingdonians, Methodists did not separate from the Church of England until after John Wesley's death. Whitefield and the Wesleys called for a more methodical practice of worship. Methodist ministers tended to be more evangelical, energetic, and emotional in their style of preaching than most of their fellow Anglicans, and they often addressed audiences that were socially very inclusive, preaching outside of churches, as well as within them, to bring religion to the poor. In the July 30, 1763, entry in his *Life of Samuel Johnson,* James Boswell (1740–1795) reports a conversation with Johnson that helps explain the appeal of Methodism to the lower classes: "JOHNSON. 'Sir, it is owing to their expressing themselves in a plain and familiar manner, which is the only way to do good to the common people, and which clergymen of genius and learning ought to do from a principle of duty, when it is suited to their congregations; a practice, for which they would be praised by men of sense.' " As the satiric print *Credulity, Superstition and Fanaticism* (London, 1762) by William Hogarth (1697–1764) illustrates, Methodism was especially attractive during the eighteenth century to people of African descent. By 1767 there were approximately 24,000 Methodists in Britain. Unlike the Wesleys, whose Arminian doctrine held that all who believed in Christ and repented of their sins could be saved, Whitefield preached the doctrine of John Calvin (1509–1564), who taught that very few Christians were among the elect—predestined, or elected, by the grace of God to be saved. Everyone else was a reprobate, doomed to eternal damnation, despite faith or acts of charity. Grace could only be freely given by God and could not be earned by the good works of professed believers. Whitefield's position was consistent with Article 17, the most Calvinistic of the Thirty-Nine Articles of the Church of England that loosely constituted its creed. As an evangelist, Whitefield made seven tours of North America, dying on his last at Newburyport, Massachusetts, on September 30, 1770, a week after having preached in Boston. Because of the Wheatleys' association with Whitefield's patron, the Countess of Huntingdon, Whitefield may have stayed at the Wheatley residence when he was in Boston. See the variant versions of this poem.

On the Death of a Young Lady of Five Years of Age.

Included in her 1772 Proposals, dated 1770. Published 1773. Variant versions were published in the December 1781 issue of John Wesley's *Arminian Magazine* (London) and in the Philadelphia *Arminian Magazine* (1789).

On the Death of a Young Gentleman.

Included in her 1772 Proposals, undated. Published 1773. A variant version was published in the December 1781 *Arminian Magazine* (London).

To a Lady on the Death of Her Husband.

Included in her 1772 Proposals, undated. Written 1771, published 1771. The "Lady" was Thankfull Hubbard Leonard, daughter of Thomas Hubbard. Her husband, Dr. Thomas

Leonard (1744–1771), died June 21, 1771. See the variant version of this poem, "To Mrs. Leonard, on the Death of her Husband."

Goliath of Gath.

Included in her 1772 Proposals. Written 1772?, published 1773. Eliab (line 76) was David's eldest brother. "The son of Ner" (line 204), Saul's cousin and general, Abner.

Thoughts on the Works of Providence.

Not included in her 1772 Proposals. Written 1772–1773, published 1773. A variant version was published in the December 1781 *Arminian Magazine* (London).

To a Lady on the Death of Three Relations.

Not included in her 1772 Proposals. Undated, published 1773.

To a Clergyman on the Death of His Lady.

Not included in her 1772 Proposals. Written 1772, published 1772. See the variant version of this poem, "To the Rev. Mr. Pitkin, on the Death of His Lady."

An Hymn to the Morning.

Not included in her 1772 Proposals. Undated, published 1773.

An Hymn to the Evening.

Not included in her 1772 Proposals. Undated, published 1773.

Isaiah LXIII. 1–8.

Not included in her 1772 Proposals. Undated, published 1773. Idumea (line 2), another name for Edom. Bozrah (line 3), Edom's strongly fortified capital.

On Recollection.

Not included in her 1772 Proposals. Written late 1771, published 1772. See the variant version of this poem. Mneme (line 1), probably an abbreviation of Mnemosyne. Phoebe (line 12), or Artemis, goddess of the moon, and her twin brother, Phoebus Apollo, were children of Zeus and Leto (Latona).

On Imagination.

Not included in her 1772 Proposals. Undated, published 1773. A variant version was published in the December 1784 *Arminian Magazine* (London). "Silken fetters" (line 11): compare Mark Akenside (1721–1770), *The Pleasures of the Imagination* (London, 1744), Book 2, line 562), "The silken fetters of delicious ease." Flora (line 27), Roman goddess of the spring and flowers. Sylvanus (line 29), Roman god of forests, fields, and herding. Tithon (line 43), Tithonus, mortal lover of Aurora.

*A Funeral Poem on the Death of C.E. an Infant
of Twelve Months.*

Not included in her 1772 Proposals. Undated, published 1773. See the variant, "A Poem on the Death of *Charles Eliot*, Aged 12 Months."

To Captain H—d, of the 65th Regiment.

Not included in her 1772 Proposals. Undated, published 1773. Captain John Hanfield was a member of the British regiment sent in 1769 to pacify anti-British sentiment in Boston.

*To the Right Honourable William, Earl of Dartmouth, His
Majesty's Principal Secretary of State for North-America, &c.*

Not included in her 1772 Proposals. Written November 1772, published 1773. Wheatley celebrates the appointment in August 1772 of William Legge (1731–1801), 2nd Earl of Dartmouth, as secretary of state overseeing the North American colonies, and as president of the Board of Trade and Foreign Plantations, offices he held until 1775. Dartmouth and the Countess of Huntingdon were close friends, and he sympathized with her missionary work. See the variant version of this poem.

Ode to Neptune. On Mrs. W—'s Voyage to England.

Not included in her 1772 Proposals. Written 1772, published 1773. Citing a handwritten note in the American Antiquarian Society copy of Wheatley's *Poems*, William Robinson and Julian Mason both identify "Mrs. W—" as "Mrs. Susanna Wright [written in ink] eminent for her Wax Works etc. [written in pencil in another hand]." "Ae'lus" (line 2): Aeolus, god of the winds.

To a Lady on Her Coming to North-America with Her Son, for the Recovery of Her Health.

Included in her 1772 Proposals, undated. Published 1773.

To a Lady on Her Remarkable Preservation in an Hurricane in North-Carolina.

Included in her 1772 Proposals, undated. Published 1773. Boreas (line 5): the north wind. Nereids (line 6): nymph daughters of Nereus, Homer's "old man" of the sea.

To a Lady and Her Children, on the Death of Her Son and Their Brother.

Included in her 1772 Proposals, undated. Published 1773. Wheatley's 1772 Proposals identify the lady as Mrs. Boylston.

To a Gentleman and Lady on the Death of the Lady's Brother and Sister, and a Child of the Name Avis, Aged One Year.

Included in her 1772 Proposals, undated. Published 1773. Wheatley's 1772 Proposals identify the gentleman as James Sullivan. "The offspring of six thousand years": according to the calculations of James Ussher (1581–1656), archbishop of Armargh,

Ireland, the earth had been created in 4004 B.C., approximately six thousand years before 1772.

On the Death of Dr. Samuel Marshall, 1771.

Included in her 1772 Proposals. Written and published 1771. Related to Susanna Wheatley, Marshall (1735–1771) studied medicine in London after graduating from Harvard in 1754 and returned to Boston in 1764, where he married Lucy Tyler on October 14, 1765. Lucy joined the Old South Church on the same day as Phillis Wheatley, August 18, 1771. Dr. Marshall died September 29, 1771. Aesculapius (line 19): the Roman god of medicine, often said to be the son of Apollo. See the variant versions of this poem.

To a Gentleman on His Voyage to Great-Britain for the Recovery of His Health.

Not included in her 1772 Proposals. Written circa 1767, published 1773. Daniel Ricketson, *The History of New Bedford* (New Bedford, 1858), 262, identifies the gentleman as Joseph Rotch, Jr., brother of William Rotch, Sr. Both were Quaker merchants. Unfortunately, Rotch died soon after reaching Bristol, England.

To the Rev. Dr. Thomas Amory on Reading His Sermons on Daily Devotion, in Which That Duty Is Recommended and Assisted.

Not included in her 1772 Proposals. Written 1772, published 1773. Amory (1701–1774) wrote on religious subjects. On October 14, 1772, Reverend Dr. Charles Chauncy gave Wheatley a copy of Amory's *Daily Devotion Assisted and Recommended, in Four Sermons*, 2nd ed. (London, 1770; reprinted Boston, 1772). On March 26, 1774, Wheatley gave the book, as well as a copy of John Lathrop's *The Importance of Early Piety* (Boston, 1771), to her friend and Susanna Wheatley's grandnephew, Thomas Wallcut (1758–1840).

On the Death of J.C. an Infant.

Not included in her 1772 Proposals. Undated, published 1773. A variant version was published in the November 1784 *Arminian Magazine* (London).

An Hymn to Humanity. To S.P.G. Esq;.

Not included in her 1772 Proposals. Undated, published 1773. See Appendix A for a later version of this poem.

To the Honourable T.H. Esq.; on the Death of His Daughter.

Not included in her 1772 Proposals. Published January 1773 in Boston. See the variant poem on the death of Thomas Hubbard's daughter, Mrs. Thankfull Leonard.

*Niobe in Distress for Her Children Slain by Apollo,
from Ovid's* Metamorphoses, *Book VI. and from a
View of the Painting of Mr. Richard Wilson.*

Not included in her 1772 Proposals. Undated, published 1773. Richard Wilson (1714–1782), best known for his landscapes, based at least three paintings on the tale of Niobe and her children. "The Destruction of Niobe's Children" is now at the Yale Center for British Art. Wheatley probably saw an engraving after one of the paintings. Ovid (43 B.C.–17 A.D.) composed his unconventional fifteen-book epic, *Metamorphoses,* around 8 A.D. Niobe married Amphion, king of Thebes, which had been founded by Cadmus. She was so excessively proud of their seven sons and seven daughters that she foolishly disparaged Leto (Latona) for having had only two children, the twin gods Apollo ("the *Delian* god" of line 166) and Artemis (or Diana, or Phoebe), by Zeus (Jove), who had an oracle at Dodona. Apollo and Artemis were born on Mount Cynthus on the island of Delos. Niobe's arrogance was hereditary: her grandfathers were Atlas and Zeus, and her father was Tantalus, who was condemned to eternal torment in Tarturus for having tried to deceive the gods into eating his own son, Niobe's brother. Having heard Niobe's comment on Leto, the prophetess Manto, daughter of the prophet Tiresias, advised the Theban women to offer sacrifices to Leto and her children for forgiveness. Niobe interrupted the sacrifice by again bragging of her and her children's superiority to Leto and her offspring, even remarking that she had so many children that were a few to die she would still have more than Leto. After Apollo and Artemis killed all Niobe's sons and daughters as punishment for her hubris, Niobe wept for nine days and nine nights over their corpses because Zeus had turned all the Thebans to stone, leaving no one to bury them. At last taking pity on her, the gods themselves performed the funeral services, and Zeus turned Niobe into a weeping statue. "This Verse to the End is the Work of another Hand": William Robinson suggests Mary Wheatley was the author of lines 213–224.

To S.M. a Young African Painter, on Seeing His Works.

Not included in her 1772 Proposals. Undated, published 1773. "Celestial Salem" (line 18): the heavenly Jerusalem. Damon: a common name for shepherds in pastoral poems, e.g., in Virgil's *Eclogue* 8, and in Pope's pastoral "Spring." A variant version of Wheatley's poem to Scipio Moorhead was published in the April 1784 *Arminian Magazine* (London).

To His Honour the Lieutenant-Governor, on the Death of His Lady March 24, 1773.

Not included in her 1772 Proposals. Written and published March 1773. The lady was Mary Sanford Oliver, wife of Lieutenant-Governor Andrew Oliver.

A Farewel to America. To Mrs. S.W.

Not included in her 1772 Proposals. Written and published May 1773. Hebe (line 30): Greek goddess of eternal youth. See the two variant versions of this poem addressed to Susanna Wheatley.

A Rebus, by I.B.

Not included in her 1772 Proposals. Written and published 1773. Julian Mason and William Robinson both suggest that the "I.B." who wrote the rebus was James Bowdoin. Wheatley includes another's poem as necessary context for her response.

An Answer to the Rebus, by the Author of These Poems.

Not included in her 1772 Proposals. Written and published 1773. Wheatley explains the riddle with the words "*Quail,*" "*Unicorn,*" "*Emerald,*" "*Boston,*" "*Euphorbus,*" and "*C[hatha]m,*" whose initial letters spell out the answer: Quebec. Wheatley refers to the incident in the *Iliad* when the Greek leader Menelaus kills the Trojan ally Euphorbus for having wounded Patroclus, who had borrowed Achilles's armor (see note to Wheatley's "To Maecenas"). The adulterous relationship of Menelaus's wife, Helen, and the Trojan prince Paris led to the Trojan war. William Pitt (1708–1778), Earl of Chatham, had been prime minister during the Seven Years' War, known in North America as the French and Indian War, and was perceived as being sympathetic to the colonists' cause.

EXTANT POEMS NOT PUBLISHED IN
POEMS ON VARIOUS SUBJECTS

Atheism—.

Not included in her 1772 Proposals. Probably an early draft of the following poem. Preterperfect (line 11): more than perfect. Minerva (line 44): Roman goddess of wisdom, invention, martial prowess, and the arts; equivalent to the Greek goddess Pallas Athena. Pluto (line 45): Roman god of the underworld; equivalent to the Greek god Hades. Pheobus [*sic*] (line 53): Phoebus Apollo, god of the sun. Cynthia (line 55): Diana or Phoebe or Artemis, goddess of the moon.

An Address to the Atheist, by P. Wheatley at the
Age of 14 Years—1767—.

Included in her 1772 Proposals.

Deism.

Probably an early draft of the following poem.

An Address to the Deist—1767.

Included in her 1772 Proposals. "Who trod the wine-press of Je-
hovah's wrath?": cf. Isaiah 63:3.

On Messrs Hussey and Coffin.

As Julian Mason notes, this is very probably the poem "On two
friends, who were cast away" listed in Wheatley's 1772 Propo-
sals. Boreas (line 3): the north wind. Eolus (line 7): Aeolus, king
of the winds. Gulph (line 11): gulf, Cape Cod Bay.

America.

Included in her 1772 Proposals. Riecho (line 33): probably re-
echo. Agenoria (line 35): Britain.

To the Hon.ble Commodore Hood on his Pardoning a Deserter.

Included in her 1772 Proposals, dated 1769. Probably occasioned
by the account reported in the February 1769 issue of *The Gen-
tleman's Magazine* (London) of a deserter sentenced to die who
was pardoned by Samuel Hood (1724–1816), commander of the
North American station, 1767–1770.

On Friendship.

Included in her 1772 Proposals, dated 1768. Amicitia (line 1):
Latin for friendship. Amor: Latin for love.

On the Death of Mr. Snider Murder'd by Richardson.

Included in her 1772 Proposals, dated 1770. On February 23, 1770, Ebenezer Richardson, a loyalist, shot and killed eleven-year-old Christopher Snider when he fired into an anti-British mob trying to break into his house. The boy's funeral became a political event. Richardson was convicted of murder and sentenced to die, but Governor Hutchinson refused to sign the death warrant, saying he had acted in self-defense. King George III pardoned and freed him after a two-year imprisonment. Although in her 1772 Proposals this poem is dated 1770, either Wheatley or her London publisher wisely chose not to include it in her *Poems.*

Ocean.

Included in Wheatley's 1779 Proposals, the manuscript of "Ocean" was thought lost until it was offered for sale in 1998. The buyer, Mark E. Mitchell, has very kindly allowed me to include it in the Penguin edition of Wheatley's works. Many of the classical allusions in "Ocean" are identified in the note on "To Maecenas," above. The "mighty Sire of Ocean" (line 17) is Neptune, and the following line is adapted from Pope's translation of Homer's *Iliad*, which Wheatley acquired in London. "Syb's, Eurus, Boreas" (line 24): the south, east, and north winds. "Eolus" (line 27): Aeolus, god of the winds. Lines 31–32 allude to the Greek myth in which Zeus, disguised as a snow-white bull, tricks the maiden Europa into getting on his back so that he can take her across the sea to Crete, where he transforms himself into an eagle and rapes her. "[P]luto's dreary shore" (line 44): Pluto, or Hades, was the god of the underworld, land of the dead. "Iscarius" (line 55): perhaps Wheatley's combination of the names Judas Iscariot, betrayer of Jesus, and Icarus (Icarius), who fell into the sea when the wax holding his artificial wings melted because he flew too close to the sun trying to escape from Crete. Or perhaps Wheatley's "Iscarius" is simply a misspelling of Icarius.

An Elegy, to Miss Mary Moorhead, on the Death of her Father, the Rev. Mr. John Moorhead.

Not included in her 1779 Proposals. Shade (line 5): spirit, ghost. Doom (line 41): judgment. Tophet (line 42): cf. Isaiah 30:33. "Moses' Serpent": the brazen serpent Moses fashioned in the wilderness (Numbers 21:8–9). Line 66: Moorhead apparently was also a poet.

[To a Gentleman of the Navy].

Included in her 1779 Proposals as "To Lieut. R ——— of the Royal Navy." "Lieut. R ———" was probably John Prime Iron Rochfort, promoted to lieutenant December 30, 1775. Greaves has not been identified. Achaian (line 11): Greek. Albion (line 19): Britain. Cerulean (line 33): sky-blue.

The Answer [By the Gentleman of the Navy].

Included in her 1779 Proposals as "To the same." Line 26 is adapted from Alexander Pope, *Windsor Forest* (London, 1713), line 2: "At once the Monarch's and the Muse's Seats." "Great Sir Isaac" (line 33): Sir Isaac Newton (1642–1727), English mathematician, scientist, and religious writer. "Nature's bard" (line 41): John Milton (1608–1674), English epic poet, author of *Paradise Lost* (1667), to which the unknown author of "The Answer" refers.

Philis's [sic] *Reply to the Answer in our last by the Gentleman in the Navy.*

Not included in her 1779 Proposals. "Guilded shore" (line 15): Guinea, or the Gold Coast. "Cancers torrid heat" (line 19): Africa, under the zodiacal sign of Cancer. "At British Homer's and Sir Isaac's feet" (line 16): at the feet of Milton and Newton.

To his Excellency General Washington.

Included in her 1779 Proposals. Wheatley enclosed this poem in a letter to Washington (1732–1799) dated October 26, 1775. Washington responded from Cambridge on February 28, 1776:

[Miss] Phillis, Your favor of the 26th of October did not reach my hands, 'till the middle of December. Time enough, you will say, to have given an answer ere this. Granted. But a variety of important occurrences, continually interposing to distract the mind and withdraw the attention, I hope will apologize for the delay, and plead my excuse for the seeming but not real neglect. I thank you most sincerely for your polite notice of me, in the elegant Lines you enclosed; and however undeserving I may be of such encomium and panegyrick, the style and manner exhibit a striking proof of your poetical Talents; in honor of which, and as a tribute justly due to you, I would have published the Poem, had I not been apprehensive, that, while I only meant to give the World this new instance of your genius, I might have incurred the imputation of Vanity. This, and nothing else, determined me not to give it place in the public Prints.

If you should ever come to Cambridge, or near Head Quarters, I shall be happy to see a person so favored by the Muses, and to whom Nature has been so liberal and beneficent in her dispensations. I am, with great Respect, your obedient humble servant.

Washington sent Wheatley's poem and letter to his former secretary, Colonel Joseph Reed on February 10, 1776, telling him,

I recollect nothing else worth giving you the trouble of, unless you can be amused by reading a letter and poem addressed to me by Miss Phillis Wheatley. In searching over a parcel of papers the other day, in order to destroy such as were useless, I brought it to light again. At first, with a view of doing justice to her poetical genius, I had a great mind to publish the poem; but not knowing whether it might not be considered rather as a mark of my own vanity, than a compliment to her, I laid it aside, till I came across it again in the manner just mentioned.

Reed apparently took Washington's hint and sent the poem and letter with his own headnote to the editors of the *Virginia Gazette*, who published them on March 20, 1776. Thomas Paine (1737–1809) republished them in the April 1776 issue of his *The Pennsylvania Magazine or American Monthly Museum*.

On the Capture of General Lee.

Included in her 1779 Proposals. Wheatley was unaware that Major General Charles Lee (1731–1782) was very jealous of Washington's position as commander-in-chief of the Continental army and that he may even have become a traitor to the American cause after he was captured by the British in Morristown, New Jersey, on December 13, 1776.

To Mr. and Mrs.—, on the Death of their Infant Son.

Julian Mason very plausibly suggests that this may be the poem "To P.N.S. & Lady on the death of their infant son" included in her 1779 Proposals. Although this poem was first published in the September 1784 issue of the *Boston Magazine*, it is signed with Phillis's maiden name, indicating a composition date before her marriage in April 1778. An editorial note in the *Boston Magazine* says, "[t]he Poem . . . was selected from a manuscript Volume of Poems, written by PHILLIS PETERS, formerly Phillis Wheatly [*sic*]—and is inserted as a Specimen of her Work: should this gain the Approbation of the Publick, and sufficient encouragement be given, a volume will be shortly Published, by the Printers hereof [Greenleaf and Freeman], who receive subscriptions for said work."

On the Death of General Wooster.

Included in her 1779 Proposals. A New Haven, Connecticut, merchant, Major General David Wooster (1710–1777) died on May 2, 1777, having been mortally wounded by the British. This poem was enclosed in a letter Wheatley sent to his widow, Mary, on July 15, 1778.

Prayer.

Not included in her 1779 Proposals.

*An Elegy Sacred to the Memory of the
Rev'd Samuel Cooper, D.D.*

Cooper baptized Wheatley on August 18, 1771.

*An Elegy, Sacred to the Memory of that Great Divine,
the Reverend and Learned Dr. Samuel Cooper.*

On Cooper, see the note to "To the Publick," above.

Liberty and Peace, a Poem.

Lines 3–4 are quoted directly from lines 9–10 of Wheatley's
poem to Washington. Hibernia (line 37): Latin name for Ireland.

LETTERS.

To the Countess of Huntingdon (October 25, 1770).

Wheatley sent this letter as a cover for a non-extant manuscript
version of her poem on the death of Whitefield.

To Abigail May? (November or December 1771).

Julian Mason suggests that Wheatley sent this letter to Abigail
May, who joined Boston's Old South Church on the day Wheat-
ley was baptized.

To John Thornton (April 21, 1772).

Thornton (1720–1790), a wealthy English merchant and philan-
thropist, was a supporter of the Countess of Huntingdon's evan-
gelical activities and a member of her circle. The Reverend
Samson Occom was his guest during his 1766–68 fund-raising
visit to England. Thornton sent money to John and Susanna
Wheatley for Indian missions, and they kept him informed of
their progress.

To Arbour Tanner (May 19, 1772).

Elsewhere, the recipient's first name is spelled Abour or Obour. The Reverend Samuel Hopkins baptized her into the First Congregational Church on July 10, 1768. She married Barra Tanner on November 14, 1789, and died in Newport on June 21, 1835.

To Arbour Tanner (July 19, 1772).

William Whitwell (1714–1795), a Boston merchant, was also a member of the Old South Church.

To the Earl of Dartmouth (October 10, 1772).

Thomas Wooldridge (d. 1795) kept Dartmouth informed of colonial opinion on various matters and visited Wheatley, watching her compose the poem to Dartmouth.

To the Countess of Huntingdon (June 27, 1773).

Huntingdon had been interested in Phillis Wheatley since receiving her eulogy on the death of Whitefield. On May 25, 1772, Richard Carey wrote the Countess to tell her "[t]he Negro Girl of Mr. Wheatley's, by her virtuous Behaviour and conversation in Life gives Reason to believe, she's a Subject of Divine Grace—remarkable for her Piety, of an extraordinary Genius, and in full Communion with one of the Churches; the Family, & Girl, was Affected at the kind enquiry your Ladyship made after her." On April 3, 1773, Carey assured the Countess that he would introduce her friends visiting Boston to "Phillis, the Christian Poetess, who continues in well doing." On April 30, 1773, Susanna Wheatley wrote the Countess that Phillis was coming to England with Nathaniel Wheatley on the advice of her doctors and asked Huntingdon to advise them when they arrived. Phillis brought with her a letter of introduction from Carey:

This will be delivered your Ladyship by Phillis, the Christian Poetess, Whose Behaviour in England I wish may be as exemplary, as it has been in Boston. This appears remarkable for her Humility, and spiritual-mindedness, hope she will continue an ornament for the Christian name and profession, as she grows older and has more experience, I doubt not her writings will run more in Evangelical strain. I think your Ladyship will be pleased with her.

Phillis was not able to deliver Carey's letter in person, however, because the ailing Countess had retired to her home in Talgarth, South Wales, where in 1768 she had established a college at Trevecca to teach ministers the doctrine of her Connexion.

To the Countess of Huntingdon (July 17, 1773).

"Your Brother": probably James Albert Ukawsaw Gronniosaw (1710?–1772?), whose *A Narrative of the Most Remarkable Particulars in the Life of James Albert Ukawsaw Gronniosaw, an African Prince, as Related by Himself* (Bath, 1772) was dedicated to the Countess of Huntingdon. Her clergyman cousin, Walter Shirley (1725–1786), wrote the Preface to the *Narrative*.

To David Wooster (October 18, 1773).

Wheatley's letter to Wooster includes her first known reference to her manumission. On Lord Dartmouth, see the note to Wheatley's poem addressed to him. John Kirkman (1741–1780), a silk merchant, was an alderman of the City of London from 1768 to 1780. Henry Fiennes Pelham Clinton (1750–1778) was known by his courtesy title, the earl of Lincoln. Dr. Daniel Solander (1736–1782) was a Swedish-born botanist who accompanied Sir Joseph Banks (1743–1820) as a researcher in the South Pacific from 1768 to 1771, aboard the *Endeavor*, commanded by Captain James Cook (1728–1779). Lady Cavendish and Lady Carteret Webb, sisters, were followers of Lady Huntingdon. Mary (Reynolds) Palmer (1716–1796) was the sister of the famous painter Sir Joshua Reynolds (1723–1792). Dr. Thomas Gibbons (1720–1785), a dissenting minister, taught rhetoric at the Mile End Academy. He published *Juvenalia: Poems on Various Subjects of Devotion and Virtue* (London, 1750) and a

Latin poem on the death of Whitefield in 1771. Israel Mauduit (1708–1787) had been agent for Massachusetts in London since 1763. Benjamin Franklin (1706–1790) promoted American interests in London from July 1757 to March 1775, acting as agent for the colonies of Pennsylvania, Georgia, New Jersey, and Massachusetts. He visited Wheatley and offered her his services at the prompting of Jonathan Williams, his nephew-in-law in Boston, who in turn had been encouraged by Susanna Wheatley to mention Phillis in his letters to his uncle. Wheatley's proposed but never published second volume of poems and letters was to have been dedicated to Franklin. Brook Watson (1735–1807), future lord mayor of London (1796–1797), was a merchant. During her brief London trip, Phillis also visited the ailing statesman and man of letters Baron George Lyttelton (1709–1773), who died the month after she left for America. According to Margaretta Matilda Oddell, great grandniece of Susanna Wheatley, Phillis was to be presented to King George III, but her mistress's illness intervened. On the significance of Wheatley's meeting the abolitionist Granville Sharp (1735–1813), see the Introduction to this edition. The royal menagerie, the royal armories, and the Crown Jewels were kept at the Tower of London. Presumably, someone other than Wheatley paid the very expensive entry fee of ten and a half shillings for her to see the collection of gigantic jeweled automatons created by the jeweler James Cox (d. 1791 or 1792) displayed in Spring Gardens, Westminster (adjacent to present-day Admiralty Arch) and valued at £197,000. Samuel Johnson declared Cox's collection, which was displayed between 1772 and 1775, "[f]or power of mechanism and splendour of show a very fine exhibition." Sadler's Wells was the site of a medicinal well and a newly fashionable theater. In just six weeks, Wheatley toured much of greater London—from Westminster in the west to the City of London in the east, Greenwich in the south, and Sadler's Wells in the north. The books Wheatley mentions and their present-day locations include: Alexander Pope (1688–1744), translation of Homer's *Iliad* (Dartmouth College), his four-volume translation of Homer's *Odyssey* and the nine volumes of his own works (University of North Carolina at Charlotte); Tobias Smollett (1721–1771), translation of Cer-

vantes's *Don Quixote* (volume two is in the Schomburg Center
for Research in Black Culture of the New York Public Library);
John Milton (1608–1674), *Paradise Lost* (Houghton Library,
Harvard University); Samuel Butler (1612–1680), *Hudibras*;
John Gay (1685–1732), *Fables*. Wheatley does not mention that
Sharp also gave her a copy of his *Remarks on Several Very Im-
portant Prophecies, in Five Parts* (London, 1768), now at the Es-
sex Institute. After she returned to Boston, Mary Eveleigh gave
Wheatley the four-volume *Complete Works in Verse and Prose*
of William Shenstone (1714–1763), the last two volumes of
which are at the Schomburg Center.

To Obour Tanner (October 30, 1773).

The "young man" referred to in the postscript may be John Pe-
ters, Phillis Wheatley's future husband.

To John Thornton (December 1, 1773).

Jane, Henry, and Robert were John Thornton's children. Mrs.
Wilberforce, John Thornton's half-sister, was the aunt of the
abolitionist William Wilberforce (1759–1833).

To the Reverend Samuel Hopkins (February 9, 1774).

Taken from the *Pennsylvania Freeman*, May 9, 1839, a weekly
abolitionist newspaper published by John Greenleaf Whittier
(1807–1892). The "two negro men" Wheatley mentions are
probably Bristol Yamma (1744?–1793) and John Quamine
(1743?–1799). "The precious crumbs": Matthew 15:27. "The di-
vine royal Psalmist": King David; see Psalm 68.

To Samson Occom (February 11, 1774).

Wheatley's most direct attack on slavery was subsequently
reprinted in nearly a dozen New England newspapers as well as
in the May 3, 1774, issue of the *Nova Scotia Gazette and the
Weekly Chronicle*.

To Obour Tanner (March 21, 1774).

Susanna Wheatley died March 3, 1774, at the age of 65.

To John Thornton (March 29, 1774).

Wheatley is responding to Thornton's response to her letter of December 1, 1773.

To Obour Tanner (May 6, 1774).

Mr. Pemberton may be the Reverend Ebenezer Pemberton, who attested to the authenticity of Wheatley's *Poems*.

To the Reverend Samuel Hopkins (May 6, 1774).

Philip Quaque (1741–1816), son of an African ruler, had been brought in 1754 from Cape Coast, Africa (present-day Ghana), to England to be educated at the expense of the Society for the Propagation of the Gospel. In 1765 he was ordained by the bishop of London as priest in the Church of England. After marrying an Englishwoman, he was appointed "Missionary, Catechist and Schoolmaster to the Negroes on the Gold Coast in Africa." Except for a brief period in 1784–1785, when he returned to England to arrange for his children's education, he spent the rest of his life trying to pursue his mission at Cape Coast Castle, with very limited success. The ninth edition of Thomas Salmon (1679–1767), *The Modern Gazeteer: or, a Short View of the Several Nations of the World* (London, 1746) was published in London in 1773.

To John Thornton (October 30, 1774).

Anamaboe: the homeland of John Quamine, located in present-day Ghana.

APPENDIX A

"Hymn to Humanity" and "The Voice of Freedom"

I am indebted for much of the following information to Dr. Randall K. Burkett, African-American Studies Bibliographer for the Robert W. Woodruff Library of Emory University. One of two copybooks recently acquired by the Library contains thirty-three complete or partial poems by various hands, including "Hymn to Humanity," inscribed to "S.P. Gallowy," and "The Voice of Freedom," both in the same hand. According to Dr. Woodruff, the copybooks were originally owned by New York friends of a Boston employer of Wheatley. In an unpublished paper, Dr. Burkett points out that the other "copybook contains a 'List of Scholars in King street,' the street in Boston on which the Wheatley family lived and on which the booksellers Cox and Berry (the American purveyors of *Poems on Various Subjects*) were located. Those six students were William, Lewis, and Francis Deblois, Joshua Davis, Nathaniel Tayne(?), and Hannah Proctor. It is tempting to speculate that Phillis Wheatley learned some of her letters from the same tutor supervising these students, or that one of these was responsible for copying young Phillis's poems as a class exercise."

Dr. Burkett acknowledges that "[i]t is yet to be determined whether any portion of the copybook, including 'Hymn to Humanity,' is in Phillis Wheatley's own hand. While the slant in the signature is identical to that in several autographed copies of her work, the capital letter 'P' appears to be quite different, and the text overall is in a much more regular and elegant hand than in other known Wheatley manuscripts. This might be accounted for by the fact that the text is in a copybook, presumably written under the watchful eye of a tutor." One might add that the Emory variant is written in no more elegant a hand than the

Dartmouth variant, "A Poem on the death of Charles Eliot aged 12 months," which the Wheatley scholar Professor William W. Cook judges to have been written by Wheatley. On the other hand, Professor Julian Mason, editor of the works of Phillis Wheatley, says in private correspondence regarding the Emory variant, "it is not her handwriting." Dated December 12, 1773, the "Hymn" is a later version of the poem "An Hymn to Humanity. To S.P.G Esq" published in *Poems on Various Subjects, Religious and Moral* in September 1773. The newly discovered version includes many significant substantive changes and identifies "S.P.G." as "S.P. Gallowy," about whom nothing more is yet known. Either the newly discovered version is a very unusual instance of Wheatley's revising an already published poem, or it is a revision of Wheatley's poem by another poet.

During her lifetime, several of Wheatley's works included in her *Poems* subsequently appeared in variant versions in newspapers and magazines such as the *Arminian Magazine* (London), presumably revised by hands other than hers. If "Hymn to Humanity" in the Emory copybook is written in Wheatley's hand, "The Voice of Freedom," written in the same hand, would be a significant new political poem by her. Its epigraph is from "A Song for American Freedom" (the Liberty Song), published in Philadelphia in 1768 by John Dickinson (1732–1808). He is the "Immortal Farmer" because he was best known for his *Letters from a Farmer in Pennsylvania* (Philadelphia, 1768). The poet's assumption of the voice of the female allegorical figure of "Freedom" and the very domestic simile in line 12 suggest a female author.

Hymn to Humanity

To S.P. Gallowy Esq: who corrected some Poetic Essays of the Authoress

> Lo! for this dark terrestiral Dome
> He leaves his azure-paved Home
>   A Prince of heav'nly Birth:
> Divine Humanity! behold.

5   What Wonders rise! what Charms unfold
           At his Descent on Earth.
           In Bosoms of the Great & Good
           His own blest Image, when he view'd
           He fix'd Dominion there:

10   Him close compressing to his Breast
    The Sire of Gods & Men address['d]:
           "My Son, my heav'nly fair!
    Descend to Earth, there fix thy Throne
    To succour Man's afflicted Son

15   Each human Heart inspire
    To act in Bounties unconfin'd,
    Enlarge the close contracted Mind,
         And fill it with sacred Fire."
    Quick as the Word with swift Career,

20   He wings his Course from Star to Star
         And leaves the bright abode:
    The Virtue did his Charms impart,
    Their *Gallowy*! then thy raptur'd Heart,
         Perceiv'd the rushing God!

25   For when thy pitying Eye did see
    The languid Muse in low Degree,
         Then, then did thy bounteous Hand
    Command the all-inspiring Nine
    From bright Olympus' Height to shine

30   And ev'n my Song demand.
    Can Afric's Muse forgetful prove
    Or can such Friendship fail to move
         An ever grateful Heart?
    Immortal Friendship! Laurel-crown'd,

35   The smiling Graces all surround
         With ev'ry heav'nly Art.

                      Phillis Wheatley
                      Boston Decr. 12. 1773

The Voice of Freedom

["]By *Uniting* we stand, by *Dividing* we fall!["] Immortal Farmer.

Americans attend to Freedom's cry!
Who scorns *her* voice deserves to die.
"The wretched tools of tyranny conspire
5   "To set America's fair realms on fire;
"That *I* in *flames of discord* may expire!
"But oh my sons, should *hell* itself combine
"With foes to Freedom, in their fell design,
"If you're *united* in one faithful band,
"Like everlasting mountains you shall stand,
10   "Whose bases rest on God's almighty hand!
"Strong *Union's* blow shall drive them to the deep,
"As from the wall, your brooms the cobwebs sweep.
"But *disunited*, you will shortly mourn
"Fair Liberty from your embraces torn;
15   "And curse the fatal day that you were born.
"In galling Chains, for murd'rers you must toil,
"Who for your pain, will ne'er bestow a smile:
"In vain you'll then to heav'n for succor cry:
"When Freedom's day of grace is once past by.
20   "Base *slaves* you'll live, like *malefactors* die!["]

Jany 18 1773

APPENDIX B

Lucy Terry Prince (c.1730–1821)

Born in Africa, Lucy Terry was kidnapped into slavery and brought to Rhode Island. In 1735 she became the slave of Ensign Ebenezer Wells in Deerfield, Massachusetts. She converted to Christianity, becoming a member of her master's church in 1744. A free black, Obijah (or Abijah) Prince bought her freedom and married her in 1756. They moved to Guilford, Vermont, in 1760, where they raised their six children, and Lucy established a reputation as a raconteur. When her oldest son failed to gain admission to Williams College, Lucy unsuccessfully challenged the school's segregationist policy. Following her husband's death in 1794, Lucy Terry Prince moved to Sunderland, Vermont, where she died in 1821. Composed when she was about sixteen years old, "Bars Fight" commemorates the August 25, 1746, ambush by Native Americans of two white families living in a section of Deerfield, Massachusetts, called "the Bars," or meadows.

"Bars Fight"

August, 'twas the twenty-fifth,
Seventeen hundred forty-six,
The Indians did in ambush lay,
Some very valient men to slay,

5   The names of whom I'll not leave out:
Samuel Allen like a hero fout [fought],
And though he was so brave and bold,
His face no more shall we behold.

Eleazor Hawks was killed outright,
10 Before he had time to fight—
Before he did the Indians see,
Was shot and killed immediately.

Oliver Armsden he was slain,
Which caused his friends much grief and pain.
15 Simeon Arsden they found dead
Not many rods distant from his head.

Adonijah Gillet, we do hear,
Did lose his life which was so dear.
John Sadler fled across the water,
20 And thus escaped the dreadful slaughter.

Eunice Allen see the Indians coming,
And hopes to save herself by running;
And had not her petticoats stopped her,
The awful creatures had not catched her,

25 Nor tommy hawked her on the head,
And left her on the ground for dead.
Young Samuel Allen, Oh, lack-a-day!
Was taken and carried to Canada.

[written 1746; published
1855, in Josiah Holland,
*History of Western
Massachusetts*]

APPENDIX C

Jupiter Hammon (October 17, 1711–ca. 1806)

Jupiter Hammon was the second published African-American writer, after Briton Hammon, who had published his *Narrative of the Uncommon Sufferings and Surprizing Deliverance of Briton Hammon, a Negro Man* in Boston in July 1760. No evidence exists to suggest any relationship between Briton and Jupiter Hammon. Jupiter Hammon's exact birthdate is recorded in one of the ledgers of his owner, Henry Lloyd (d. 1763). Throughout his life, Hammon was owned by members of the Lloyd family, wealthy merchants at Lloyd's Neck (Queen's Village) on Long Island, New York, whom he served as clerk and bookkeeper. He was also an occasional preacher, having bought a Bible from his master in 1733. As the British were about to capture Long Island in 1776, Joseph, one of the few non-Loyalist members of the Lloyd family, fled to Stamford and later Hartford, Connecticut, taking Hammon with him. Hammon advertised in the December 14, 1779 *Connecticut Gazette* (Hartford) *An Essay on the Ten Virgins*, no copy of which is known to exist. He may have published verses celebrating the 1782 visit of the future British King William IV to the Lloyd Manor on Long Island. Hammon also published the sermon essays *A Winter Piece: Being a Serious Exhortation, with a Call to the Unconverted* (Hartford, 1782) and *An Address to the Negroes in the State of New York* (New York, 1787; reprinted in Philadelphia, 1787, and New York, 1806), in the latter advising his fellow slaves to bear their own condition patiently while trying to persuade their masters to manumit their children.

AN Evening THOUGHT. SALVATION BY CHRIST, *WITH*
PENETENTIAL CRIES: Composed by Jupiter Hammon, a
Negro Belonging to Mr. Lloyd, of Queen's-Village, on Long-
Island, the 25th of December, 1760.

> SALVATION comes by Jesus Christ alone,
> > The only Son of God;
> Redemption now to every one,
> > That love his holy Word.
> 5 Dear Jesus we would fly to Thee,
> > And leave off every Sin,
> Thy tender Mercy well agree;
> > Salvation from our King.
> Salvation comes now from the Lord,
> 10 Our victorious King;
> His holy Name be well ador'd,
> > Salvation surely bring.
> Dear Jesus give thy Spirit now,
> > Thy Grace to every Nation,
> 15 That han't the Lord to whom we bow,
> > The Author of Salvation.
> Dear Jesus unto Thee we cry,
> > Give us thy Preparation;
> Turn not away thy tender Eye;
> 20 We seek thy true Salvation.
> Salvation comes from God we know,
> > The true and only One;
> It's well agreed and certain true,
> > He gave his only Son.
> 25 Lord hear our penetential Cry:
> > Salvation from above;
> It is the Lord that doth supply,
> > With his Redeeming Love.
> Dear Jesus by thy precious Blood,
> 30 The World Redemption have:
> Salvation comes now from the Lord,
> > He being thy captive Slave.

Dear Jesus let the Nations cry,
  And all the People say,
35 Salvation comes from Christ on high,
  Haste on Tribunal Day.
We cry as Sinners to the Lord,
  Salvation to obtain;
It is firmly fixt his holy Word,
40 *Ye shall not cry in vain.*
Dear Jesus unto Thee we cry,
  And make our Lamentation:
O let our Prayers ascend on high;
  We felt thy Salvation.
45 Lord turn our dark benighted Souls;
  Give us a true Motion,
And let the Hearts of all the World,
  Make Christ their Salvation.
Ten Thousand Angels cry to Thee,
50 Yea louder than the Ocean.
Thou art the Lord, we plainly see;
  Thou art the true Salvation.
Now is the Day, excepted Time;
  The Day of Salvation;
55 Increase your Faith, do not repine:
  Awake ye every Nation.
Lord unto whom now shall we go,
  Or seek a safe Abode;
Thou hast the Word Salvation too
60 The only Son of God.
Ho! every one that hunger hath,
  Or pineth after me,
Salvation be thy leading Staff,
  To set the Sinner free.
65 Dear Jesus unto Thee we fly;
  Depart, depart from Sin,
Salvation doth at length supply,
  The Glory of our King.
Come ye Blessed of the Lord,
70 Salvation gently given;

O turn your Hearts, accept the Word,
  Your Souls are fit for Heaven.
Dear Jesus we now turn to Thee,
  Salvation to obtain;
75 Our Hearts and Souls do meet again,
  To magnify thy Name.
Come holy Spirit, Heavenly Dove,
  The Object of our Care;
Salvation doth increase our Love;
80 Our Hearts hath felt thy fear.
Now Glory be to God on High,
  Salvation high and low;
And thus the Soul on Christ rely,
  To Heaven surely go.
85 Come Blessed Jesus, Heavenly Dove,
  Accept Repentance here;
Salvation give, with tender Love;
  Let us with Angels share.

       Hartford, August 4, 1778

*AN ADDRESS to Miss PHILLIS WHEATLY, Ethiopian
Poetess, in Boston, who came from Africa at eight years of age,
and soon became acquainted with the Gospel of Jesus Christ.*

Miss WHEATLY; pray give leave to express as follows:

1.
O Come you pious youth! adore
  The wisdom of thy God, Eccles[iastes]. xii.
In bringing thee from distant shore,
  To learn his holy word.

2.
Thou mightst been left behind,
  Amidst a dark abode; Psal[ms]. cxxv, 2, 3.

God's tender mercy still combin'd,
    Thou hast the holy word.

3.

Fair wisdom's ways are paths of peace,
    And they that walk therein,   Psal. i. 1, 2;
Shall reap the joys that never cease,   Prov[erbs]. iii, 7.
    And Christ shall be their king.

4.

God's tender mercy brought thee here,
    Tost o'er the raging main   Psal. ciii, 1, 3, 4.
In Christian faith thou hast a share,
    Worth all the gold of Spain.

5.

While thousands tossed by the sea,
    And others settled down,   Death.
God's tender mercy set thee free
    From dangers still unknown.

6.

That thou a pattern still might be,
    To youth of Boston town,   2 Cor[inthians].
The blessed Jesus set thee free,   v, 10.
    From every sinful wound.

7.

The blessed Jesus, who came down,
    Unvail'd [sic] his sacred face,   Rom[ans]. v, 21.
To cleanse the soul of every wound,
    And give repenting grace.

8.

That we poor sinners may obtain
    The pardon of our sin;   Psal. xxxiv, 6, 7, 8.
Dear blessed Jesus now constrain,
    And bring us flocking in.

9.
Come you, Phillis, now aspire,
          And seek the living God,   Matth[ew]. vii, 7, 8.
So step by step thou mayst go higher,
          Till perfect in the word.

10.
While thousands mov'd to distant shore,
          And others left behind,   Psal. lxxxix, 1.
The blessed Jesus still adore,
          Implant this in thy mind.

11.
Thou hast left the heathen shore,
          Thro' mercy of the Lord,   Psal. xxxiv, 1, 2, 3.
Among the heathen live no more,
          Come magnify thy God.

12.
I pray the living God may be,
          The shepherd of thy soul;   Psal. lxxx, 1, 2, 3.
His tender mercies still are free,
          His mysteries to unfold.

13.
Thou, Phillis, when thou hunger hast,
          Or pantest for thy God,   Psal. xiii, 1, 2, 3.
Jesus Christ is thy relief,
          Thou hast the holy word.

14.
The bounteous mercies of the Lord,
          Are hid beyond the sky,   Psal. xvi, 10, 11.
And holy souls that love his word,
          Shall taste them when they die.

15.
These bounteous mercies are from God,
          The merits of his Son;   Psal. xxxiv, 15.

The humble soul that loves his word,
        He chooses for his own.

16.

Come, dear Phillis, be advis'd,
        To drink Samaria's flood: John iv, 13, 14.
There nothing is that shall suffice,
        But Christ's redeeming blood.

17.

While thousands muse with earthly toys,
        And range about the street,   Matth. vi, 33.
Dear Phillis, seek for heaven's joys,
        Where we do hope to meet.

18.

When God shall send his summons down,
        And number saints together,   Psal. cxvi, 15.
Blest angels chant, (triumphant sound)
        Come live with me for ever.

19.

The humble soul shall fly to God,
        And leave the things of time,   Matth. v, 3, 8.
Start forth as 'twere at the first word,
        To taste things more divine.

20.

Behold! the soul shall waft away,
        Whene'er we come to die,   1 Cor. xv, 51, 52, 53.
And leave its cottage made of clay,
        In twinkling of an eye.

21.

Now glory be to the Most High,
        United praises given,   Psal. cl, 6.
By all on earth, incessantly,
        And all the host of heav'n.

Composed by JUPITER HAMMON, a Negro Man belonging to Mr. Joseph Lloyd, of Queen's Village on Long-Island, now in Hartford.

The above lines are published by the Author, and a number of his friends, who desire to join with him in their best regards to Miss Wheatly.

"A Poem for Children with Thoughts on Death"

1

O ye young and thoughtless youth,
    Come seek the living God,
The Scriptures are a sacred truth,
    Ye must believe the word.

                              Eccles[iastes]. 12:1

2

'Tis God alone can make you wise,
    His wisdom's from above,
He fills the soul with sweet supplies
    By his redeeming love.

                              Prov[erbs]. 4:7

3

Remember, youth, the time is short,
    Improve the present day
And pray that god may guide your thoughts,
    And teach your lips to pray.

                              Ps[alms]. 30:9

4

To pray unto the most high God,
    And beg restraining grace,
Then by the power of his word
    You'll see the Saviour's face.

5

Little children they may die,
        Turn to their native dust,
Thier souls shall leap beyond the skies,
        And live among the just.

6

Like little worms they turn and crawl,
        And gasp for every breath,
The blessed Jesus sends his call,
        And takes them to his rest.

7

Thus the youth are born to die,
        The time is hastening on,
The blessed Jesus rends the sky,
        And makes his power known.

8

Then ye shall hear the angels sing
        The trumpet give a sound,
Glory, glory to our King,
        The Saviour's coming down.

9

Start ye saints from dusty beds,
        And hear a Saviour call,
'Twas Jesus Christ that died and bled,
        And thus preserv'd thy soul.

10

This the portion of the just,
        Who lov'd to serve the Lord,
Their bodies starting from the dust,
        Shall rest upon their God.

11

They shall join that holy word,
        That angels constant sing,
Glory, glory to the Lord,
        Hallelujahs to our King.

12

Thus the Saviour will appear,
        With guards of heavenly host,
Those blessed Saints, shall then declare,
        'Tis Father, Son and Holy Ghost.

                                    Rev[elation]. 1:7–8

13

Then shall ye hear the trumpet sound,
        The graves give up their dead,
Those blessed saints shall quick awake,
        And leave their dusty beds.

                                    Matt[hew]. 27:51–52

14

Then shall ye hear the trumpet sound,
        And rend the native sky,
Those bodies starting from the ground,
        In the twinkling of an eye.

                                    1 Cor[inthians]. 15:51–54

15

There to sing the praise of God,
        And join the angelic train,
And by the power of his word,
        Unite together again.

16

Where angels stand for to admit
        Their souls at the first word,
Cast sceptres down at Jesus' feet,
        Crying holy, holy Lord.

                                    Rev[elation]. 4:8

17
Now glory be unto our God
    All praise be justly given,
Ye humble souls that love the Lord,
    Come seek the joys of Heaven.

Hartford, January 1, 1782

AN
Evening's Improvement.
SHEWING
The NECESSITY of beholding the LAMB of GOD.
To Which is added,
A DIALOGUE,
ENTITLED,
The KIND MASTER and DUTIFUL SERVANT.

Written by JUPITER HAMMON, a Negro Man belonging to Mr. John Lloyd, of Queen's Village, on Long-Island, now in Hartford.

HARTFORD:
Printed for the Author,
by the Assistance of his Friends [1783].

MASTER.
1. Come my servant, follow me,
    According to thy place;
And surely God will be with thee,
    And send thee heav'nly grace.

SERVANT.
2. Dear Master, I will follow thee,
    According to thy word,
And pray that God may be with me,
    And save thee in the Lord.

MASTER.

3. My Servant, lovely is the Lord,
      And blest those servants be,
That truly love his holy word,
      And thus will follow me.

SERVANT.

4. Dear Master, that's my whole delight,
      Thy pleasure for to do;
As for grace and truth's in sight,
      Thus far I'll surely go.

MASTER.

5. My Servant, grace proceeds from God,
      And truth should be with thee;
Whence e'er you find it in his word,
      Thus far come follow me.

SERVANT.

6. Dear Master, now without controul,
      I quickly follow thee;
And pray that God will bless my soul,
      His heav'nly place to see.

MASTER.

7. My Servant, Heaven is high above,
      Yea, higher than the sky:
I pray that God would grant his love,
      Come follow me thereby.

SERVANT.

8. Dear Master, now I'll follow thee,
      And trust upon the Lord;
The only safety that I see,
      Is Jesus's holy word.

MASTER.

9. My Servant, follow Jesus now,
      Our great victorious King;

Who governs all both high and low,
    And searches things within.

SERVANT.

10. Dear master, I will follow thee,
    When praying to our King;
It is the Lamb I plainly see,
    Invites the sinner in.

MASTER.

11. My Servant, we are sinners all,
    But follow after grace;
I pray that God would bless thy soul,
    And fill thy heart with grace.

SERVANT.

12. Dear Master, I shall follow then,
    The voice of my great King;
As standing on some distant land,
    Inviting sinners in.

MASTER.

13. My Servant, we must all appear,
    And follow then our King;
For sure he'll stand where sinners are,
    To take true converts in.

SERVANT.

14. Dear Master, now if Jesus calls,
    And sends his summons in;
We'll follow saints and angels all,
    And come unto our King.

MASTER.

15. My Servant, now come pray to God,
    Consider well his call;
Strive to obey his holy word,
    That Christ may love us all.

SERVANT.

16. Dear Master, now it is a time,
       A time of great distress;
    We'll follow after things divine,
       And pray for happiness.

MASTER.

17. Then will the happy day appear,
       That virtue shall increase;
    Lay up the sword and drop the spear,
       And Nations seek for peace.

SERVANT.

18. Then shall we see the happy end,
       Tho' still in some distress;
    That distant foes shall act like friends,
       And leave their wickedness.

MASTER.

19. We pray that God would give us grace,
       And make us humble, too;
    Let ev'ry Nation seek for peace,
       And virtue make a show.

SERVANT.

20. Then we shall see the happy day,
       That virtue is in power;
    Each holy act shall have its sway,
       Extend from shore to shore.

MASTER.

21. This is the work of God's own hand,
       We see by precepts given;
    To relieve distress and save the land,
       Must be the pow'r of heaven.

SERVANT.

22. Now glory be unto our God,
       Let ev'ry nation sing;

Strive to obey his holy word,
    That Christ may take them in.

MASTER.
23. Where endless joys shall never cease,
    Blest angels constant sing;
The glory of their God increase,
    Hallelujahs to their King.

SERVANT.
24. Thus the Dialogue shall end,
    Strive to obey the word;
When ev'ry Nation acts like friends,
    Shall be the sons of God.

25. Believe me now my Christian friends,
    Believe your friend call'd Hammon:
You cannot to your God attend,
    And serve the God of Mammon.

26. If God is pleased by his own hand
    To relieve distresses here;
And grant a peace throughout the land;
    'Twill be a happy year.

27. 'Tis God alone can give us peace;
    It's not the pow'r of man:
When virtuous pow'r shall increase,
    'Twill beautify the land.

28. Then shall we rejoice and sing
    By pow'r of virtue's word,
Come, sweet Jesus, heav'nly King,
    Thou art the Son of God.

29. When virtue comes in bright array,
    Discovers ev'ry sin;
We see the dangers of the day,
    And fly unto our King.

30. Now glory be unto our God,
    All praise be justly given;
Let ev'ry soul obey his word,
    And seek the joy of heav'n.

FINIS.

APPENDIX D

Francis Williams (ca. 1700–ca. 1770)

From Edward Long (1735–1813), *THE HISTORY OF JAMAICA, OR, GENERAL SURVEY OF THE ANCIENT AND MODERN STATE OF THAT ISLAND: WITH Reflections on its Situation, Settlements, Inhabitants, Climate, Products, Commerce, Laws, and Government.* IN THREE VOLUMES. (London: Printed for T[homas]. Lowndes, in Fleet-Street, 1774), 2:475–485.

The achievements of Francis Williams, well known on both sides of the Atlantic during the eighteenth century, presented a clear problem for those who asserted the innate superiority of whites over blacks. For example, Williams is very probably the black referred to by the American Alexander Hamilton (1712–1756) in the June 19, 1744, entry in his unpublished "Itinerarium": "There, talking of a certain free negroe in Jamaica who was a man of estate, good sense, and education, the 'forementioned [white] gentleman [from the West Indies] who had entertained us in the morning about burying of souls, gravely asked if that negroe's parents were not whites, for he was sure that nothing good could come of the whole generation of blacks." The principal biographical source for Williams and the sole source for his one known extant poem is Edward Long, an apologist for slavery, who included Williams's Latin verse with Long's own English translation in an attempt to demonstrate the supposed inferiority of poetry by people of African descent. I have separated the poem from its context so that the reader may approach the verse uninfluenced by Long's biased commentary on the author and his work:

FRANCIS WILLIAMS.

I have forborne till now to introduce upon the stage a personage,
who made a conspicuous figure in this island, and even attracted
the notice of many in England. With the impartiality that be-
comes me, I shall endeavour to do him all possible justice; and
shall leave it to the reader's opinion, whether what they shall dis-
cover of his genius and intellect will be sufficient to overthrow
the arguments, I have before alledged, to prove an inferiority of
the Negroes to the race of white men. It will by this time be dis-
covered, that I allude to *Francis Williams*, a native of this island,
and son to John and Dorothy Williams, free Negroes. Francis
was the youngest of three sons, and, being a boy of unusual
lively parts, was pitched upon to be the subject of an experiment,
which, it is said, the Duke of Montague [the same Duke who
acted as Ignatius Sancho's patron] was curious to make, in order
to discover, whether, by proper cultivation, and a regular course
of tuition at school and the university, a Negroe might not be
found as capable of literature as a white person. In short, he was
sent to England, where he underwent a regular discipline of clas-
sic instruction at a grammar school, after which he was fixed at
the university of Cambridge, where he studied under the ablest
preceptors, and made some progress in the mathematics. During
his abode in England, after finishing his education, it is said (I
know not with what truth) that he composed the well-known
ballad of "Welcome, welcome, brother debtor, &." But I have
likewise heard the same attributed to a different author [the bal-
lad has been attributed to Wetenhall Wilkes (d. 1751)]. Upon his
return to Jamaica, the duke would fain have tried his genius like-
wise in politics, and intended obtaining for him a privy seal, or
appointment to be one of the governor's council; but this scheme
was dropped, upon the objections offered by Mr. Trelawny, the
governor at that time [Edward Trelawney (1699–1754), Gover-
nor of Jamaica, 1738–1752]. Williams therefore set up a school in
Spanish Town, which he continued for several years, where he
taught reading, writing, Latin, and the elements of the mathemat-
ics; whilst he acted in this profession, he selected a Negroe pupil,
whom he trained with particular care, intending to make him his

successor in the school; but of this youth it may be said, to use
the expression of Festus to Paul, that "much learning made him
mad" [Acts 26:24]. The abstruse problems of mathematical insti-
tution turned his brain; and he still remains, I believe, an unfor-
tunate example, to shew that every African head is not adapted
by nature to such profound contemplations. The chief pride of
this disciple consists in imitating the garb and deportment of his
tutor. A tye perriwig, a sword, and ruffled shirt, seem in his
opinion to comprehend the very marrow and quintescence of all
erudition, and philosophic dignity. Probably he imagines it a
more easy way of acquiring, among the Negroes, the reputation
of a great scholar, by these superficial marks, which catch their
eye, than by talking of Euclid, whom they know nothing about.

Considering the difference which climate may occasion, and
which Montesquieu has learnedly examined, the noble duke
would have made the experiment more fairly on a native African;
perhaps too the Northern air imparted a tone and vigour to his
organs, of which they never would have been susceptible in a hot
climate; the author I have mentioned will not allow, that in hot
climates there is any force or vigor [sic] of mind necessary for
human action, "there is (says he) no curiosity, no noble enter-
prize, no generous sentiment" [Long quotes Charles de Secon-
dat, Baron de La Brède et de Montesquieu (1689–1755), *The
Spirit of the Laws* (1748; Thomas Nugent's London ed., 1750),
bk. 14, sec. 2].

The climate of Jamaica is temperate, and even cool, compared
with many parts of Guiney; and the Creole Blacks have undeni-
ably more acuteness and better understandings than the natives
of Guiney. Mr. Hume, who had heard of Williams, says of him,
"In Jamaica indeed they talk of one Negroe as a man of parts and
learning; but 'tis likely he is admired for very slender accom-
plishments, like a parrot who speaks a few words plainly" [Long
quotes David Hume (1711–1776), "Of National Characters," in
Essays and Treatises on Several Subjects (London and Edin-
burgh, 1764), 234n]. And Mr. Estwick, pursuing the same idea,
observes, "Although a Negroe is found in Jamaica, or elsewhere,
ever so sensible and acute; yet, if he is incapable of moral sensa-
tions, or perceives them only as beasts do simple ideas, without
the power of combination, in order to use; it is a mark that dis-

tinguishes him from the man who feels, and is capable of these moral sensations, who knows their application, and the purposes of them, as sufficiently, as he himself is distinguished from the highest species of brute" [Samuel Estwick (ca. 1736–1795), *Considerations on the Negroe Cause Commonly So Called, Addressed to the Right Honourable Lord Mansfield, Lord Chief Justice of the Court of King's Bench, &c. By a West Indian* (London, 1772; 2nd. ed. 1773), 79n, only in second and subsequent eds.] I do not know, if the specimen I shall exhibit of his abilities will, or will not, be thought to militate against these positions. In regard to the general character of the man, he was haughty, opinionated, looked down with sovereign contempt on his fellow Blacks, entertained the highest opinion of his own knowledge, treated his parents with much disdain, and behaved towards his children and his slaves with a severity bordering upon cruelty; he was fond of having great deference paid to him, and exacted it in the utmost degree from the Negroes about him; he affected a singularity of dress, and particularly grave cast of countenance, to impress an idea of his wisdom and learning; and, to second this view, he wore in common a huge wig, which made a very venerable figure. The moral part of his character may be collected from these touches, as well as the measure of his wisdom, on which, as well as some other attributes to which he laid claim, he had not the modesty to be silent, whenever he met with occasion to expatiate upon them. Of this piece of vanity, there is a very strong example in the following poem, which he presented to Mr. Haldane [George Haldane (1722–1759), Governor of Jamaica, April–July 1759], upon his assuming the government of the island; he was fond of this species of composition in Latin, and usually addressed one to every new governor. He defined himself "a *white* man acting under a *black* skin." He endeavoured to prove logically, that a Negroe was superior in quality to a Mulatto, or other cast. His proposition was, that "as a simple white or a simple black complexion was respectively perfect: but a Mulatto, being a heterogeneous medley of both, was imperfect, *ergo* inferior."

His opinion of Negroes may be inferred from a proverbial saying, that was frequently in his mouth; "Shew me a *Negroe*, and I will shew you *a thief.*" He died, not long since, at the age of seventy, or thereabouts.

[Here follows William's Latin verse and Long's translation.]

There is, in this performance, a strain of superlative panegyric, which is scarcely allowable even to a poet. *Buchanan* is compared with *Virgil,* and Mr. *Haldane* made equal to *Achilles;* nay, exalted still higher, for he is hailed the *Caesar* or emperor of *America.* The author has taken care, whilst he is dealing about his adulation, not to forget himself. His speech is represented erudite and modest; his heart is filled with wisdom; his morals are immaculate; and he abounds with patriotism and virtue.

To consider the merits of this specimen impartially, we must endeavour to forget, in the first place, that the writer was a *Negroe;* for if we regard it as an extraordinary production, merely because it came from a *Negroe,* we admit at once that *inequality* of genius which has been before supposed, and admire it only as a rare phaenomenon. . . .

We are to estimate it as having flowed from the polished pen of one, who received an academic education, under every advantage that able preceptors, and munificent patrons, could furnish; we must likewise believe it to be, what it actually was, a piece highly laboured; designed, modeled, and perfected, to the utmost stretch of his invention, imagination, and skill.

Should we, or should we not, have looked for something better from one, upon whom [all learning has been bestowed]? or, is it at all superior, in classic purity and numbers, in sentiment and propriety, in poetic images and harmony, to any composition we might expect from a middling scholar at the seminaries of Westminster or Eaton [sic]? It is true, *poeta nascitur, non fit* [poets are born, not made]: but the principal forte and excellence of this man lay in versification; however, as I mean not to prejudge the cause, I shall leave it to the fair verdict of a jury of critics. The Spaniards have a proverbial saying, *"Aunque Negros somos gente";* "though we are Blacks, we are men." The truth of which no one will dispute; but if we allow the system of created beings to be perfect and consistent, and that this perfection arises from

an exact scale of gradation, from the lowest to the highest, com-
bining and connecting every part into a regular and beautiful
harmony, reasoning them from the visible plan and operation of
infinite wisdom in respect to the human race, as well as every
other series in the scale, we must, I think, conclude, that,

> The general *order*, since the whole began,
> Is kept in *nature*, and is kept in *man*.
> *Order* is heaven's first law; and, this confest,
> *Some are*, and *must be*, *greater* than the rest. [Alexander Pope
> (1688–1744), *An Essay on Man* (London, 1733–1734), 1:171–172,
> 4:49–50.]

> "To That most upright and valiant Man, GEORGE HALDANE, Esq;
> Governor of the Island of Jamaica; Upon whom All military and
> moral Endowments are accumulated."

An ODE.

    AT length revolving fates th' expected year
    Advance, and joy the live-long day shall cheer,
    Beneath the fost'ring law's auspicious dawn
    New harvests rise to glad th' enliven'd lawn.
5   With the bright prospect blest, the swains repair
    In social bands, and give a loose to care.
    Rash councils now, with each malignant plan,
    Each faction, that in evil hour began,
    At your approach are in confusion fled,
10   Nor, while you rule, shall rear their dastard head.
    Alike the master and the slave shall see
    Their neck reliev'd, the yoke unbound by thee.
    Ere now our guiltless isle, her wretched fate
    Had wept, and groan'd beneath th' oppressive weight
15   Of cruel woes; save thy victorious hand,
    Long fam'd in war, from Gallia's[1] hostile land;
    And wreaths of fresh renown, with generous zeal,

Had freely turn'd, to prop our sinking weal.
Form'd as thou art, to serve *Britannia's* crown,
20 While *Scotia*[2] claims thee for her darling son;
Oh! blest of heroes, ablest to sustain
A falling people, and relax their chain.
Long as this isle shall grace the Western deep,
From age to age, thy fame shall never sleep.
25 Thee, her dread victor *Guadaloupe* shall own,
Crusht by thy arm, her slaughter'd chiefs bemoan;
View their proud tents all level'd in the dust,
And, while she grieves, confess the cause was just.
The golden *Iris*[3] the sad scene will share,
30 Will mourn her banners scatter'd in the air;
Lament her vanquisht troops with many a sigh,
Nor less to see her towns in ruin lie.
Fav'rite of *Mars*![4] believe, th'attempt were vain,
It is not mine to try the arduous strain.
35 What! shall an *AEthiop* touch the martial string,
Of battles, leaders, atchievements sing?
Ah no! *Minerva*,[5] with th'indignant *Nine*,[6]
Restrain him, and forbid the bold design.
To a *Buchanan* does the theme belong;[7]
40 A theme, that well deserves *Buchanan's* song.
'Tis he, should swell the din of war's alarms,
Record thee great in council, as in arms;
Recite each conquest by thy valour won,
And equal thee to great *Peleides'* son.[8]
45 That bard, his country's ornament and pride,
Who e'en with *Maro* might the bays divide:[9]
Far worthier he, thy glories to rehearse,
And paint thy deeds in his immortal verse.
We live, alas! where the bright god of day,
50 Full from the zenith whirls his torrid ray:
Beneath the rage of his consuming fires,
All fancy melts, all eloquence expires.
Yet may you deign accept this humble song,
Tho' wrapt in gloom, and from a falt'ring tongue;
55 Tho' dark the stream on which the tribute flows,
Not from the *skin*, but from the *heart* it rose.

To all of human kind, benignant heaven
(Since nought forbids) one common soul has given.
This rule was 'stablish'd by th'Eternal Mind;
60   Nor virtue's self, nor prudence are confin'd
To *colour;* none imbues the honest heart;
To science none belongs, and none to art.
Oh! *Muse,* of blackest tint, why shrinks thy breast,
Why fears t'approach the *Caesar* of the *West!*
65   Dispel thy doubts, with confidence ascend
The regal dome, and hail him for thy friend:
Nor blush, altho' in garb funereal drest,
Thy body's white, tho' clad in sable vest.
Manners unsullied, and the radiant glow
70   Of genius, burning with desire to *know;*
And learned speech, with modest accent worn,
Shall best the sooty *African* adorn.
An heart with wisdom fraught, a patriot flame,
A love of virtue; these shall lift his name
75   Conspicuous, far beyond his kindred race,
Distinguish'd from them by the foremost place.
In this prolific isle I drew my birth,
And *Britain* nurs'd, illustrious through the earth;
This, my lov'd isle, which never more shall grieve,
80   Whilst you our common friend, our father live.
Then this my pray'r—"May earth and heaven survey
A people ever blest, beneath your sway!"

1. Gallia: France.
2. Scotia: Scotland, Haldane's native land.
3. Iris: the goddess of the rainbow.
4. Mars: the chief Italian god after Jupiter and the Roman name for the Greek god of war, Ares.
5. Minerva: the Roman name for the Greek war goddess Athena, who was also the goddess of wisdom.
6. The nine Muses, or Greek female deities of the arts and sciences.
7. George Buchanan (1506–1582), author of a Latin *History of Scotland* (1582).
8. Peleides' son: Achilles, hero of Homer's *Iliad.*
9. Maro: Virgil (70–19 B.C.), author of the *Aeneid,* virtually completed by the time of his death, which celebrates the exploits of Aeneas and, indirectly, the achievements of Caesar Augustus (63 B.C.–A.D. 14).